WE'RE GOING TO RUN THIS CITY

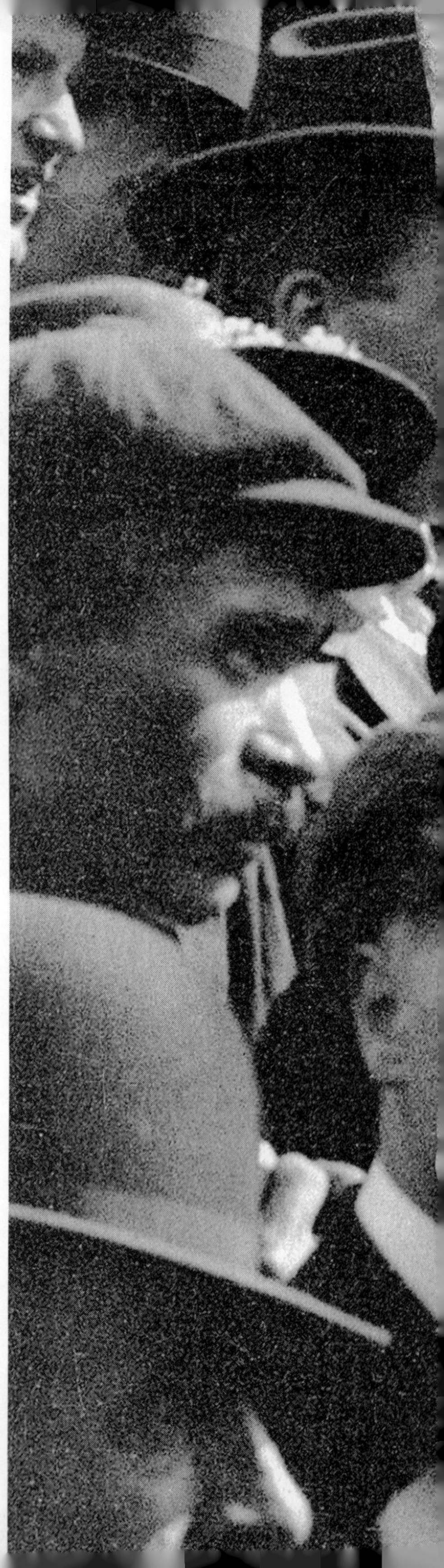

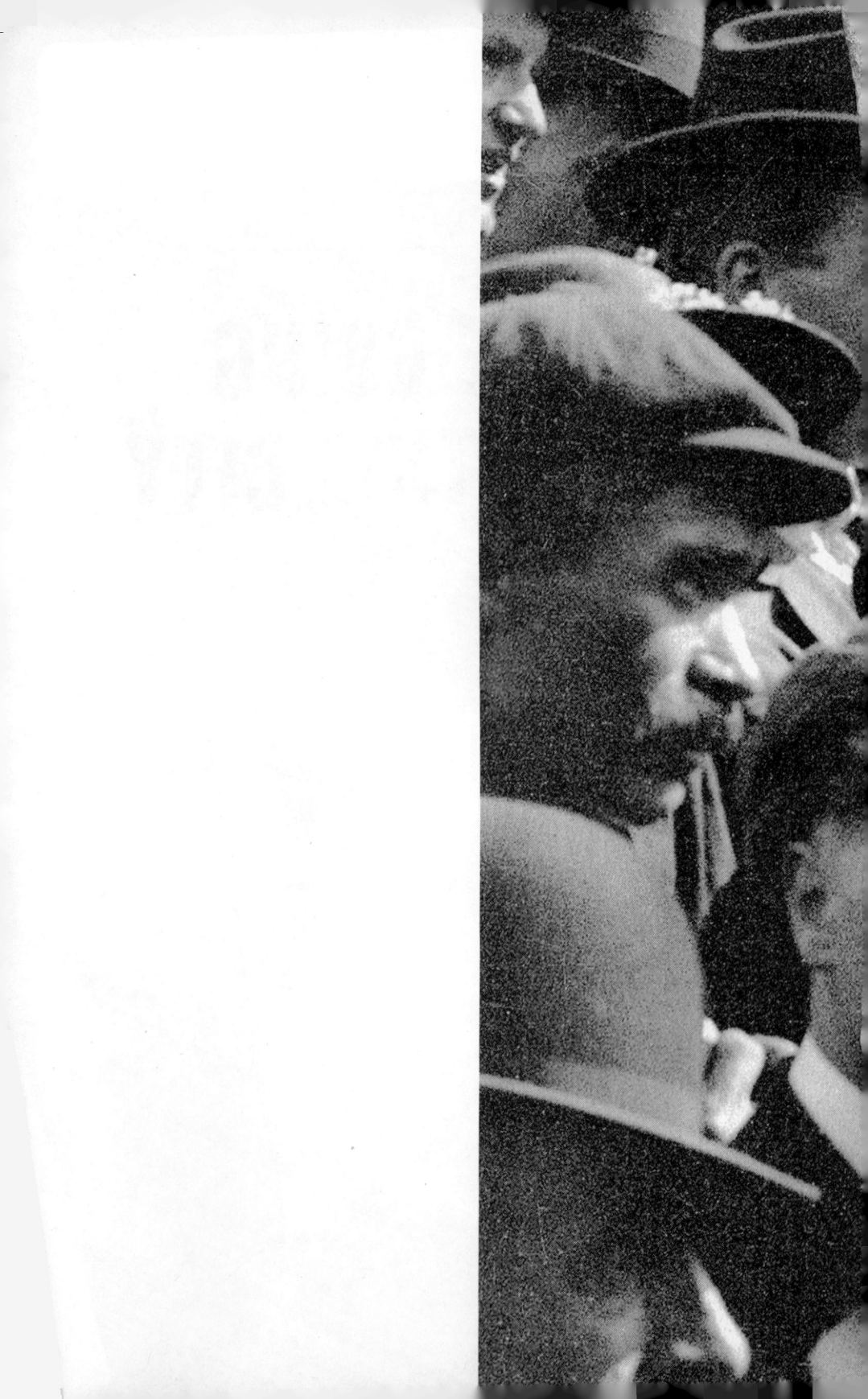

WE'RE GOING TO RUN THIS CITY

Winnipeg's Political Left after the General Strike

Stefan Epp-Koop

UMP
University of Manitoba Press

*To my parents
For giving me a passion for learning
and the desire to write.*

University of Manitoba Press
Winnipeg, Manitoba
Canada R3T 2M5
uofmpress.ca

© Stefan Epp-Koop 2015

Printed in Canada
Text printed on chlorine-free, 100% post-consumer recycled paper

19 18 17 16 15   1 2 3 4 5

All rights reserved. No part of this publication may be reproduced or transmitted in any form
or by any means, or stored in a database and retrieval system in Canada, without the prior
written permission of the University of Manitoba Press, or, in the case of photocopying or
any other reprographic copying, a licence from Access Copyright
(Canadian Copyright Licensing Agency). For an Access Copyright licence,
visit www.accesscopyright.ca, or call 1-800-893-5777.

Cover photo: Winnipeg General Strike meeting at Victoria Park, 13 June 1919.
Photo by L.B. Foote. Archives of Manitoba, N2747.
Cover design: TG Design
Interior design: Jess Koroscil

Library and Archives Canada Cataloguing in Publication

Epp-Koop, Stefan, 1984–, author
We're going to run this city : Winnipeg's political left
after the General Strike / Stefan Epp-Koop.

Includes bibliographical references and index.
Issued in print and electronic formats.
ISBN 978-0-88755-784-2 (pbk.)
ISBN 978-0-88755-475-9 (pdf)
ISBN 978-0-88755-473-5 (epub)

1. Right and left (Political science)—Manitoba—Winnipeg—
History—20th century. 2. General Strike, Winnipeg, Man., 1919.
3. Winnipeg (Man.)—Politics and government—20th century. I. Title.
II. Title: We are going to run this city.

FC3396.4.E66 2015   971.27'4302   C2015-903496-5
                                      C2015-903497-3

The University of Manitoba Press gratefully acknowledges the financial support
for its publication program provided by the Government of Canada through the Canada
Book Fund, the Canada Council for the Arts, the Manitoba Department
of Culture, Heritage, Tourism, the Manitoba Arts Council,
and the Manitoba Book Publishing Tax Credit.

CONTENTS

LIST OF ILLUSTRATIONS
ix

PREFACE
xi

INTRODUCTION
1

CHAPTER 1
The Second Round
18

CHAPTER 2
The Reign of the Furies
40

CHAPTER 3
The Revolutionary Party on the Parliamentary Map
58

CHAPTER 4
A Victory for Those Engaged in the Struggle for Better Conditions
84

CHAPTER 5
For Freedom's Cause, Your Bayonet's Bright
106

CHAPTER 6
A Bombshell to Many Citizens
116

CONCLUSION
145

ACKNOWLEDGEMENTS
151

NOTES
153

BIBLIOGRAPHY
183

INDEX
192

LIST OF ILLUSTRATIONS

1. Overcrowded, poor quality housing was a reality for many Winnipeggers, especially the city's Eastern European immigrants. (Archives of Manitoba, N2438) / **2**

2. Jailed leaders of the Winnipeg General Strike. Back row, left to right: Roger Bray, George Armstrong, John Queen, R.B. Russell, R.J. Johns, and William Pritchard. Front row, left to right: William Ivens and A.A. Heaps. (Archives of Manitoba, N12322) / **4**

3. A 1931 demonstration outside city hall calling for the release of political prisoners. Notice the heavy police presence, a common feature of communist rallies. (AUUC-WBA Archives) /**16**

4. Winnipeg mayor Ralph Webb. (Archives of Manitoba, Legislative Assembly 1932–1936, A0242) / **24**

5. Mayor John Queen shortly after taking office in 1935. (Archives of Manitoba, N20731) / **30**

6. A May Day rally in 1932 with city hall in the background. (AUUC-WBA Archives) / **36**

7. Adults were not the only people to march in Winnipeg's lengthy May Day parades. Here, children waving red flags march in the parade. (AUUC-WBA Archives) / **36**

8. Winnipeg's municipal wards after 1921. Adapted from Alan Artibise, "Patterns of Population Growth and Ethnic Relationships in Winnipeg, 1874–1974." Map by Elise Epp / **38**

9. The May Day march in 1936. William Kolisnyk is second from right in the first row. (AUUC-WBA Archives) / **65**

10. Protests by unemployed Winnipeggers were common throughout the 1930s in response to low levels of unemployment relief. (AUUC-WBA Archives) / **78**

11. Winnipeg's city council in 1930 led by Mayor Ralph Webb. This was also William Kolisnyk's final year on city council. (Archives of Manitoba, N686) / **78**

12. Communist alderman Jacob Penner, pictured during the 1933 municipal election campaign. (Archives of Manitoba, N8915) / **90**

13. A plan for public housing in Winnipeg from 1934. The plan was the first of many plans for housing in Winnipeg during the 1930s that were not implemented. (*Journal of the Royal Architectural Institute of Canada*, July–August 1934): 111 /**132**

PREFACE

As a resident of Winnipeg's West End, it is not hard to experience the legacy of the city's municipal politics of the 1930s. I occasionally walk past Jacob Penner Park, or down Agnes Street where the Independent Labour Party held rallies at a labour hall, or cross the Arlington Street Bridge into the North End, still home to many small Eastern European shops that are reminiscent of an earlier era. And, as I do, my mind once in a while drifts back to vivid newspaper descriptions or political circulars from eighty years ago; to imagine the school gymnasiums of my neighbourhood packed with people to hear John Queen or S.J. Farmer; to imagine a parade of thousands of workers coming down Main Street waving red banners and singing Soviet songs; or to walk down the elm-lined streets of Wolseley or River Heights and imagine dinner conversations denouncing the dangers of the Reds and radicals.

As an adopted Winnipegger, my exploration of this history occurred as I came to know and understand the city in its current form. There were moments, such as one walking to the City of Winnipeg Archives on a bitterly cold December day, where I wondered why I could not have been interested in something just a bit more exotic. But it was the localness of the work that excited me; the ability to connect actual places with the lived experience of people in Winnipeg and to begin to understand contemporary Winnipeg better through the lens of its history.

Even though nearly eighty years have passed since the municipal campaigns discussed in this book, there is more that remains the same in Winnipeg than a few landmarks and my imaginings. Many of the challenges and conflicts outlined in this book remain today, albeit in different forms. For example, while there may be less animosity between business and labour nearly one hundred years after the General Strike, the city remains deeply divided. Divisions of race, ethnicity, and socioeconomic status continue to shape the city and its politics. The North End, which plays a central role in this book, remains the home of people on the political margins. Now, however, the marginalized Ukrainian and Jewish populations that called the North End home in the 1920s and 1930s have been replaced by Aboriginal Canadians and newcomers from Asia and Africa. These new communities face many of the same challenges as their predecessors in the neighbourhood: racial discrimination, limited employment opportunities, and little political power, being a few.

Winnipeg remains a city where the political left has maintained a strong presence. Yet despite success in provincial and federal elections, the left has rarely succeeded in wresting control of municipal power from the Liberal and Conservative descendants of the business leaders who united to fight the General Strike in 1919. This informal alliance has been effective at controlling the municipal agenda in Winnipeg for most of the past eighty years. Similarly to the 1920s and 1930s, the left can count on roughly a third of seats in city council, a figure usually increased only in exceptional circumstances. This often means that these councillors essentially become the unofficial opposition rather than being central to the formation of municipal policy, a role that would have been familiar to Independent Labour Party (ILP) or Communist aldermen for most of the 1920s and 1930s.

Winnipeg's mayoral races continue to be depicted as battles between the left and the right, and many parallels can be drawn between the campaigns of the 1920s and 1930s and those today. First, the city remains deeply divided between areas that support the candidates on the left and right. The electoral result in most neighbourhoods is easily predicted, with neighbourhoods won handily by one candidate or another. Second, the candidate on the left often faces accusations of being beholden to a political party, the New Democratic Party (NDP), while the candidate on the right is generally not perceived of as having party ties, even if they too are actively involved in a political party. This was regularly the case in the 1920s and 1930s, when accusations of partisanship were levelled against the ILP, but not against their business-oriented opponents, who in many ways acted as a party in all but name. And finally, there is often a great deal of fear generated about what might happen if the candidate on the left were to win. Just as in the 1920s and 1930s, the potential victory of a left-leaning candidate is cast as a harbinger of tax hikes and economic stagnation. This leads to movements to unite the right to prevent this from occurring, a phenomenon that has been a factor in Winnipeg's municipal politics for the past eighty years.

While many of the issues that city council faced in the early years of the twentieth century have long since been settled, divisions continue over issues such as taxation, public transportation, the arguably disproportionate lack of municipal services in core neighbourhoods, and the role of government in addressing societal issues. In particular, a key issue in recent years has been the relationship between public and private services. This debate has been similar to the debates of earlier decades, with its focus on public control of services, workers' rights, the long-term nature of contracts with private companies, and the profiting of these companies from municipal services. Even over a span of eighty years, the dividing lines in the city over these issues have remained essentially the same.

A key difference in the geography of the city between the twenty-first century and the twentieth century is the role of suburban politics, a change that began with the unification of Winnipeg and its surrounding municipalities in 1972. Less than half of municipal wards today were even part of the City of Winnipeg prior to amalgamation. As a result, instead of the north-south split of the early twentieth century, the city's current divisions now better resemble a donut. No longer is the essential political division in the city along Portage Avenue or the Assiniboine River. Indeed, often the central neighbourhoods that used to comprise the City of Winnipeg, neighbourhoods that would have once found themselves on opposite sides of nearly every election, vote similarly to each other. There are still divisions in the city, but the political landscape has shifted as the suburbs have gained political power.

In comparison with its past, there is also a distinct lack of big-picture political and socioeconomic debate within Winnipeg's contemporary municipal politics. Campaigns are tepid affairs spent debating the adequacy of snow removal or the location of dog parks. While many of the political activities outlined in this book were pragmatic and rooted in the realities of Winnipeg's working class, many municipal campaigners also had a larger goal in mind, whether it was a cooperative commonwealth or proletarian revolution. There is now, it would appear, limited space in public discourse for broader conversations of our socioeconomic relationships with each other.

I do not think that this is a history whose importance is limited to Winnipeg. There is much that can be learned about the history of the left, the role of the left in municipal politics, and the relationships between those of different political stripes. There is much that is similar between what occurred in Winnipeg and events that transpired in other Canadian cities. Nevertheless, while this story is applicable beyond the city limits of Winnipeg, it is a history rooted in neighbourhoods and the people who lived in them. It is also a history that parallels many contemporary events. As uncovering this history was for me part of coming to learn about my adopted city, I hope that this book will not only shed light on the history of the political left but also help people come to understand and imagine Winnipeg, both its past and its present, in new ways.

WE'RE GOING TO RUN THIS CITY

INTRODUCTION

Tensions were high as thousands of Winnipeg workers gathered in Market Square, just outside city hall, on 21 June 1919. Only days earlier key strike leaders had been arrested and imprisoned. It would be that fateful Saturday, "Bloody Saturday," that marked a final turning point of the six-week-old strike. After Mayor Charles Gray read the Riot Act, the North West Mounted Police charged the crowd of workers, the thunder of horse hoofs, the crack of rifles, the thud of billy clubs and baseball bats emanating across downtown. The power of the state, supported by several hundred deputized "special police," was on full display. As night fell, the strike was essentially broken. Along with it, two strikers had been killed and thirty injured. The Winnipeg General Strike, a six-week struggle that had inspired sympathy strikes across the country and empowered Winnipeg's workers to essentially take control of their city, was over.

For most, this is where the story ends. Five days later workers returned to their jobs and Winnipeg slowly returned to capitalist normality. Generations of historians have since been left to debate whether the strike was a success or failure, whether its goal was reform or revolution. It has been the focus of monographs and essays, documentary films, artwork, songs, and even a musical. There is something about the audacity, length, and size of the General Strike that continues to capture public and scholarly attention. It is a unique story in Canada's labour history. Yet, in the history of Winnipeg's political left, the strike slots in somewhere closer to the beginning of the story, rather than as a definitive end. It may be hard to see past the shadow of such an event, but there would be much more to come in the decades to follow.

When the strike ended in the summer of 1919, its underlying causes did not disappear. Workers in Winnipeg continued to experience a city profoundly divided along class lines. Housing shortages that had begun during the First World War would worsen throughout the interwar years. Many were forced to live in high-cost, overcrowded apartments and tenements. When workers lost their jobs, which many did in the economic downturn after the First World War and again a decade later during the Great Depression, restrictive municipal regulations limited their ability to access unemployment relief. For recent immigrants, accessing relief could even result in deportation. Meanwhile, business taxes remained among the lowest in Canada, while taxes were comparatively high for working-class homes.

1. Overcrowded, poor quality housing was a reality for many Winnipeggers, especially the city's Eastern European immigrants. (Archives of Manitoba, N2438)

Consequently, even after the strike ended, battle lines remained. But unlike the spring and summer of 1919, these issues would not be fought again through industrial action, at least not to the same degree that they had been that fateful summer. Instead, municipal politics became a focal point for the struggle of working-class Winnipeggers and the political left. It was in the municipal political arena where the Independent Labour Party (ILP) and the Communist Party of Canada (CPC) would work towards an alternative vision of Winnipeg than the one advanced by decades of pro-business municipal leaders. Rooted in working-class neighbourhoods, and led by many of the same individuals who had been instrumental in the General Strike, the political left would focus on municipal politics as a way to create change in the city.

A familiar opponent remained. The "Citizens," the political descendants of the Citizens' Committee of One Thousand from the General Strike, would continue to advance pro-business policies that would affect the lives of working-class Winnipeggers. It would be in the council chamber in city hall that old rivals would clash once again.

Canadians seem to be, for the most part, apathetic toward municipal politics. Most Canadian mayoral elections are decided with turnouts well under 50 percent. Except for the occasional municipal scandal, federal and provincial politics take up most of the news headlines and citizens rarely engage in an active way with local politics. You might see protests against federal or provincial policies, but rarely do you see a march on city hall. In contemporary politics, potholes, photo radar, and snow clearance dominate municipal affairs—necessary, but not usually inspiring or transformative.

Nevertheless, there are many reasons why we should pay attention to municipal politics or even place the "city at the centre rather than the periphery" of history.[1] First, it is the level of government that most affects the lives of Canadians. Municipal governments deal with practical issues that affect our day-to-day lives: the roads we drive on, the water we drink, the collection of our trash. This was even more true in the 1920s and 1930s, when the scope of municipal jurisdiction was broader than it is today. Winnipeg City Council was responsible for issues that are now federal or provincial responsibilities, unemployment relief being one of the most significant. The city also had a role to play in the provision of social services and employment programs in addition to the array of services we have come to expect from our municipal governments. Consequently, control over municipal decision making could make a difference in the lives of working-class Winnipeggers, something that the political left in the city recognized.

2. Jailed leaders of the Winnipeg General Strike. Back row, left to right: Roger Bray, George Armstrong, John Queen, R.B. Russell, R.J. Johns, and William Pritchard. Front row, left to right: William Ivens and A.A. Heaps. (Archives of Manitoba, N12322)

A second reason why we should explore municipal politics in a historical context is that people in the 1920s and 1930s cared about municipal politics. Analysis of this pivotal period in Canadian history would be incomplete without it. The mainstream press provided detailed reporting of city council meetings and municipal election campaigns. News reports were filled with stories of packed houses to listen to lively political debates and dirty tricks to interrupt opponents' meetings. *The Weekly News*, the newspaper of Winnipeg's Independent Labour Party, also dedicated significant coverage to labour's municipal representatives and their campaigns. This meant that municipal elections were opportunities to debate public policy, extending beyond the issues of the day and into broader political questions about the nature of the capitalist economy. The political left recognized this: municipal politics could be used to raise key issues, create public support, and demand change.

Third, we should try to understand municipal politics as we study the history of the political left in Canada, because it was at the municipal level that the left experienced electoral success in the 1920s and 1930s. Although municipal elections were usually won by pro-business Citizen candidates, Winnipeg elected a labour mayor in 1922, only three years after the General Strike. Twelve years later, the political left elected enough aldermen and a mayor to hold a majority of seats on city council. In Winnipeg we can see what a labour party did when in power, something that had happened only rarely in Canadian history prior to that point. This is a unique opportunity to understand the challenges that the political left faced when in power, the deep divides between different factions of the left, and how the policies advanced by the political left were able to make real changes in the lives of working-class Winnipeggers.

Winnipeg was not the only city throughout the 1920s and 1930s where the left actively engaged in municipal politics. Indeed, in 1920 alone one report indicates that across Canada 271 labour candidates ran for office in forty-four municipalities and 111 candidates were elected.[2] In the Maritimes, the left achieved successes in small mining communities such as Glace Bay, Nova Scotia, as well as larger communities such as Moncton, New Brunswick. In Ontario, several communities elected municipal candidates from the political left, including Hamilton, St. Catharines, Peterborough, and Welland. Meanwhile, in Edmonton, the Dominion Labour Party–endorsed mayoral candidate, Joe Clarke, won the election in 1918 and again in 1919.[3] While labour-affiliated candidates would lose some momentum with the economic rebound of the late 1920s, the 1930s saw labour candidates winning in places like Toronto, Edmonton, Calgary, and Regina. Across the country, in cities large and small, the political left won victories in municipal elections.

As such, the study of the political left at the municipal level gives historians a new vantage point from which to explore and understand the left's activities and ideology. In his work on communists, James R. Barrett describes local studies as having an "unparalleled and largely unfulfilled opportunity to grasp the Communist Party as most participants and those around them experienced it."[4] It would have been through municipal campaigns and politicians at a local level that many Winnipeggers would have come to know of the Communist Party and accepted or rejected its politics. This was not only true for communists. It was at the municipal level that many Winnipeggers across the political left engaged with and experienced politics.

Yet despite the potential insights that can be gained through an examination of the role of the left in municipal politics, little has been written about the role of the left in municipal politics during this era. There are some exceptions; Brandon, Regina, and Calgary being notable in western Canada.[5] Often, however, the presence of the left on municipal councils is mentioned but not discussed, as historians focus on provincial or federal politics or industrial action.

Finally, exploring the role of the political left in Winnipeg's municipal politics also provides a lens into a key question about the very nature of parliamentary political activity—could a party seeking an alternative future do so through existing government systems, could parties on the left remain true to their ideals as they fought elections or played politics in the council chamber? Or, as Ian McKay has written, "how could leftists withstand the co-optive strategies of the liberals and hang on to the core vision of a new world?"[6] Would political parties on the left be drawn to the glow of immediate political power while setting aside bigger visions for a co-operative commonwealth or dictatorship of the proletariat? Would the parties on the left be able to effect change while working within a system created by, and in many ways for, their opponents? These are among the many questions that can be asked as we explore the role of the left in municipal politics.

In a 1918 strike that served as a precursor to the larger strike of 1919, Sam Blumenberg, a prominent local socialist who would be deported after the General Strike in 1919, declared, "We are going to run this city."[7] Seats on city council likely were not what Blumenberg had in mind. But by 1935, the political left did "run the city," and many of those elected to council were veterans of Winnipeg's earlier labour conflicts. It may have been imperfect control, limited in many ways by structures shaped through decades of rule by pro-business councils. It may not have lasted long, as within two years Citizens once again would hold a majority of seats on city council, but control it was. Not long after the placards from the General Strike were discarded, it was through the ballot box that the political left would seek control of the city.

As soon as the General Strike in Winnipeg ended in 1919, people began trying to interpret what it had meant. Indeed, Nolan Reilly has suggested that "no other single event in Canadian labour history has received the attention historians have showered upon the Winnipeg General Strike."[8] Was it a revolutionary moment? A pragmatic new tactic in the fight for collective bargaining? A sign of a uniquely western radicalism? These debates have been the fodder for substantial historiographical discussion. They also can affect how we understand municipal politics in Winnipeg in the years following the Strike.

In the early days after the Strike, both the Citizens and labour movement tried to define what exactly had occurred in the summer of 1919. For the Citizens, the General Strike had not just been a simple labour dispute but an attempt to overthrow the state, although they allowed that not all the participants in the strike were necessarily aware of their role in bringing on a soviet Canada. Conversely, labour publications after the Strike emphasized union recognition and collective bargaining and denied any attempts to overthrow the government.[9] Naturally, both had something to gain from these interpretations. Citizens sought to legitimize their anti-Strike actions, just as labour sought to legitimize the Strike itself.

For many years, historians largely agreed that the General Strike was not a revolutionary act, but rather was a reaction to local economic conditions. This argument was made by D.C. Masters in the first monograph published on the Strike in 1950 and later that decade by W.L. Morton in *Manitoba: A History*. In the 1970s, Norman Penner articulated that the Strike was "really a trade-union struggle" making very specific economic demands.[10] David Bercuson also clearly stated that the Strike was not revolutionary, saying it "was not a revolution and was never planned to be one."[11] Instead it was rooted, he said, in the effects of immigration, economic depression, and war, which had further polarized classes in Winnipeg, and in an attempt to achieve union recognition and increased wages. Furthermore, wrote Bercuson, the Strike was essentially Western Canadian in nature, rooted in a western radicalism that was opposed by more conservative eastern Canadian unionists.[12] In achieving its pragmatic goals, Bercuson said, the strike was a complete failure, resulting in neither better wages nor union recognition.

Since then, historians have re-evaluated the nature of the General Strike. Several historians have argued that the Strike was not indicative of a uniquely western radicalism (as opposed to eastern conservatism in the labour movement) but was part of a radical politics growing across the country.[13] This argument further suggests that there was revolutionary potential in the actions of 1919. Craig Heron suggested that "while revolt is not necessarily a revolution, it is implicitly and overtly a challenge to the structures of bourgeois power and the forms of workers' subordination."[14] This challenge was exemplified in the General Strike, which was one of the most public manifestations of what has been described as a nationwide revolt by labour.

In his book, *Reasoning Otherwise*, Ian McKay points out that while the Winnipeg General Strike—or as he refers to it, the "Winnipeg Revolt"—was certainly at least in part about labour issues, these could have, as they had been before and were elsewhere, been handled without a General Strike. As such, he says, the Strike was "at least partly an attempt to form a new historical bloc—to expand a vocabulary (and identity) based on the working-class."[15] In doing so, the Strike was for collective bargaining while still being a revolutionary act. McKay suggests that Winnipeg demonstrated a city run by workers was not chaos and, as the Strike organizers operated in a remarkably democratic and participatory manner, the Strike represented "a conscious attempt to imagine what new relations of freedom would look like in the post-capitalist future."[16]

What do these differing interpretations of the Strike mean for understanding what came after? While the General Strike of 1919 has drawn academic and popular attention, it would be the struggle in the city council chambers over the decades that followed that defined Winnipeg during the 1920s and 1930s. Indeed, one of the key outcomes of the Strike was the mobilization of Winnipeg's political left in the municipal political arena. D.C. Masters, for example, argued that the Strike gave labour a "sense of solidarity and effectiveness" and put power in the hands of those who favoured electoral, rather than industrial, action.[17] J.E. Rea, one of the few historians to study the Strike's political aftermath in detail, also indicated that even when the Strike was over, "the passions it provoked would not be allayed for many years to come."[18] More recently, Michael Dupuis has identified that one of the positive outcomes of the Strike was establishing labour as a political force in the city.[19] Yet, despite the frequent mentions of the solidarity and passions of future years, little scholarship has been done on the post-Strike period.

David Bercuson has criticized the perspective that the Strike was so cataclysmic as to define the politics of the city for decades to come. The problem with saying that the Strike caused decades of division, he wrote, was that class polarization in Winnipeg existed long before the Strike. The Strike did not create a polarized environment, it was a sign of it.[20] Indeed, Bercuson argues that the "strike brought only defeat and the sapping of the strength of the Winnipeg labour movement for years to come so that it could offer little or no resistance to the employer counter-offensives of the 1920s."[21]

It is true that the tactic of a General Strike was never again used in Winnipeg, that the labour movement in Winnipeg was divided by the legacy of the Strike, and that the Strike did not create the class divisions that divided Winnipeg. However, while the Strike did not create divisions, it reinforced them and was a catalyst for political action based on those divisions. As Alan Artibise has written, the Strike "crystallized in one occurrence the tensions that had been developing in the community since its inception."[22] After the Strike, political parties on the left were far more successful than they had been before it. The Strike served as a unifying force for the city's diverse working-class community, and while there would be divisions between ethnic groups and between different parties on the left, it served as a reminder of the division between Winnipeg's business elites and the working class for years to come. Much of the rhetoric used by both the political left and their opponents over the next twenty years would point back to this key moment.

The Strike also created opportunities for a new generation of leadership. Leaders like F.W. Dixon, J.S. Woodsworth, S.J. Farmer, and John Queen all would play prominent roles after the General Strike, whereas Arthur Puttee, the first ever Labour MP, would be sidelined by this new generation of leadership.[23] Puttee—who had played a prominent role in local politics before the

Strike, having been involved in the founding of the Trades Council, *The Voice* newspaper, and the city's first Labour party—was never a factor afterwards.[24] He sought the Dominion Labour Party's nomination for mayor in 1920 but was defeated by S.J. Farmer. Conversely, Woodsworth, Farmer, and Queen would all go on to have long political careers municipally, provincially, and federally.

The General Strike, and the polarized atmosphere that continued in Winnipeg municipal politics afterwards, also seemed to foreclose the possibility of broader reform movements in Winnipeg in the 1920s and 1930s, at least at a municipal level. While active reform movements in Winnipeg and other Canadian cities in the early part of the twentieth century had drawn leadership from professionals, businessmen, middle-class women, and churches, and had often included the participation of working-class people, this was rarely the case in the 1920s and 1930s.[25] Indeed, the General Strike and the subsequent rise of the political left were strongly opposed by many of the professional and business leaders who had earlier called for reforms. While Winnipeg's elites did not agree on all issues, all were committed to the success of the liberal and capitalist state and sustaining the existing social order.[26] On issues ranging from unemployment relief to municipalization of utilities, Citizen aldermen tended to vote as a bloc for the status quo. There was little room on a divided council for collaboration.

In short, those six weeks in the summer of 1919 would have a dramatic effect on Winnipeg, with its repercussions reverberating through municipal politics for the next twenty years. It defined the vocabulary that the political left (and their opponents) used, polarized the political landscape to the point that there would be disagreement on almost every key issue in the city, and created the political space for the leadership that would define the ILP and CPC in the 1920s and 1930s. As Mitchell and Naylor have suggested, the Strike would shape the world view of Winnipeg's working class for years to come.[27]

The contest of Winnipeg municipal politics throughout the early twentieth century was defined by the social and economic divisions that dominated the city. Winnipeg's elite in the early twentieth century had imagined the city as a place that was prosperous and meritocratic, a place with strong roots to Britain and empire.[28] This vision, however, did not come to pass. By the 1920s and 1930s, Winnipeg was a city divided along ethnic, class, and political lines. Divisions between rich and poor, those of British origin and those from elsewhere, were manifested in many ways in the types of housing, education, work, and recreation that Winnipeggers could enjoy. These overlapping divisions would have a profound effect on the city, its residents, and possibilities for political change.

Winnipeg had grown rapidly in the early decades of the twentieth century. The city had all the appearances of a boom town, tripling in size in the first decade. Businesses flocked to the city to service the growing population of Winnipeg and the Canadian West. Manufacturers, wholesalers, and retailers opened in the city, establishing it as the preeminent commercial hub of western Canada. The city also profited from the growing agricultural production of the Prairies as the home of the grain exchange and many companies producing agricultural implements and supplies. Optimism abounded, anything was possible. Civic boosters imagined Winnipeg as the "Chicago of the North," a world-class city.

That became the commonly accepted narrative of the city's growth. Indeed, many Winnipeggers did become quite wealthy during those boom years and there was significant economic opportunity for those who were able to access it. But many of those drawn to Winnipeg would not share in this prosperity. Those that worked in the railway yards, manufacturers, and industries that sprung up to support this new city and its growth remained vulnerable in low paying jobs with little job security. Often, these people were also recent immigrants to Winnipeg as, by 1921, Winnipeg was Canada's most diverse city.[29]

Ethnic diversity would be a key component to Winnipeg's social and political life. First, the city was geographically divided based on ethnicity. The North End would be the new home for many recent arrivals to the city, particularly from Eastern Europe. Nearly 90 percent of Winnipeg's Jewish population lived in the North End, along with the majority of the city's Ukrainian community.[30] Meanwhile, British labourers and the city's elite tended to live south of the railway tracks that divided the North End from the rest of the city.[31]

Occupation had strong connections to ethnicity. In a study comparing occupation with ethnic origin, Daniel Hiebert found that 89 percent of people classified as "capitalists," 88 percent of managers and professionals, and 88 percent of other white-collar workers were of British origin, even though 72 percent of city residents were British. Meanwhile, 30 percent of the city's Ukrainian men worked in railway yards, 10 percent in iron shops, and 10 percent in meat packers—in short, blue-collar, unskilled jobs. The Jewish community was highly overrepresented in some manufacturing and retail sectors. Even though only 6.5 percent of Winnipeg's population was Jewish, 68 percent of furriers, 72 percent of hawkers and peddlars, 35 percent of tailors, and 33 percent of retail merchants were Jewish.[32]

Life was not easy for these Eastern European immigrants. Ethnic discrimination was common, particularly after the First World War and the Russian Revolution. Many community members of British origin blamed the challenges faced by immigrants on the perceived moral failings of the immigrants themselves, who they thought had brought with them un-British social ills from their home countries.[33] And since many of these immigrants were working in low-paying, blue-collar jobs, "most individuals faced ethnic discrimination, class exploitation, or a combination of the two."[34] Immigrants often struggled to find steady, adequately paying employment, but were also at risk of deportation should they be forced to rely on relief. People lived in poor-quality housing, worked in dangerous jobs, and faced other challenges such as high disease rates. For example, in the North End in 1912, the infant mortality rate amongst central and southern Europeans was 372 per 1,000 births, well over three times the rate of the city's south (predominantly British) side.[35]

A study of housing conditions in Winnipeg demonstrates the clear differences between the North End and more affluent parts of the city. The report, published by the Assistant Chief Health Inspector, examined five case study districts across the city. In District 1, located in what is now the Wolseley neighbourhood, 96 percent of the population was Canadian, British, or American born. The heads of families in this neighbourhood worked primarily at white-collar jobs such as office workers, clerks, agents, and as professionals such as doctors and dentists. As a result, 60 percent of men earned $150 or more per month, while only 6 percent earned less than $100 per month. Since these families earned substantial incomes they also lived in relatively large houses. Fewer than one in five families had three rooms or less, with an average of 6.1 rooms per family.

By comparison, District 5 in the study, located between Alfred and Selkirk Avenues and McKenzie and Salter Streets in the heart of the North End, was overwhelmingly non-British, low-income, and lived in much smaller houses. Only 13 percent of residents in this district were British, Canadian, or American born, while over two-thirds were categorized as Russian (although many of these would have been Ukrainian or other Eastern Europeans). Nearly half of families lived in three rooms or less, and the average population per room was almost twice as high as in District 1—an average of 1.1 people per room. Meanwhile, North End residents earned substantially less money than those in south Winnipeg. Over half of men earned less than $100 per month, with only 8 percent earning more than $150 per month. Not surprisingly, these men worked primarily in blue-collar jobs, with over a quarter of men described as labourers and many others working in building trades, or as railway employees, mechanics, and plumbers.[36]

Ethnic societies were key to the lived experience of Winnipeg's North End residents. By 1921, each major ethnic group had a mutual savings and health benefit society, and many had educational programs, choirs, theatre groups, newspapers, social societies, religious orders, and left-wing groups.[37] These groups were integral to not only the social lives of recent immigrants but would also play key roles in the establishment of, and support for, political action, much of which was rooted in organizations such as the Ukrainian Labour Farmer Temple Association (ULFTA). However, Winnipeg's immigrants were grossly underrepresented in local politics. Between 1874 and 1914, only five aldermen were non-Anglo-Saxon, of which two were Jewish, two were Icelanders, and one was Ukrainian.[38]

With the dawn of the First World War, immigration, which had contributed to nearly all of Winnipeg's population growth in the first decade of the twentieth century, slowed substantially. It would recover somewhat during the 1920s but a decade later, as the city faced economic depression, immigration would slow to a trickle. As a result, between 1921 and 1941 the percentage of people in Winnipeg who were foreign born would drop from 47 percent to 35 percent.[39] Immigration slowed during the 1920s before coming to an almost complete halt during the 1930s. Not only had the major source of population growth in the city itself slowed, but the need for the many services Winnipeg businesses had provided to new immigrants across the Canadian West had as well. Winnipeg was still a major centre, but without much of the buoyant optimism that had marked its earlier growth.

Winnipeg struggled economically after the First World War. A recession set in from 1919 that did not lift until the mid-1920s. There were several reasons for this. With the development of the Panama Canal and increased shipping through Vancouver, the railway through Winnipeg was no longer as essential to the Canadian economy. Other western Canadian cities were also growing, increasing competition for Winnipeg's manufacturers and wholesalers who had previously supplied much of western Canada. Finally, locally owned retailers were being challenged by national and international chain stores, the result often being reduced employment opportunities.[40] This not only affected local businesses but also the labourers who worked in them. Unemployment increased in Winnipeg in the early 1920s, putting stress on the city's unemployment relief system.

Winnipeg's economy would pick up again in the late 1920s, as railway construction resumed and resource and agricultural development continued in rural and northern Manitoba.[41] Winnipeg's strong economic performance in the late 1920s, however, was overshadowed by the even faster growth of other western Canadian cities. Soon new firms were challenging Winnipeg wholesalers and manufacturers. New transportation structures made it cheaper for firms to ship directly from eastern Canada to western cities rather than shipping first to a wholesaler in Winnipeg. The result was that the wholesale industry, which had been a staple of the Winnipeg economy for the first two decades of the twentieth century, began to decline, particularly relative to the growth of other western Canadian centres. But the growth of other cities was not all bad news for Winnipeg. The construction boom across the Canadian West meant new markets for construction products and manufactured goods produced in Winnipeg.

The boom of the 1920s was to be short-lived. By the end of the decade, Winnipeg was surpassed by Vancouver as the biggest city in western Canada. Rapidly growing urban centres in Alberta and Saskatchewan challenged Winnipeg's once dominant role in the economy of western Canada. Consequently, the 1920s and 1930s were a period of adjustment in Winnipeg. Gone were the days of rapid population growth, massive building projects, and visions of grandeur. Gone were the days when all roads led to Winnipeg. Yet Winnipeg also would continue to play a major role in western Canada's economy, shaping and being shaped by the economic and social forces around it as the Great Depression settled in.

When the Great Depression swept across North America, Winnipeg was hit hard. While the 1930s were economically challenging times across Canada, a 1937 report by Graham Towers, the president of the Bank of Canada, found that Manitobans had been worse affected than most of the rest of the country.[42] At first the city went relatively unscathed through the early shockwaves of 1929 and even into the early months of 1930, but the signs of decline were many. Winnipeg had built its economy on servicing resource industries that were among the hardest hit by the economic depression. As Alan Artibise has described it, there was a "virtual cessation of developmental activity throughout the west."[43] The result was economic collapse. Businesses closed and many workers lost their jobs or were significantly underemployed. For example, in 1929, the value of industrial products produced in the city was $109.3 million. By 1932, this had fallen to $56.4 million, just over half as much as a few years earlier. While this would grow slightly over the next few years, it would take the Second World War for industrial production to hit 1920s levels again.[44]

A prominent example of the economic collapse in Winnipeg was a new office tower planned by James Richardson for the corner of Portage and Main. The new building was to be a foundational component of Winnipeg's famed central artery. All was well when work started in the summer of 1929. The building that had previously been on the site was demolished and excavation work began for the foundation of the building that fall. By winter, however, construction was halted. Richardson had lost significant amounts of money in the stock market crash and the construction project was cancelled. Eventually the excavation would be filled in, a gas station taking the place of the skyscraper.[45]

James Richardson was not the only person to cancel construction plans in Winnipeg. Throughout the city, construction plunged. The average number of buildings built per year in the 1930s was less than half that of the 1920s, and about a third of what it had been during the boom years in the early part of the century. For example, at the peak of development in 1912, 5,328 buildings were constructed with a total value of $20.6 million. By comparison, in 1935 only 884 buildings were constructed with a total value of approximately $700,000.[46]

Construction may have stopped on James Richardson's tower, but it would be Winnipeg's working-class families, many of whom lived in the North End, who would suffer most from the Depression. Unemployment rose quickly, and many families were now dependent on unemployment relief while many more were underemployed. As wages fell, Winnipeggers also struggled to pay for basic necessities. A housing shortage led to increasing rents and many were forced to live in increasingly deplorable and crowded conditions. Not surprisingly, this had a major impact on the city. Unemployment relief was a municipal responsibility. Economic instability and poor housing would be a reality for Winnipeg's working class, particularly the North End's large unskilled labour force, during the 1930s.

This book will trace the history of the political left in Winnipeg through the interwar years, culminating with the two years it held power in 1935 and 1936. Throughout, it will focus on the parties on the political left in Winnipeg, their key leaders, and the motivations and challenges that these parties faced. Additionally, it will address the deep divides that existed in Winnipeg between the ILP and CPC. While the membership of these two parties shared some historic connections, and while they often worked with each other and voted together in city council, there was also tremendous animosity within the left during much of this period.

After providing an introduction to the key parties in Winnipeg municipal politics, the book will pick up the story of the political left with the election of S.J. Farmer to the mayoralty of Winnipeg in November 1922. Farmer, who was the city's first labour mayor, would hold two one-year terms. Coming only three years after the General Strike, Farmer's opponent in the 1922 election described a Farmer mayoralty as a potential "reign of fury" that threatened catastrophe for the city. Farmer was mayor for two years, but a reign of fury never came. In many ways Farmer was a moderate and respectable mayor who was able to win the support of Winnipeggers. Yet he was also able to in some small ways create change in the city, even when faced with a strongly pro-Citizen council.

Whether it was eliminating the pauper burial ground or advancing the cause of public ownership of municipal utilities, Farmer worked to address some of the key social inequities that existed in early 1920s Winnipeg, but the change that he was able to achieve was limited.

At this point, the book will shift attention from the ILP to the newcomers on the political left in Winnipeg, the CPC, exploring the aldermanic careers of their aldermen in the 1920s and 1930s. Two years after the defeat of Farmer, another historic event happened in Winnipeg's municipal election. Winnipeg elected William Kolisnyk, reputed to be the first communist elected to office in North America. Kolisnyk would remain on council for four years, where he advanced a variety of key communist issues, from unemployment relief to reducing deportations. Kolisnyk was a leader in the city's large Ukrainian community, and ethnic politics were an important part of his strategy. However, he would also be frequently embroiled in controversy, even within his own party, and was defeated in 1930.

The next communist aldermen would have much longer aldermanic careers. Jacob Penner (first elected in 1933) and Martin Forkin (elected in 1934) would each serve as aldermen for the North End for nearly thirty years, becoming fixtures in local politics. This chapter will focus on their earliest years on city council, exploring the position of the communist aldermen vis-à-vis others on the political left and how the communist aldermen understood their role on city council. The careers of Penner and Forkin highlight how profoundly loyal party members could also be dedicated to and driven by a local constituency, in this case the North End, rather than orders from thousands of miles away, a challenge to traditional historiography that focused on Soviet domination over local independence.

While communists invested a lot of energy in municipal politics, the issue of "revolution" was one that frequently came up during the 1920s and 1930s. Revolution was an explicit part of the communist promise. Their goal was not to tinker with the existing system but to overthrow it entirely. This book will explore the revolutionary rhetoric employed by local communists, both elected municipal officials and other Party members, as well as claims by provincial and federal police that Winnipeg communists had more revolutionary plans than sitting on city council. In short, while some local communists did speak of insurrectionary revolution in an imminent sense, elected officials like Penner saw revolution as a long-term project, one that they did not even necessarily think they would see in their lifetime.

3. A 1931 demonstration outside city hall calling for the release of political prisoners. Notice the heavy police presence, a common feature of communist rallies. (AUUC-WBA Archives)

Throughout these chapters focused on communist aldermen and the CPC, the ILP remains ever present. The communists and ILP were frequently in conflict but often cooperated on city council. While these parties employed different language, strategies, and philosophies, they both advanced a vision of the city alternative to that proposed by their Citizen opponents. Therefore, while the focus of the book shifts from one party to the other, both parties are represented in each chapter.

The climax of this story is the election of a council in Winnipeg in November 1934 that included both a labour mayor, John Queen, and a labour majority on city council. This result, which came as a shock to Winnipeg's business community, would have profound implications as over the next two years, labour had, in one sense, control of the city. This chapter will explore what the political left did with this unprecedented opportunity. Much was possible. New programs were introduced that humanized unemployment relief and raised taxes on big businesses. But there was also significant disappointment. The structures that were in place limited the political left's ability to create change and the fiscal restraints of the Great Depression limited their ability to fully implement an alternative vision.

We often forget that municipal politics are a place where profound change can be made. By winning in municipal politics, the political left believed it could improve conditions for the unemployed, support organized labour, rebalance the city's tax burden, reduce deportations and police intimidation, call for more inclusive voting rights, and address an acute housing shortage. Whether these politicians came from the ILP or the CPC, the individuals in this book genuinely believed that a more just world was possible and were willing to make tremendous sacrifices to make it happen. This may not have been flashy or glamorous. There will be no musical or documentary films made about twenty years of motions and resolutions in city council. Yet it has been suggested that "the counter-hegemonic challenge (of the General Strike) had not been killed that day (Bloody Saturday) on 21 June 1919."[47] Over the next twenty years, members of the ILP and CPC would continue the counter-hegemonic challenge, envisioning a different kind of city, and they would do it through their involvement in municipal politics.

CHAPTER 1

THE SECOND ROUND

Less than five months after the General Strike came to an end, the city was once again embroiled in class conflict, although this time the fight was to be waged at the ballot box instead of the picket line. This was not the first time that labour candidates were running for office. However, between 1874 and 1914 only three of 515 elected aldermen could be considered to be labour representatives and there was not a history of running a labour candidate in mayoral elections.[1] In the early twentieth century, labour parties regularly ran unsuccessful municipal election campaigns, constrained by disinterest amongst workers and restrictive voting rules that prevented many Winnipeg workers from voting.[2] It was not until the election of Dick Rigg in 1913, under the banner of the Labour Representation Committee, a combined effort of the Social Democratic Party and labourites, that labour would have a regular presence on city council.[3] While this number would grow during the First World War, with the election of future leaders such as John Queen (1882–1946) and A.A. Heaps (1885–1954), labour still remained in the minority at city hall.

This would be the first of many elections that would be fought along the lines that had been defined in the General Strike: Citizens and labour. In an election described as "one of the most fiercely contested municipal elections in the history of twentieth century Canada,"[4] a newly empowered working class would nearly upset the balance of power in the city through the ballot box. Labour saw the importance of this election, as government had played an important role in defeating the General Strike of that summer. A letter to the editor in the *Western Labour News* by P. Callaghan pointed to the importance of electoral victory: "Wake up Mr. Worker! You put the present government in. You are to blame. Are you going to repeat your blunder, or have you learned your lesson through the strike?"[5] The strike had drawn attention to the key role that municipal and other levels of government could play in supporting, or damaging, the goals of labour.

Early in his campaign, labour's mayoralty candidate S.J. Farmer (1878–1951) acknowledged what everyone already knew. "This civic election," he declared at a large campaign gathering, "is the second round of the strike which took place last May and June."[6] Furthermore, he declared on a different occasion, "the strike taught labor the necessity of representation on the city council.

We will set a beacon on fire in Winnipeg that will be seen by all workers in Canada."[7] This effort drew the unprecedented unity of several labour parties, the Dominion Labour Party, Social Democratic Party, and the Ex-Soldiers' and Sailors' Labour Party, which all joined forces in a single campaign.

For labour candidates, the November 1919 election was a chance to right some of the losses from the Strike and to improve the living standards of Winnipeg's working class. Labour candidates trumpeted tax relief for any property valued at less than $3,000, a measure which would have lifted much of the working class off the municipal tax rolls and shifted the tax burden on to larger home owners. They also sought to re-hire 200 civic employees who had been fired for their role in the summer's Strike and called for the ability of civic employees to participate in outside unions. Additionally, Farmer called for municipal trading (such as milk distribution), a municipal house-building scheme, and the elimination of tax exemptions for the city's railways. But beyond the immediate issues at hand, labour candidates often spoke of an end to a broad system of bondage and discrimination in which property was held superior to human well-being. Farmer declared that the real issue of the campaign was "whether the people of Winnipeg are content to be dominated by an old system which keeps them in slavery and maintains itself by fraud, or whether they will turn to progressive people in the community and march onward with truth."[8]

S.J. Farmer had not actually been labour's first candidate for mayor. William Ivens, the leader of the Labour Church and a long-time labour advocate, was the first choice of the voting delegates, winning by a narrow margin of 222 to 206. Ivens, who was on a speaking tour of Ontario at the time, refused the nomination and threw his support behind Farmer, telegraphing back to the convention gathered in Winnipeg, "Thank you for the vote of confidence. It was a complete surprise. Cannot possibly accept the nomination."[9] Farmer, who had narrowly lost the first ballot, was selected as labour's mayoral candidate for 1919 in his place. Interestingly, neither Farmer nor Ivens were labourers themselves, although both had long histories of involvement in local labour politics.

Farmer would be joined by a diverse group of labour candidates. The *Manitoba Free Press*, which was vocally anti-labour throughout the campaign, dismissed the slate as an "oil-and-water mixture of Socialists with Single Taxers," an alliance they claimed "could not last when confronted with the practicalities of administration."[10] Many of these candidates had had a role in the General Strike as leaders and grassroots strikers. Some, like incumbent alderman John Queen, already had experience in politics while others were political neophytes. Several of these candidates, such as Queen, Thomas Flye, and John Blumberg, would spend decades involved in municipal politics, providing a link between the earliest post-Strike campaign and the eventual victory of labour in municipal politics sixteen years later.

Labour would be opposed by the Citizens' League, comprised of fifty-six leading business and professional men.[11] The Citizens referred to the Strike even more regularly than to labour, frequently reminding *Manitoba Free Press* readers in full-page ads of the indignities of life during the General Strike. "Citizens of Winnipeg," one advertisement read, "should not forget the days when they were told that the strike committee permitted them to secure bread and milk. When the peril was facing them, the citizens united to combat it and they defeated it...Let us drive this menace from our midst." Another ad portrayed a volunteer firefighter looking hopelessly at a burning building with thirty pounds of pressure clearly indicated on his ineffective fire hose. "Is Thirty Pound Citizenship Good Enough for Winnipeg?" asked the caption, a reference to reduced water pressure during the strike.[12]

The Citizens declared that this was a critical moment in Winnipeg's history. The *Manitoba Free Press*, which sided quite publicly with the Citizens, wrote in an editorial that the election was of "vital importance to the future welfare of this city." More was at stake than a year of control of city council. The *Free Press* suggested that "a vote for the radical candidate tomorrow will be a vote in favour of an eventual radical-socialist autocracy,"[13] employing a tactic used during the General Strike of dismissing labour as radical, wild, and Soviet. One of the Citizens' many prominent full-page newspaper ads went further to describe Winnipeg under labour control as a "Would-Be Soviet."[14] The future of British-style democracy was at stake, with the results of the election to be felt "all over Canada, indeed all over the Anglo-Saxon world." In defending his mayoralty, Mayor Charles Gray declared "there is only one issue [in this campaign], whether the city is to be administered by the British traditions of law and order and equity, or by one class who are fanatics."[15] If labour candidates were to win, it was argued, not only would British traditions be in danger, but Winnipeg, as the seed of this dissent, would be an embarrassment around the world.

Consequently, according to the Citizens, Winnipeggers had a choice to make: constitutional rule or rule by radical labour. The *Manitoba Free Press* declared that "a vote cast for any of the radical-labor candidates...is a vote in favour of substituting eventual class domination for public control of the public property and services."[16] Frequently, both the media and the Citizens used the One Big Union as a bogeyman figure. The OBU, they claimed, controlled the labour candidates and, if elected, would control the city as well. Why would Winnipeggers, they asked, hand over control of their city to a class of radical outsiders, suggesting, for example, that OBU control would effectively mean that the city could not control its own police force or workers. The result, warned the *Free Press*, was "threatened or actual lawlessness, starvation, and deprivation of the public services."[17]

Finally, in a theme that would be repeated in Winnipeg for decades, Citizen supporters declared that labour candidates were dangerous for the economy, could not be trusted with money, and would scare investors away from the city. Aldermanic candidate Frank Davidson suggested, "you could not sell a bond of the city if these ultra-radicals were in control, nor would the banks retain their confidence in civic integrity for a moment."[18] Labour's promise to eliminate taxes on homes valued at less than $3,000 was seized upon by Citizens as not only financially irresponsible but as class warfare. Such an action, they declared, would have ominous consequences for the middle class and businesses that would have to make up for the lost revenue.

As election day neared, tensions were running so high that police recruited forty special police constables to keep order. Despite the concerns, election day passed peacefully and order, as the Citizens saw it, was maintained, albeit with a smaller margin than they likely hoped. Charles Gray, the mayor that led Winnipeg through the General Strike, won 56 percent of the vote over S.J. Farmer. The aldermanic results point to the divided nature of the city. Labour candidates won three of the seven seats up for grabs in the election and won 58 percent of the vote in the three northern wards. Yet the four southern wards were won convincingly by Citizen candidates, with 70 percent of the votes in those ridings. It would not be long before these results pushed city council to change the election boundaries, reshaping the city's political geography and curtailing labour's chance for political success.

The conflicts that divided Winnipeg in the summer of 1919 were alive and well not only that fall but for the coming decades. The terminology used to refer to the different sides was borrowed from the Strike. "Citizens" represented the pro-business interests of Winnipeg's elites.[19] Many of the leaders from the 1919 Strike Committee and Citizen's Committee of One Thousand would play defining roles in municipal politics. And many of the issues would remain the same, as pro-labour and pro-business representatives put forward radically different conceptions of the city. General R.Y. Patterson, a prominent local Conservative, proclaimed in a campaign speech that Winnipeg was a battleground in the fight between established institutions and socialists.[20] These divisions would continue to polarize the city throughout the 1920s and 1930s.

Municipal politics was about more than sidewalks and sewers. Key foundational understandings of the role of the city, the nature of public institutions, and even the existence of the capitalist system were all fodder for debate during local campaigns or city council meetings. Municipal politics became a venue for intense ideological debate, a place to talk about grand social visions, not just day-to-day issues. Yet it was that too. A place where grand rhetoric or revolutionary bravado ran into the very real concerns of constituents, where there was still a city to be run.

Three main political bodies would define municipal politics in Winnipeg throughout the 1920s and 1930s. On the political right were the Citizens, which existed not as a party per se, but as an alliance of Liberals and Conservatives intent on preserving the status quo: low taxes and minimal civil services. On the political left, the largest party was the Independent Labour Party (ILP). The Communist Party of Canada (CPC) also developed a strong following in the city, primarily in the North End. It is these two parties that this book will focus on, but it is also important to understand the political philosophy of their primary opponents, the Citizens.[21]

The Citizens

The political descendants of the Citizens' Committee of One Thousand, the organization formed by the local business community to fight the General Strike, took on various names during the following decades. Whether known as the Citizens' League (1919–1921), Citizens' Campaign Committee (1922), the Winnipeg Civics Association (1923–1924), the Civic Progress Association (1929–1932), the Citizens' Group (1932–1935), or the Civic Election Committee (1936–1959),[22] this alliance of Liberals and Conservatives was commonly known as the Citizens. The name, and its connection to the General Strike, is no coincidence. Many of the key leaders in the Citizens' Committee during the Strike would take on leadership roles in municipal politics as Citizens in the years to come.

The Citizens of the 1920s and 1930s shared similar aims to those of their General Strike predecessors. Their goal was to put forward a united slate of candidates to defeat labour politicians and ensure that the city was kept safely in the hands of pro-business elected officials.[23] Lloyd Stinson, who would serve as a Co-operative Commonwealth Federation (CCF)–affiliated councillor in Winnipeg, wrote, "everyone knew that the major group at City Hall was Establishment-oriented and favoured real estate and business interests as opposed to those of Labour."[24] While Citizen organization would vary over the years, "the more threatening the challenge of Labour, the more cohesive and effective the response of the Citizens' League" became.[25]

Winnipeg had had a citizens' group before in municipal politics. In 1884, the first citizen group called for improved financial management of the city. The focus was not much different nearly forty years later. The most important thing a municipal government could do, according to the Citizens, was to run a business-like, efficient administration that maintained low tax rates and minimal civic expenditures. In the words of J.G. Sullivan, "in municipal affairs I am of the belief that no municipality or government should do for me anything I can do for myself or have done by others as efficiently and more cheaply than the community or government will charge for the service."[26] As a result of Citizen dominance in municipal politics, Winnipeg maintained one of the lowest business tax rates in the country, provided tax breaks to key industries, and had restrictive unemployment relief policies.

One of the most common election refrains from the Citizens group was that governance of the city should remain non-partisan. Yet while the Citizens were not officially a political party, they shared many common characteristics, including nominating and supporting slates of candidates. Citizens stated that there was no party control—a Citizen alderman could vote how he or she wanted once they were in office—but Citizen aldermen regularly voted as a bloc, particularly on issues where the ILP took a strong opposing stance. The result was that votes on council were often split sharply along business-labour lines, with Citizens taking one side and the ILP the other.

P.H. Wichern has suggested a different interpretation of the political activities of the Citizens. He suggests that "civic boosterism," rather than anti-socialism, was the most important political goal of the Citizens.[27] Indeed, as will be seen with the career of Mayor Ralph Webb, civic boosterism was an important part of the message of the Citizens. However, Wichern moves too quickly to dismiss the anti-labour drive of Citizens. The Citizen groups were formed in response to a perceived threat from the political left (and efforts were renewed each time a new perceived threat emerged), their politicians frequently campaigned by pointing out the supposed dangers of their opponents, and Citizens generally were united against proposed policies brought forward by the ILP or CPC.

Winnipeg was not the only city to have a citizens' group active in municipal politics. In Vancouver, for example, the Non-Partisan Association (NPA) brought together Liberals and Conservatives to oppose the rise of the CCF in municipal politics in the late 1930s. Similar to Winnipeg's Citizens, the NPA condemned the participation of political parties in municipal politics (while acting much like one themselves) and sought to protect business interests in the city.[28] The business elite in other western Canadian cities such as Edmonton, Calgary, and Regina responded similarly. The rise in labour as a political force

4. Winnipeg mayor Ralph Webb. (Archives of Manitoba, Legislative Assembly 1932–1936, A0242)

was a catalyst for unity in business communities seeking to protect themselves from this new potential threat.

If the essence of Citizen ideology was captured in one man, it would have been Ralph Webb, whose lengthy reign as mayor (from 1925 to 1927 and 1930 to 1934) exacerbated political rifts between Winnipeg's business leadership and working class.[29] Similar to many in Winnipeg's political elite, Webb was of British origin, having been born on a ship from India to England in 1880. After coming to Canada as a boy, he spent over a decade involved in the lumber trade in Ontario and British Columbia. Webb enlisted in the First World War, where he was a decorated soldier, winning a Distinguished Service Order medal, Military Cross, and Croix de Guerre.[30] Webb would lose a leg in the War and, after returning from Europe, he became involved in the tourist trade, eventually becoming the manager at the Marlborough Hotel and a member of the Board of Trade. Within twenty months of arriving in Winnipeg, he was mayor.

Webb's politics emphasized self-reliance and loyalty to the British Empire. In regards to the Great Depression, he called for a return to self-reliance and individual initiative, arguing "we have been blaming all governments for not doing enough...instead of realizing what we ourselves can do to help ourselves and others."[31] While he was not an outsider to the establishment, he would occasionally cast himself as one if it was politically beneficial to do so. He was also known for his municipal boosterism, leading at one point a "Pine to Palm" motor cavalcade to New Orleans to promote Winnipeg as a tourist destination. As a result, Webb has been described as "Winnipeg's best salesman until the arrival of Stephen Juba."[32] He was also vehemently anti-communist, taking a tour at another point to drum up opposition to communists across Canada and lobbying the federal government to take a harder line against communists in Canada. His support for suppression of communism will be explored later in more detail.

Independent Labour Party

The ILP was the largest labour party in Winnipeg, and established itself as the leading alternative to the Citizens throughout the 1920s and 1930s. It was founded in November 1920 under the leadership of F.J. Dixon and S.J. Farmer as a successor to the Dominion Labour Party (DLP). At the time, the local DLP branch was suffering from "irresolvable tensions" between labour factions over the General Strike. Post-Strike, organized labour was split in the city between the OBU and the more conservative Trades and Labour Council (TLC). At a meeting in August 1920, Bill Hoop of the TLC said that, during the Strike, "the OBU was out to smash the state and put in its place a Russian soviet system."[33] Hoop's statement angered many in the party, particularly since this implied that strike leaders were guilty of the conspiracy that Citizens were accusing them of. The TLC's leadership also argued that the DLP should have more formal ties to union leadership, even though many prominent DLP members were not actually union members.

When Hoop was nominated by the DLP for election in 1920, Dixon, Farmer and the rest of the executive resigned from the party and created a new one, which would become the ILP. The ILP would be open to both factions of the city's labour movement. Not all were happy about this. Alderman W.B. Simpson accused Dixon of denouncing divisions on one hand while creating a "secessionist party." The DLP, now a shell of its former self, was in the hands of the TLC, but with many of its key leaders gone it shortly folded. Other future ILP leaders were in prison at the time for their role in the strike, but would take on key roles in the party upon their release.[34]

Members of the ILP initially came from a variety of political backgrounds, ranging from neo-Georgian single taxers to social gospellers to radical unionists.[35] For example, F.J. Dixon was a prominent single taxer who worked closely with middle-class reformers, churches, farmers, and labour for reform. Rooted in Christian morality and a concern for justice, Dixon saw a tax on land value and direct legislation as key components of creating a more just society.[36] Other ILP members came from backgrounds in the Social Democratic Party, which combined revolutionary aspirations with demands for immediate reforms from the city's diverse union movements. There were some similarities between these two approaches—both, for example, sought public ownership of utilities—and for the most part the ILP, despite its diverse origins, worked well together.

The politics of the ILP that emerged were rooted in a British-style socialism that proposed establishing a "cooperative commonwealth" to solve society's problems, a politics based more on the philosophy of J.S. Mill than Karl Marx.[37] Similar to their opponents on the political right, ILP leaders tended to be of British descent.[38] During the 1930s, 70 percent of all ILP aldermen were born in Great Britain and their political philosophy was rooted in the socialist environment of British working-class politics.[39] Interestingly, though, many of the ILP's leaders were not blue-collar workers themselves and were not union members. Both ILP mayors during this period, S.J. Farmer and John Queen, worked white-collar jobs.

British roots were manifested in the ILP in a variety of ways. As James Naylor has written, the CCF tradition in Winnipeg represented by the ILP "reflected a clear and pervasive Britishness."[40] Indeed, despite the large Eastern European and German populations in Winnipeg working-class neighbourhoods, the ILP did not elect a single alderman of German, Polish, or Ukrainian descent between 1919 and 1945. J.E. Rea, a prominent scholar of municipal politics in Winnipeg, criticized the ILP for their reluctance or inability to create an ethnic constituency, relying presumably instead on appeals to class.[41] Additionally, the ILP maintained close connection with the British Independent Labour Party. Articles in the *Weekly News*, a newspaper founded by S.J. Farmer and Alderman W.B. Simpson in 1925, frequently discussed issues facing labour in the United Kingdom and the actions of the British Labour Party and British ILP. The paper also highlighted labour parties in other parts of the former British Empire, particularly Australia. Yet, despite its close connection to the British ILP, the ILP in Manitoba did not display the same kind of radicalism or anti-capitalism as their British counterparts.[42]

The ILP was rooted firmly in urban Manitoba. By 1930 there were seventeen ILP branches with nearly 1,000 members, almost entirely in Winnipeg and Brandon.[43] The party, therefore, was shaped by the urban environment and a longstanding suspicion of farmers. Indeed, until 1927, the ILP prohibited members of the United Farmers of Manitoba from even joining the party.[44] There were several reasons for this. Rural communities were often seen by the ILP as more conservative and reactionary; it was farmers who had been used to stack the jury against labour leaders in the trials that followed the General Strike. And rather than adopt the more radical politics expressed by farm organizations in some other provinces, rural Manitobans eagerly adopted the Progressive Party, which in many ways was little different than the Liberal Party.

While the ILP can be understood as a reformist party, the language used to describe their ultimate objectives did carry revolutionary overtones. ILP manifestoes regularly included statements proposing that "social ownership of the means of production, distribution, and exchange is essential to the permanent solution of the problems arising out of our social and economic ills."[45] Big changes were necessary to right the wrongs with the capitalist system. Alderman James Simpkin posited that "there is no cure (for the economic depression) short of a complete change in our economic and social system."[46] A cooperative commonwealth, ILP members proposed, would eliminate the profit motive, private ownership, and individual struggle, and replace them with a system of cooperation in which goods would be produced for the needs of the people rather than for profit.[47]

ILP leaders often pointed to Winnipeg's economic disparity as a sign of the failure of the capitalist system. One article in the *Weekly News* described a local man building a $15,000 private swimming pool, juxtaposing this with an update on Winnipeg's slum conditions. "A community which would tolerate such extremes," the article said, "which would look upon them with complacence and satisfaction, is doomed and dying."[48] John Queen also pointed to these divisions, saying, "I don't think there ever was a period when there was so much distress, human agony, hunger and privation, though there is abundance of food and other commodities and great wealth."[49] If co-operation could replace competition, the ILP argued, there was plenty of wealth for everyone.

Yet while the ILP called for social ownership and replacing private struggle with a system of cooperation, they were not revolutionaries, at least in the insurrectionary sense. For the ILP, transformational change was required to achieve a cooperative commonwealth. Yet, this was to be done peacefully through the ballot box. They rejected all possibilities of violent overthrow of the state to achieve their means, saying "now, at least, we have the ballot and it is criminal folly to think and talk of bloody revolution when the mighty weapon of the secret ballot is in our hands."[50] A cooperative commonwealth, they said, would not be created through violence, but through persuasion, as it was only possible to "appeal to such majorities by the force of argument."[51]

Despite the calls for transformative change, in many ways the ILP essentially behaved as a municipal reform party and signs of radicalism were scarce.[52] Party founders F.J. Dixon and S.J. Farmer argued that change was "gradual, evolutionary, and practical."[53] ILP politicians frequently talked about "humanizing" the existing system, finding ways to make life easier for the working class and shifting the balance of power between business and workers, but not eliminating the capitalist system. They criticized the Citizens for supporting a purely private system, while simultaneously critiquing the communists for their revolutionary rhetoric. Consequently, ILP election platforms emphasized efforts to ameliorate the worst conditions in the city: improving unemployment relief and working conditions, a city housing program to relieve slum districts, public ownership of transportation and other services where beneficial, and shifting the tax burden from workers to businesses.[54]

In addition to rejecting revolutionary rhetoric, the ILP did not frequently talk about class divisions, even while calling for shifts in power between labour and business. The *Weekly News*, the ILP's official newspaper, wrote an editorial claiming that the party "makes no appeal to class feeling.... The Independent Labour Party seeks the good of all."[55] Indeed, for leaders such as S.J. Farmer, class would not have been a central focus. This point was frequently critiqued by communists. For example, after John Queen made a radio address in 1932, the *Workers' Election Bulletin* pointed out that Queen frequently referred to "citizens" but failed to distinguish the "workers" from others.[56] At a different time, the *Weekly News* explained that "the Labour members at all times treat questions that come before the council and school board from a viewpoint which will benefit the majority of the people and are opposed to special privileges for anyone."[57]

If Ralph Webb was the defining figure of Citizen ideology, then John Queen was equally representative of the ILP. John Queen fit the mould of an ILP leader. Born in Scotland in 1882, Queen immigrated to Canada in 1906, where he would become known in Manitoba socialist circles.[58] He was a prominent member within the Social Democratic Party (SDP) in Winnipeg and active in the city's socialist circles, at one point teaching a "Socialist Sunday School" with fellow SDP member and future communist Jacob Penner. The SDP was a diverse party including both revolutionary demands (arguing for the overthrow of capitalism and the establishment of the co-operative commonwealth) as well as practical demands (such as improved working hours and universal adult suffrage). They argued that immediate reforms would address the real, practical concerns of workers while mobilizing workers to ultimately achieve revolution.[59]

Although Queen's political career often saw him take pragmatic positions, he was known to have solid radical credentials. Bercuson, for example, holds Queen up as an advocate for the General Strike and the role of unions as a vanguard for ushering in socialism.[60] Indeed, for some in the pre-Strike labour movement, Queen was too radical. When Queen was nominated by the SDP to run in a federal election in 1917 along with S.J. Farmer of the Anti-Conscription League, the TLC decided to run their own candidates, arguing that Queen and Farmer would be too radical to be elected. Eventually, Queen and Farmer would withdraw.[61] Two years later, like many in Canada's political left, Queen was intrigued by the early events happening during the Russian Revolution. He chaired a large rally at the Walker Theatre in Winnipeg in 1919, where he called for three cheers for the Russian Revolution.[62] Upon the completion of the Strike, Queen was one of the leaders arrested and would serve one year in prison for his role as advertising manager of the *Western Labour News*.[63]

Despite these solid leftist credentials, Queen was known for being able to adapt to a variety of situations. John Queen was also not employed as a labourer for much of his time in electoral politics—a point of great interest to his communist opponents. Although he was trained as a cooper, John Queen spent much of his life working in white-collar professions. For example, when he was elected to the mayoralty in 1935, Queen was working as a car salesman. Jules Preud'homme, the city solicitor, described Queen as having "the knack of adjusting himself to any situation, and fitting into his surroundings. Among the communists, he could talk their language; and at a cocktail party, he could meet the social elite and the highest of the military caste, and make them feel he was one of them."[64]

5. Mayor John Queen shortly after taking office in 1935. (Archives of Manitoba, N20731)

John Queen began his political career in 1916, a few years before the General Strike, and would go on to have a long career as a provincial and municipal politician, serving as mayor of Winnipeg (1935 to 1936 and 1938 to 1941), alderman (1916 to 1921), Member of the Legislative Assembly (1920 to 1941), and provincial leader of the ILP (1930 to 1935). According to fellow ILP politician Fred Tipping, Queen was not a natural politician, at least not at first. He described Queen as having "very, very little to say" and was nominated to run for the first time when "most of those present hadn't any claim to property so that no candidate could be found, and then someone thought of John Queen, the silent John. He had title to property and a huge mortgage at the time, but he was eligible to run and John was promptly nominated." Tipping went on to say, though, that "one of the most remarkable things about [Queen] was his development—how quickly he developed as a thinker and as a speaker when he became a member of the City Council."[65]

It was this ability that would make Queen one of the pre-eminent Manitoban labour politicians in the first half of the twentieth century. In describing his political philosophy, Queen explained that he was "interested in the organization of all the forces of society for better living for the people: not by individual, but by organized effort."[66] As the policies he would implement would show, he believed rebalancing was necessary and that the city should play an active role in that redistribution. He would champion a variety of reform measures to improve the quality of life of Winnipeg's working class. These ranged from allowing trains to run on Sundays to give workers the ability to visit local beaches, to advocating on behalf of the right to "peacefully picket," to developing public housing in Winnipeg.

John Queen was married to Katherine Ross Queen, who was also from Scotland and had her own radical political history. Ross Queen had been a member of the SDP and the Women's Labour League during the fight for female suffrage. As part of the Labour Women of Greater Winnipeg, she lobbied for birth control clinics and equal opportunities for women.[67] She died in 1934, only two months before John Queen was elected as mayor of Winnipeg. A radical to the end, her coffin was draped in a red flag. John and Katherine had five children, one of whom, Gloria Queen-Hughes, became a prominent Winnipeg politician in her own right.

John Queen was not the first ILP mayor of Winnipeg. Seymour J. Farmer was elected as an ILP mayoral candidate in 1922. Farmer was born in Cardiff, Wales, the son of a Baptist minister. Prior to coming to Canada he studied engineering and immigrated in 1900, arriving first in southwestern Manitoba. In 1909 he moved to Winnipeg, where he found work as an accountant for the International Elevator Company. He would become secretary of the Manitoba

Labour Party in 1910 and later was involved in the leadership of the Dominion Labour Party. He would also take a leadership role in the Anti-Conscription League during World War I.

Similar to Queen, Farmer had a British background and worked in a white-collar profession. Unlike Queen's, Farmer's politics were originally rooted in the "single tax" vision of Henry George rather than a cooperative commonwealth. George argued that poverty was not permissible in a just society and that the reason for poverty was speculation, suggesting that if society reached its productive capacity everyone's needs could easily be met. Therefore, land value should be taxed to encourage people to put land to use.[68] While Allen Mills describes Farmer's politics as essentially "liberal," focused on individual freedom and welfare, he also indicates that he was primarily concerned about the "common man," and in doing so "believed he was, in working to end privilege and poverty, seeking the best interests of the industrial worker." By the time that Farmer was involved in the founding of the ILP, his economics had become more socialist—for example, an interest in cooperative commonwealth—and less liberal.[69]

Farmer worked well with people from a variety of political backgrounds and played an instrumental role in developing the ILP. Although his election opponents often tried to portray him as radical and dangerous (*Winnipeg Free Press* editor J.W. Dafoe would describe Farmer as a "dangerous man")[70] he had a public reputation for moderation and dependability. In this way, Farmer's political career fits with that of many other municipal leaders in Canada nominated by labour parties, who refuted charges of radicalism with the nomination of moderate, respectable candidates.[71] Farmer was described, in an endorsement from the *Western Labour News* as "intellectually thorough, an eloquent and incisive speaker, a hard worker, modest to a degree in pushing himself forward, but absolutely without fear in advancing the ideas he believes to be true."[72] Allen Mills has described him as a thoughtful speaker, although not necessarily a great orator, diligent, hard working, and a good manager.[73] In addition to serving two one-year terms as mayor, Farmer would also serve as an MLA from 1922 to 1949.[74] S.J. Farmer became the first provincial CCF leader in Manitoba and eventually sat in the provincial cabinet during the Second World War.[75]

It is worth noting that while much of the ILP was British, the party also provided a "political home for Jewish humanists."[76] For example, John Blumberg was a long-time alderman who served on city council for decades and would eventually serve as Deputy Mayor under John Queen. Blumberg, a Jew born in Hull, England, entered politics after the arrest of John Queen and A.A. Heaps in 1919 after the General Strike. Another prominent Jewish ILP member was Marcus Hyman, an occasional mayoral candidate for the ILP. Hyman had been part of the legal defence team for those arrested in the aftermath of the General Strike. He was the son of a Polish rabbi who had immigrated to the United Kingdom. Before coming to Winnipeg, Hyman studied at Oxford and became a lawyer. In addition to his leadership role in the ILP, he also taught at the Manitoba Law School and was active in a variety of Jewish communal organizations.[77] It should be noted, however, that both of these influential Jewish leaders in the ILP had connections with Britain and would have been familiar with the British roots of the party.

To situate the ILP within the pantheon of Canadian labour history, it is important to note that the ILP would eventually join, albeit somewhat grudgingly, the Co-operative Commonwealth Federation (CCF). Several members of the ILP were instrumental in the creation of the CCF. J.S. Woodsworth, for example, became its first national leader and S.J. Farmer became the CCF provincial leader in Manitoba. John Queen was at the Calgary Convention, where he unsuccessfully proposed the name "United Socialist Federation."[78] But many in the ILP, including Queen, were resistant to the "broadening out" that the new CCF called for. They had no interest in diluting their successful political brand and were suspicious of the politics of farmers, who did not espouse the same kind of socialist politics. As one Brandon ILP member said, "it was not that old country Scotch socialism that the farmers were talking about."[79]

The issue came to a head in 1937 when the Manitoba ILP passed a resolution to disaffiliate from the national CCF. Many, especially those involved in municipal politics, had become frustrated with the new party and its broad strategy. There may have also been personal politics involved, with some suggesting that key members of the ILP were opposed to the new CCF because they had been overlooked for party positions and wanted to maintain the influence they held in the ILP.[80] Others have suggested that many in the ILP's leadership were opposed to the national leadership and politics of J.S. Woodsworth.[81] After pleading from Woodsworth, who threatened to resign from the ILP if it followed through with disaffiliation, and after negotiations with the ILP leadership, the party changed its mind and backed off from disaffiliation. By 1943 the ILP was formally disbanded, although it was said that many ILP aldermen remained apathetic about their new party affiliation and did little to get involved with the CCF.

Communist Party of Canada

The final party on the Winnipeg political scene was the CPC, which was rooted in the North End, a working-class neighbourhood with a large number of recent immigrants. Although the CPC regularly launched membership campaigns in the central and southern regions of the city, these had little success and, in

1933, nearly 60 percent of Winnipeg party members lived in the North End.[82] Unlike other parties in Winnipeg, but similar to the Communist Party across the country, the vast majority of members were non-English immigrants. Of the 415 members reported in 1934, 236 were Ukrainian while only thirty-two were English, Canadian, French, or Irish.[83] This is particularly interesting when compared to the ILP, which was mostly British, pointing to an ethnic division within Winnipeg's political left. The party was nearly ninety percent male and over half of its members were unemployed.[84] Of those who were employed, most were labourers, including several members who worked for the railroads. Most recruits were younger than thirty years of age, and nearly all were younger than forty.[85] The average Winnipeg communist, therefore, was a young, unemployed Ukrainian male, living in the city's poorest working-class neighbourhood, the North End.[86]

Communists saw the composition of the party membership as a cause for concern. One party document declared that Winnipeg communists must "overcome the 'lopsided development' of the [party], mainly in North Winnipeg among the foreign-born workers. It means the transformation of the [party] composition by the recruitment of at least 150 Canadian workers in the central and other Canadian sections of the city."[87] The focus from party leadership was "Canadian workers" as opposed to the Ukrainians, Russians, Poles, Jews, and Germans that dominated the party membership. It has even been suggested that while Tim Buck, Stewart Smith, and Leslie Morris (all key communist leaders on the national level) enjoyed celebrating Jacob Penner's victories, they thought he was not the Party's ideal standard bearer on city council because he was not Anglo-Saxon.[88]

This book will explore the ideology of the Communist Party in municipal politics in more depth in later chapters, but it is important to mention here how their politics were distinguished from the ILP on the political left. Communists, such as Jacob Penner (1880–1965), argued that the communist party must be involved in a "sharp uncompromising struggle to unseat the dictatorship of the bourgeoisie" and that "social revolution is the only remedy for the prevailing economic crisis."[89] Winning seats on city council was not the ultimate goal, the workers revolution was. However, as will be seen throughout this book, the dream of revolution did not impede communist aldermen's ability to represent their constituents or to advocate on behalf of causes to improve the lives of workers here and now.

A second major difference between the Communists and the ILP was the use of class as a significant component of their rhetoric. While the ILP had a strong working-class identity, their election campaigns and public statements spoke of "putting humanity first," something that communists said ignored class consciousness. Communist election papers warned workers that they should not be "fooled by the election ballyhoo of the candidates of the boss class. If you are a worker, remember that your class has interests distinct and separate from those of the boss."[90] There was no such thing as "the people," according to the CPC, but rather society was divided between the proletariat and the bourgeoisie. Thus, it was impossible to "put humanity first" when humanity was composed of two groups with inherently opposed interests: the bosses and the workers.

Throughout the 1930s, Winnipeg CPC members established or participated in a variety of economic and cultural organizations such as cooperative dairies, lumberyards, ethnic associations, athletic clubs, choirs, and theatre groups.[91] An array of national organizations such as the Canadian Labour Defence League, Young Communist League, and National Unemployed Workers Association were established in the city. Other organizations such as the Ukrainian Labour-Farmer Temple Association included many members who were sympathetic to communist politics, even if they were not card-carrying party members. Reports throughout the 1920s and 1930s suggest that many Winnipeggers were willing to join communist demonstrations. For example, on the International Day Against Unemployment in 1931, 12,000 Winnipeggers marched through the streets.[92] Annual May Day parades attracted thousands of workers, while speeches in Market Square regularly drew hundreds or thousands of listeners. Certainly there was an active communist base in the city, whether visible in the Workers' and Farmers' Cooperative, May Day parades, ethnic clubs, or in associations for the unemployed.[93]

While the Communist Party often ran candidates throughout the city, as well as candidates for mayor, it was only in the North End that it had much of a chance electorally. A combination of a large Eastern European population, dire poverty, and a recognition that communist aldermen got stuff done for their constituents made the North End fertile ground for communist candidates for decades. Indeed, not only would the North End elect North America's first communist elected official (William Kolisnyk), they would continue to elect communists straight through the Cold War until the early 1980s.

Political Geography

It is important to give some sense of the political geography of the city and how the electoral map affected political campaigning and governing. Throughout this period, mayoral elections were held annually in Winnipeg, and each adult with sufficient property was given the vote (extending the franchise would become one of the major priorities of the ILP in 1935 when labour aldermen achieved a majority of seats on council).

6. A May Day rally in 1932 with city hall in the background. (AUUC-WBA Archives)

7. Adults were not the only people to march in Winnipeg's lengthy May Day parades. Here, children waving red flags march in the parade. (AUUC-WBA Archives)

The city was also divided into three wards for the purposes of aldermanic elections. There were six aldermen per ward, each of whom sat for two-year terms. The terms were staggered, however, so that three aldermanic seats were available per ward each year. This meant that there were eighteen seats on council with the mayor having the tie-breaking vote.

Political boundaries were by no means accidental. After the General Strike, pro-Citizen aldermen worried that labour parties could actually win a municipal election. The election of 1919 was the last to use a seven-ward system. Less than three months after the November 1919 election, Citizen aldermen changed ward boundaries dramatically. To ensure that middle- and upper-class candidates could dominate city council, the seven-ward system was transformed into a three-ward system—with the wards won by labour candidates mostly folded into one ward. As Alan Artibise has described it, the three-ward system amounted to little more than "a gerrymander by the city's establishment."[94] John Queen denounced the boundary changes at the time, arguing that "representation should be by population. There is nothing much wrong with the present ward boundaries. But you see the Citizen's committee is afraid so, of course, council had to make the change."[95]

The changes disadvantaged the political left in several ways. First, southern Winnipeg, which tended to strongly favour the Citizens, received an extra four aldermanic seats. The transferrable ballot system with the vote for property owners also meant that Citizens could count on at least one seat in Ward Three, the strongest ward for the political left. Additionally, non-resident property owners also had the right to vote, further limiting the ability of labour candidates to win elections. Finally, wards became quite a bit larger, and therefore more resource intensive to run a campaign in, further pressuring candidates on the left who were less likely to have significant financial resources.[96]

Ward One, south of Portage Avenue, was mostly affluent and predominantly British. As a Communist Party election bulletin explained, "Portage Avenue is more than the main business thoroughfare of Winnipeg. It is the sharp line of demarcation between the wealthy and the poor, or the bourgeoisie and the proletarians of the city." It would go on to say that the region south of Portage Avenue was the site of "stately mansions presided over by well-fed, prosperous business men and haughty social dames, whose slightest whims are obeyed by a corps of obsequious servants."[97] The description may have been somewhat hyperbolic and not entirely true (there were working-class neighbourhoods in sections of Fort Rouge near the railroad shops), but it was true that this ward was populated by the city's commercial elite. Not surprisingly, the Ward was almost the exclusive domain of the Citizens, although the ILP was occasionally successful in capturing one of the six seats in the Ward.

In 1925, the ILP's *Weekly News* published a description of some polling divisions in Ward One, pointing out that while labour was often critiqued for class-based politics, "when you review some of the polling divisions in Ward One you will certainly agree that 'class vote' was very apparent among those who cry 'away with class.'" For example, at the Kelvin School polling station earlier that fall, Citizen mayoral candidate Ralph Webb had beaten ILP candidate

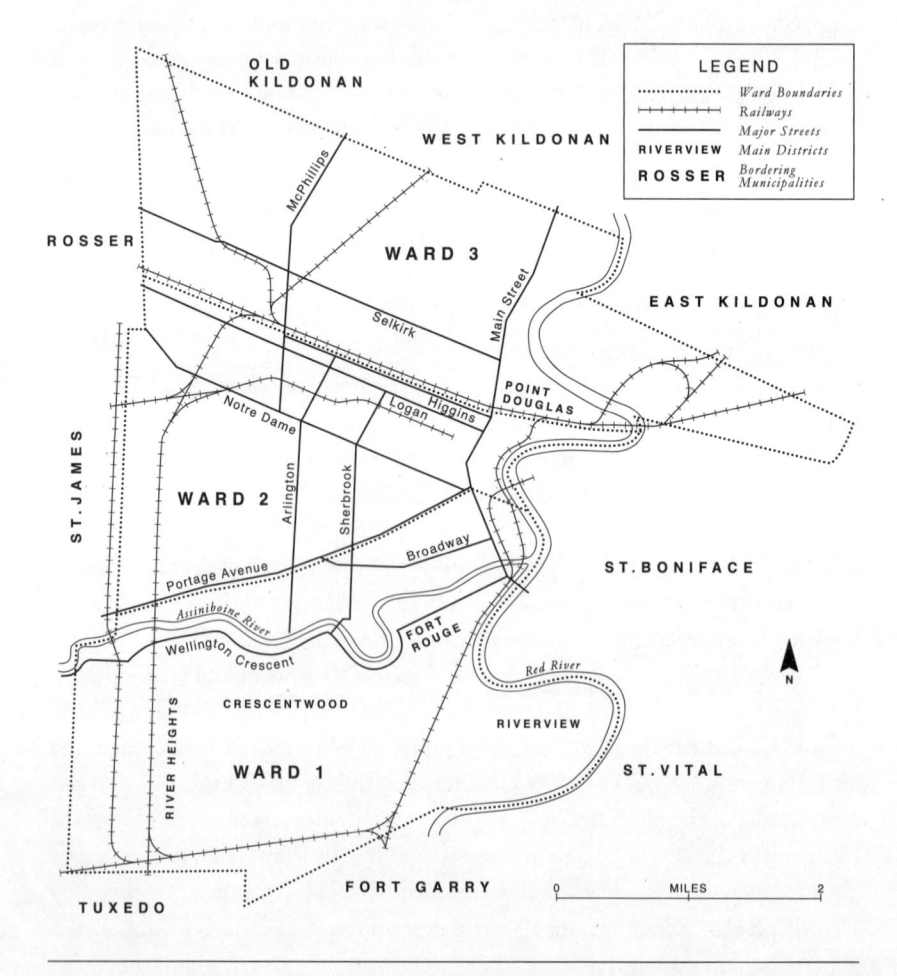

8. Winnipeg's municipal wards after 1921. Adapted from Alan Artibise, "Patterns of Population Growth and Ethnic Relationships in Winnipeg, 1874–1974." Map by Elise Epp.

Fred Tipping by 1,386 votes to 44. The *Weekly News* went on to suggest that "if the Archangel Gabriel came down from Heaven and ran as a Labour candidate in Ward One, Kelvin, Mulvey, and Laura Secord would pile up huge majorities against him."[98] Thus, while there were pockets of working-class people in Ward One, it was predominantly known for its upper-class population.

Ward Two, stretching from Portage Avenue in the south to the CPR tracks in the north was a mixed ward that encompassed both working-class and middle-class neighbourhoods. This diverse population made the ward competitive for much of this period. Both the Citizens and the ILP won seats regularly, although the Citizens had a slight edge. However, the ILP had a strong base in the community, particularly in the predominantly British working-class neighbourhoods of the West End, where the ILP had their main labour hall. In many elections, Ward One would swing largely to the Citizens and Ward Three to the ILP, leaving Ward Two to decide the election.

The final ward in the city, Ward Three, extended north from the CPR tracks to the city's northern boundary. Commonly known as the North End, this ward had a large population of recent immigrants, particularly from Eastern Europe, and was the home of labour radicalism in the city. Many of Winnipeg's ethnic minorities lived in Ward Three. In 1921, 60 percent of Winnipeg's Germans, 86 percent of Ukrainians, 84 percent of Jews, and 76 percent of Poles lived in Ward Three. This was also the ward in which both the communists and the ILP had their greatest success, although Citizen candidates also had some support in the Ward, in large part because absentee landlords were given the vote in wards in which they owned property.

CHAPTER 2

THE REIGN OF THE FURIES

Despite gerrymandered election boundaries and voting rules that limited the right to vote, it would not take long for Winnipeg's political left to achieve its first significant political victory. In November 1922, only three years after the General Strike, S.J. Farmer was elected as mayor of the city. Now, for the first time, the city's most prestigious position was in the hands of a labour man. Many in Winnipeg's business community predicted that calamity would unfold, that even though Citizens still held a majority on city council, the presence of a labour mayor would scare away capital, drive up taxes, and lead to a public takeover of private enterprise. They need not have worried. S.J. Farmer would turn out to be a moderate mayor, recognized by his opponents as a respectable figure who represented the city well. In his two-year stint as mayor, Farmer was never in a position to reorient a city that was still politically dominated by its business community. Farmer did manage to play a leadership role in campaigns for the public ownership of utilities, but the mayor's role was in many cases ceremonial or procedural, giving him few opportunities to implement an agenda different than his business opponents'.

S.J. Farmer was not the ILP's first choice for mayor in 1922, possibly not even its second or third choice. Even though he had run in the two previous elections as a mayoral candidate, rumours abounded and the press speculated about the ILP nomination. The North Winnipeg branch first nominated Fred Dixon, but at a large public meeting Dixon declined the role, not once or twice, but four times saying that he could not hold two jobs.[1] As a popular MLA, Dixon did not feel he could adequately serve both municipally and provincially. Attention then turned to A.A. Heaps, who would also turn down the nomination multiple times. At this point, the press suggested that John Queen would be the candidate for the ILP, before the ILP finally settled on S.J. Farmer, also an MLA-elect, as their mayoral candidate.[2] Farmer, it seemed, did not have qualms about holding multiple elected positions.[3]

Farmer's opponent, the Citizen candidate in 1922, was J.K. Sparling. If any candidate set the race up as another rematch of the 1919 General Strike, it was Sparling. While he had not served on the executive of the Citizens' Committee of One Thousand during the Strike, he shared their goals and had met with them frequently. In his position as the Police Commission chair he had played an instrumental role by giving the police an ultimatum to sign a loyalty oath or lose their jobs. Sparling, it has been described, was the most important figure at city hall during the General Strike, with the exception of the mayor.[4] Throughout the campaign, Sparling would return to the type of language employed during the Strike, categorizing his opponent as radical, dangerous, and revolutionary.

A single issue dominated the 1922 campaign, creating conditions that outgoing Mayor Frank Fowler described as "unusually lively."[5] The franchise provided to the Winnipeg Electric Company (WEC) for its operation of the street railway service enabled the city to take over the service during certain windows. While this window was not to occur until between 1926 and 1927, the company stated that it was unable to raise debentures unless it received assurances from the city that its franchise would be extended. Many Citizen aldermen opposed a public takeover of the street railway, citing risk, expense, and an aversion to public ownership in principle as reasons to avoid it. Despite this opposition, there was interest on council in a referendum to settle the question of whether the city should take over ownership.

This is where the Citizen-dominated council misstepped. On 2 November 1922, less than a month before the election, council voted to let only the 24,000 ratepayers, rather than the entire electorate, vote in the referendum on the fate of the street railways by declaring it to be a money bylaw. The lead voice in favour of this plan was none other than J.K. Sparling, while all ILP aldermen opposed it. Their decision was controversial for two reasons. First, most Winnipeggers were disenfranchised from making this key decision about the future of the city. Many working-class Winnipeggers relied on the street railway but were denied the opportunity to speak regarding potential changes to this essential service. Secondly, there was already significant public resentment and suspicion towards the WEC, which frequently claimed poverty when dealing with the city but embarked on expensive expansion projects and lucrative shareholder dividends.

As a result, what should have been a quiet election turned into a referendum on the street railway question. As a *Manitoba Free Press* editorial stated, "this city council, by limiting the voting on the proposition to property holders… has made it certain that the question will make the maximum of disturbance." The editorial went on to state that the referendum should be open to the entire electorate as "to this contract, all the citizens are a party." Consequently, the *Free Press* argued, "the mayoralty election will turn itself into a referendum" on the street railway.[6]

The election campaign did exactly that. J.K. Sparling, who was left trying to defend the nearly universally disliked referendum, wavered under the pressure. Labour aldermen even threatened to take the city to court to prevent the referendum from going ahead. By 16 November, council decided to push back the referendum to an undisclosed later date. Citizen Alderman John McKerchar commented in the *Free Press* that the referendum question should not be an issue; after all, he said, the interests of the company and the city were interwoven.[7]

The damage, however, was already done. Labour candidates went on the offensive. Nearly every ILP rally focused squarely on the street railway, linking Citizen candidates to the unpopular WEC. A capacity crowd at the Isaac Brock Community Centre heard S.J. Farmer denounce the WEC for seeking "concessions (each year) or the company could not finance the work. Now 1922 comes along and we have them saying that unless they have an extension of the franchise they cannot raise debentures.... How do you expect them to keep their promises now?"[8] Not only was the electorate to be suspicious of the WEC, declared Farmer, but it should defeat those aldermen who had sought to disenfranchise them. In a Ward Two rally, Farmer condemned city council, asking, "would the electors of Winnipeg return those aldermen who had disenfranchised them on such an important issue?"[9]

This appeal likely gained Farmer and the ILP many votes outside the traditional labour constituency. Even the *Manitoba Free Press*, the same paper that suggested three years earlier that a Farmer victory would result in a Soviet Winnipeg, subtly endorsed Farmer's candidacy, encouraging voters to use the mayoral election as a referendum on the WEC franchise (although it made clear that people should vote for aldermen based on other issues). Looking back on the election, the pro-Citizen newspaper *The North Ender* suggested that the WEC had lost public confidence by spending millions of dollars on power development while claiming it could not pay the City of Winnipeg its taxes, launching a new power scheme that appeared to pose a threat to the publicly owned City Hydro system, and that the referendum antagonized non-ratepayers.[10] Meanwhile, the focus on the unpopular referendum also limited Citizen candidates from focusing on other issues. Nearly all the media coverage of the campaign focused on the referendum debacle, even after council pushed off the referendum to a later date.

The *Manitoba Free Press* suggested that the street railway question was "bound to exacerbate class feeling in this city; of this there has been far too much for the city's good and wise citizens have been rejoicing to see its steady abatement in recent months. Now the fires are newly lit."[11] While Farmer and the ILP did appeal somewhat to class consciousness with their bid to non-ratepayer (mostly working-class) electors, it was J.K. Sparling and the Citizens who resorted to language that seemed like it could have been cut and pasted from the General Strike. With little positive momentum of his own, Sparling was left to warn voters of the dangers of this "group of radicals" with "no regard for the manner in which the taxpayers' money was expended."[12] Sparling's campaign tried to change the election's narrative, saying that the key issue was not the street railway referendum, but the appropriateness of having labour representatives in a position of power. An ad in the *North Ender* told voters: "Do not be confused. The real issue in this election is only this. An attempt is being made to elect an administration of irrepressible elements dangerous to any community—under the smoke-screen of Municipal Ownership."[13]

In an ad that ran in the *Manitoba Free Press* the day before the election, Sparling made it even clearer to voters that he saw the election as a continuation of the labour-business conflict of the General Strike. He told voters that "Winnipeg Faces Another Crisis Tomorrow in the Civic Election." Voters had a choice: "Sparling and Stability" or "Farmer and the Reign of the Furies." He went on to ask, "do you think the ultra radical leaders in this city are not working to these ends, that they may fiddle, Nero-like, while Rome burns?" Furthermore, the ad declared, "anything less than the defeat of a ticket for this City headed by names such as FARMER, HEAPS, BRAY, [and] ARMSTRONG would be a Civic Disgrace. We do not intend to place them in CONTROL of our lives, our property, the education of our children, and the measure of our taxes." Just in case any reader had missed the connection to long-standing labour-business conflict, Sparling's ad ended with a clear, capitalized message: "LET US SETTLE THIS THING ONCE MORE, AND FOR ALL!"[14]

The message could not have been clearer. Sparling and the status quo, or Farmer and dangerous, incendiary revolution; business or labour. By warning of labour control, Sparling seemed to be reminding readers of the Strike Committee's efforts to restrict business operations during the General Strike, equating control of the city during the Strike with the efforts of the political left to win city council. Sparling had a clear message for Winnipeggers. The Citizens may have won in 1919, but another victory was needed, one large enough to defeat the labour nuisance once and for all.

The "Civic Disgrace" of a Farmer election did come to pass—he won 57 percent of the vote—but there would be no "reign of the furies." Six ILP aldermen joined Farmer on city council, not nearly enough for a majority. There was also no sense in the local media that Farmer's victory was unexpected or calamitous. Interestingly, the *Free Press*, which had attacked Farmer mercilessly when he ran for mayor in 1919, merely declared that his victory was a rejection of Sparling's approach on the referendum question. There was no sense that the city had fallen to the radicals, but rather that Farmer's victory could be logically explained. This election, it was suggested, was not a sign of a leftward shift amongst the electorate. Even though a labour mayor was something new in Winnipeg, it could be dismissed by those who wanted to as inconsequential rather than as a sign of things to come. The *Western Labour News* concurred, saying that the election had focused almost entirely on the street railway question and that the "personality of the candidates counted for very little."[15] And besides, with a strong Citizen majority on council, the mayoralty was in many ways a more symbolic than practical win. This would be the challenge for Farmer: how to advance ILP and labour policies within the confines of a pro-Citizen political structure.

During the election, Sparling had foretold disaster should Farmer be elected mayor of Winnipeg. However, after the election, press accounts painted a picture of Farmer doing much what a Citizen mayor would have done. He joined the Board of Trade, welcomed visitors to the city, and presided over curling events, IODE gatherings, and Red Cross appeals. Readers of the *Free Press* could well have been left wondering what the fuss had been about. Farmer would even take up the sport of golf, *The North Ender* reporting that he was hooked after being introduced to the game by A.A. Heaps. "His Worship is having difficulty in bringing his score down toward the century mark," *The North Ender* reported, tongue firmly in cheek, "but he is becoming very expert at cutting neat divots without touching the ball." It went on to make a more serious point: "some labor supporters of Mr. Farmer are insinuating that his enthusiasm for his new McLaughlin 6-cylinder sedan and his zeal for golf are incompatible with the ideals and practice of a genuine labor leader."[16]

The North Ender was a strongly and openly pro-Citizen publication. There was never any public concern expressed by ILP members that Farmer was adopting bourgeois practices or that he was not adequately representing labour interests. Yet it was true that Farmer did not accomplish much beyond cutting ribbons in his first months on city council. The office of the mayor was relatively powerless without a supportive majority on council. Much of what Farmer did was attend galas, open festivities, and bring greetings, not radically change the direction of a city council that continued to be dominated by business leaders.

There were two issues during his first year in office, however, that were profoundly shaped by Farmer's politics. The first was the ongoing question of the street railway. Early in his term in office, Farmer declared the WEC to be "unscrupulous" and a "direct menace to the interests of the people."[17] He sought payment from the company for services provided by the city, including snow removal and paving charges. Council was not split precisely along labour-Citizen lines on the question of demanding these funds from the street railway. There were Citizen aldermen who wanted to ensure that the WEC was paying for what it got out of the city. This reflected more a matter of good business practice than any interest in municipalization. But it was primarily Farmer and ILP aldermen who tenaciously insisted that the WEC pay its bills to the city—seeking, by November 1923, $400,000 from the company.

The WEC had a long, complicated, and often adversarial relationship with the City of Winnipeg. It had obtained its first franchise for street railway service in 1892 and by 1900 had a monopoly on gas, electricity, and public transit. Controlling these three essential services proved lucrative for the Toronto-based syndicate—led by William Mackenzie—that owned the WEC, with earnings increasing by over 30 percent a year in the early 1900s. It would not take long before Winnipeg business leaders were concerned that the power rates they were paying to the WEC were cutting into their bottom line and restricting the city's growth. In 1906, it was the municipal elite who pushed the city to get into the electrical business, forming Winnipeg Hydro. According to Alan Artibise, lowering the cost of power through a municipal provider was no great social act. He describes it as "beyond the capacity of Winnipeg's governing elite (in the early twentieth century) to think of the city in terms of a public environment and care for all men, not just successful men. Their first duty remained the private search of wealth, and public ownership merely served in this one instance as the best means for achieving that goal."[18] When Winnipeg Hydro began competing with the WEC in 1911 it had what were thought to be the lowest power rates in North America.[19]

While it was local businesses that had pushed for municipalization in 1906, much had changed by the 1920s. First, in 1919 the Winnipeg Electric Company was sold to Winnipeg-based owners. No longer were profits going to eastern capitalists, profits were staying within Winnipeg's business community. Second, the polarization of the General Strike made Winnipeg's business community much less interested in public ownership. What was once good business was now a suspect idea from the political left. For example, even though Winnipeg's business community had lobbied for the creation of a municipal hydro company, it supported the private development of the Seven Sisters dam for the WEC in the 1920s while labour fought for public ownership of Seven Sisters through Winnipeg Hydro.[20]

Winnipeg was not the only Canadian city dealing with the question of private ownership of streetcars. Across the country, creating a profitable street railway tended to come at the expense of alienating riders and workers. Vancouver had sought to "be free of the shackles of the BC Electric Railway Company" but the railway was "generally able to hoodwink an indignant but directionless municipal government."[21] After an attempted municipalization in 1917, the private street railway survived by appealing to federal legislation, and by the early 1920s was more established than ever. In Montreal, the city spent five years in contentious negotiations with Montreal Tramways Corporation, before finally agreeing to an arbitrated service-at-cost contract that guaranteed the company profit on its capital investment.

While private ownership survived in Montreal and Vancouver through the 1920s, the story was different in Toronto. After years of struggling to get the Toronto Railway Company (TRC) to improve service and build new track, the City of Toronto agreed to purchase the TRC and Toronto Electric Light Company from William Mackenzie for $30 million in 1913. After contentious negotiations over the cost and World War I interrupted financing, Torontonians voted by an eleven to one margin to take over the street railway network when the TRC's franchise expired in 1921.[22] In September 1921, two years prior to the debate in Winnipeg, the Toronto Transportation Commission (TTC) was formed—an example that would be cited by Winnipeg's ILP in local debates around municipalization. In November 1923, Farmer illustrated the need for municipalizing the city's street railway by arguing in part that Toronto had benefited from municipalization and that the TTC had already made $100,000 in profit.

While Winnipeg was similar to other major Canadian cities in its debates around municipalizing street railways, its situation was unique in the Prairies, as other major cities such as Calgary, Edmonton, Saskatoon, and Regina all had municipally owned street railway services. This was not due to any particular radicalism or municipally minded policy development in these cities. Rather, private enterprises had not been interested in developing street railways in those cities and the service was required to support rapidly growing cities and industries. As a result, the municipalization debate, which played a significant role in Winnipeg's municipal politics in the 1920s, was less present in many other western Canadian cities.[23]

While the mayor was not able to vote on issues in city council, he was able to rule on meeting procedure. It was this tool that he would use to great effect at times to limit the ability of Citizen aldermen to get their bylaws and motions heard. In late January 1923 Alderman Robert Shore moved the second reading of a bylaw to extend the WEC's railway franchise. The first reading had been brought forward in October, prior to the election. Farmer quickly ruled the bylaw out of order as it had not been approved by the city's voters and because no notice had been given to other aldermen. Many of the aldermen, he said, were new and had not heard the bylaw when it had first been read in October. Had the bylaw gone to a vote, it is likely it would have passed, given the strong Citizen majority on council. However, Farmer's ruling effectively quashed the street railway question for the time being.

The issue of public ownership of utilities would also define the other prominent issue of Farmer's first year in office. B.W. Parker, a local engineer, sought a municipal franchise for developing a central steam-heating facility in the Fort Rouge neighbourhood. According to a city report, there were several advantages to central steam heat: cheaper heating, reduced smoke nuisance, reduced fire risk, thermostatic control, and the elimination of the need for individual residents to handle coal and the subsequent ashes.[24] An independent study from a Chicago-based consulting firm also suggested that Winnipeg would benefit from a central heating system, a finding backed by the City Hydro manager.[25]

Despite these advantages, when Parker brought forward his proposal in 1923, the city was split sharply on the issue of whether to allow his project to proceed along business-labour lines. The issue was not the relative benefit of central steam-heating technology or the cost of installing such a system—as this was to be borne by Parker himself. Rather, the debate centred on the larger question of public and private ownership of local utilities. The question for city council, was if central heating was so needed and advantageous, should it ultimately be owned by private interests?

For Citizen aldermen, the answer was clearly yes. Alderman E.T. Leach suggested that since the proposal would provide citizens with a needed service and the city with a market for off-season power, a contract should quickly be prepared with Parker. John McKerchar, another Citizen alderman, argued that while the service was needed, the city could not possibly afford to provide it, so private capital was an excellent solution. Conversely, ILP aldermen like Herbert Jones dismissed the franchise, suggesting "Parker and his friends no doubt had big visions of big profits. Such profits would be going into the hands of a few. The city should go into business and every citizen should be a shareholder in it." ILP Alderman James Simpkin indicated that private franchises were a "corrupting influence in public life wherever granted."[26]

The stage was set for a confrontation between the ILP and Citizens. By the time that Farmer ruled Citizen motions to approve the franchise out of order in mid-July, claiming that proper notice had not been provided, battle lines had already been drawn. Farmer's ruling effectively delayed the debate for a couple of weeks, at which point Farmer was quoted in the newspaper saying that he would refuse to sign the Parker franchise, arguing that municipal governments could not delegate use of public highways, streets, and lanes without a referendum.[27] Furthermore, he argued, selling publicly produced power at cut-rate prices to a private enterprise was not an appropriate practice.

Farmer was backed by labour supporters both inside and outside of council. The TLC declared that they were unqualifiedly against the franchise for Parker, saying that the deal offered little protection or benefit to the city, and commended Farmer for his efforts.[28] Meanwhile, labour aldermen in council "bombarded the chairman of the Utilities committee with a fusillade of technical questions" declaring that they were going to "force the issue." Citizen Alderman McKerchar dismissed the questions as insincere while his colleague Alderman Sullivan called them "political bumkum."[29] Eventually, Citizen Alderman Shore pressed for a suspension of the rules to go on to the next order of business, but Farmer insisted that all questions be heard. He was overruled, however, with all Citizen aldermen uniting to vote to suspend debate on the Parker franchise question. Eventually council could agree on one thing, creating a special committee to investigate and decide on the Parker franchise.

Labour Alderman William Simpson followed up on that meeting by submitting twenty-four technical questions to City Hydro. In response, John Glassco, the manager of City Hydro, explained that Parker had agreed to buy all excess power produced at a fixed price up to 25,000 horsepower during the winter months. While the rate to citizens for off-peak power was more than twice that offered to Parker, Glassco explained, it also ensured that the municipally owned hydro company could sell any power that was not used. Glassco also expressed that the plan had the benefit of allowing a private company to develop costly and risky infrastructure, which the city could take control of after five years should the experiment prove successful.[30] However, Parker would only buy power from October to April and not during the summer months, when the most excess power was available. Additionally, Glassco noted, the franchise would potentially also reduce revenue for water heating in the Fort Rouge area that was being earned by City Hydro.[31]

Farmer would continue to play a prominent role in the debate over the Parker franchise when it went to the special committee a few days later. He insisted that prior to any arrangement being made, the electorate should have an opportunity to vote in a referendum on the proposal. When other aldermen dismissed this possibility, Farmer once again threatened to refuse his signature for the franchise proposal. Farmer and ILP Alderman William Simpson denounced the proposal, calling it a threat to the city's public power system, questioning the franchise's plans to dig up streets to lay the requisite piping, and insisting that the terms for potential city expropriation after five years were too favourable to Parker. Simpson would describe these arrangements as a "heads I win, tails you lose" proposition, as Parker could buy power cheaply and sell it for a profit while not being required to buy power in the summer months when he did not need it.

The Parker scheme would never actually come up for a vote. By the end of August, Parker decided he had heard enough. He wrote Alderman Herbert

Gray indicating that he was "compelled by circumstances" to withdraw his application, calling the negotiations "unduly protracted." Furthermore, he claimed that, given the circumstances, it would be impossible to obtain the necessary capital, as "capital invested in such an undertaking will be under continuous attack from the opponents of private ownership." While saying that his plan would have put to use Winnipeg's energy surplus and made life more comfortable for Winnipeggers, he declared "there are strong influences insisting that the City have the right to expropriate my undertaking and to strip me of the business which I may develop."[32]

The withdrawal fit well into narratives of both the Citizens and the ILP. For the Citizens, this was an indication that labour politicians could not responsibly encourage new investment in the city and that having a labour mayor endangered economic growth. Conversely, the ILP described the withdrawal as being in the best interest of the citizens of Winnipeg. They argued that public interests had been defended against an attempt by private capital to monopolize a public service—just as the WEC had with the street railway. After all, it was their hope that more, not fewer, services would be municipalized.

There was some question whether there would even be a mayoral election in 1923. After all, Farmer's supporters insisted that there was a tradition of allowing a mayor an uncontested second term. Citizens, however, were not about to let a labour mayor go uncontested. They argued that the precedent for the second term no longer applied, as it was only relevant "before party politics entered the fray."[33] The Winnipeg Civics Association endorsed Hon. Robert Jacob, a lawyer, MLA, and former school board member, as the Citizen mayoral candidate, in the process supposedly collecting 5,000 signatures to support the candidacy.

Class divisions, or the supposed lack thereof, would become a key message in Jacob's campaign. Whereas labour argued that there were class divisions in the city, Jacob and his fellow Citizens whitewashed class divisions. Launching his campaign, Jacob declared that "at all times our mayor should represent all classes of the community...I shall make it my first duty to promote harmony and cooperation among all citizens."[34] Harmony would remain a frequent refrain at Jacob campaign rallies, occasionally drawing heckling from unfriendly crowds. During one Elmwood meeting, the *Free Press* reported that the audience repeatedly burst into laughter at the mention of "harmony," with one woman yelling out, "how can you bring harmony when people are starving?"[35] Yet Jacob insisted that there was no true division between business and "honest labour." To illustrate this, Jacob often told the story of his own working life, which had started at the age of thirteen as a farm labourer, before ultimately becoming a lawyer and MLA.

Jacob conjured up similar campaign images to those used by Sparling a year earlier to scare voters about the dangers of labour government. *The North Ender* described Farmer as uniting with the four horses of the apocalypse—the Workers' Party, One Big Union, Socialist Party, and trade unionism—to destroy rich and free men.[36] Jacob himself would say that the ILP would further the political ambitions of communism. Returning to language that would have been familiar to Citizens in 1919, he accused the ILP of holding views "repugnant to a large number of citizens" including "extreme radicalism and socialism."[37]

One way that the Citizen campaign tried to raise questions about this "extreme radicalism" was by questioning Farmer's respect for Armistice Day ceremonies. Many wondered what Farmer, who had opposed World War I, would do during these ceremonies. Farmer had spoken publicly against the war; on one instance, for example, telling a large public rally that he was returning his draft registration card unsigned.[38] During a speech to the Caledonian Club, A.E. Hoskin, the president of the Civics Association, suggested that Farmer had disrespected veterans by keeping his hat on for the "Last Fife" and "God Save the King." Farmer reacted angrily to the accusation, denouncing it as "malicious, villainous and contemptible canard." He went on to say, "I may have appeared awkward to some critics, but that does not alter the fact that I have just as much respect for those who died overseas as Mr. Hoskin or anybody else and I refuse to use their memory as a political football."[39]

Another, more practical result of Farmer's supposed radicalism, claimed Jacob, was that private capital had been scared away. Citing the Parker case as an example, Jacob and his Citizen allies denounced Farmer and the ILP for chasing investment from the city and causing economic hardship. *The North Ender* urged Winnipeg to wake up, suggesting that if the ILP gained control of the city, "within a few years private industry and private business will be abolished."[40] Jacob himself declared:

> There is something wrong with Winnipeg at the present time. Cities to the east of us and cities to the west of us have been going ahead in 1923. What about Winnipeg? We are actually going backward instead of forward. Not in my experience in Winnipeg for the past eighteen years has the horizon been so cloudy as during 1923. During the mayoralty terms served by Mr. Ashdown, Mr. Evans, Mr. Waugh, and Mr. Deacon before the war, Winnipeg went ahead by leaps and bounds....

Why with the same clear blue sky shining over this whole continent should a dark cloud be over Winnipeg?[41]

The answer, to Jacob, was simple: "there is no hope of any money coming in here for investment because the financial centres of the world felt there is no assurance of protection."[42] According to Citizens, labour and Farmer were to blame for Winnipeg's economic troubles.

Not surprisingly, Farmer disputed Jacob's economics, commenting, "one would imagine that the four years had nothing to do with [the economic challenges]. I am evidently held responsible for the collapse of European markets. Mr Jacob presumably believes that it is through the influence of a labour mayor that the crop in Manitoba did not come up to expectations."[43] It was, he argued, an issue of global scale, not the fault of a pro-labour mayor. "Terrible things were going to happen if labour was elected a year ago," said Farmer. He continued, "I ask you if any one of those terrible things has happened. You know that they have not. You were told that taxes would go up and they have not. A year ago it was either 'Farmer and the Reign of Furies' or 'Sparling and Stability.' Now it is 'Farmer and a Funeral' or 'Jacob and a Jamboree.' There is no foundation to the statements that either a labour mayor or labour aldermen had anything to do with the existing business depression."[44] Farmer countered that Jacob's campaign was a well-financed machine, funded by the corporate elites that wanted to erase labour from government, declaring, "we have had enough of corporation dictatorship, let the rule of the people continue!"[45] Two days later he described the Citizens as a "well-oiled political machine, organized on a gigantic scale [spending money] as if it were water in an effort to defeat labour."[46] In short, said Farmer, the Citizens were simply trying to gain back the control they had lost when he had been elected, describing a "feverish desire of certain interests to get back the control over civic affairs that was wrenched from their hands a year ago."[47]

Beyond just defeating labour, Farmer accused the Citizens of attempting to win in order to preserve the private ownership of public utilities. His opponents, he said, would pick apart existing public utilities while maintaining the Winnipeg Electric Railway's franchise. Farmer was clear. Public ownership of utilities was essential and only the ILP could save them. Jacob, too, said that he would maintain public ownership, but was accused by Farmer of having a hidden agenda and many of Jacob's supporters were vocally against public ownership.

As the votes were counted on 23 November 1923 the results quickly became clear, with Farmer winning the largest majority in city history. In celebration, Farmer was carried shoulder-high along Portage Avenue to the *Free Press* building on Carlton, where a crowd had gathered to watch the results. There he was met with "a thunderous ovation by thousands of citizens who were awaiting the progressive returns of the city vote."[48] Labour had also managed to win an additional aldermanic seat, increasing their presence on council from six to seven. The ILP even won first place in Ward One, the Citizen stronghold in south Winnipeg, although after preferential ballots transferred votes to the Citizen candidates, the ILP only narrowly won the seat.

S.J. Farmer had made public ownership of utilities a central component of his re-election campaign, but without a majority backing him on city council, there was little he could do to extend the city's reach into public ownership. It was not until the fall that he was able to take a strong stand on an issue related to public ownership. The *Manitoba Free Press* reported that the Norman Dam, a privately held dam providing electricity to the city, was in bad shape and was seeking public funds for repair. Farmer saw this as an opportunity for the public to take ownership of the dam and was quick to condemn a federal government plan to pay for the needed repairs and for the right to control the dam's generators, while maintaining private ownership of the dam itself.

Farmer was not alone in making this stand. Some of his Citizen opponents and several provincial politicians declared that they were against the deal, saying it would limit power availability, increase costs, and discourage growth. But it was Farmer, in his role as mayor, who would take the lead in opposing the use of public funds for the Norman Dam.

More awkwardly, Farmer found himself representing the city and its notorious Slave Pact for municipal workers against labour opposition. In June 1924, the International Brotherhood of Electrical Workers (IBEW) wrote to the city to complain about the "Slave Pact," the rule that prohibited city workers from affiliating with outside unions. The IBEW declared that this arrangement limited freedom of association and was depriving municipal workers of the sick and death benefit funds they had paid into when they had been union members prior to the General Strike.[49] City council was split on how to respond. Labour aldermen proposed that the IBEW's accusations should be given due consideration, while Citizens sought to dismiss them outright, which is what the city did.

The complaint did not die there. Federal Minister of Labour James Murdock wrote Farmer, saying that he would force a Board of Conciliation on the city if it did not agree to one voluntarily. Murdock appealed to Farmer as someone "sympathetic to organized labour for many years" to address the city's "entirely indefensible," "un-British and un-Canadian attitude."[50] Farmer found himself in the peculiar position of being a pro-labour mayor defending the Slave

Pact to an infuriated federal minister. It is unclear what Farmer thought about the issue. He had a long history of opposing the Slave Pact but never spoke publicly on this particular issue as mayor, and there were some ILP aldermen who joined with the Citizens to dismiss the bid, saying there was little interest in it from local union members. Nevertheless, this peculiar position shows the limitations of his position. While he was in the centre of the Slave Pact debate, there was little that he could actually do about the Slave Pact.

If Farmer was unable to effect real change for workers while they were alive, he did manage to change their fate after death. A free grave section had been available at Brookside cemetery. This area was located apart from the rest of the cemetery and the city buried people there who could not afford to be buried elsewhere. Even the simplest of funerals could cost $100, a steep price for Winnipeg's poorest workers.[51] A pauper burial, however, meant a gravesite that was poorly cared for and where no monuments were allowed for the dead. Even in death, Winnipeg's poor were geographically and socially divided from the rest of the city.

Farmer was the key public voice in opposing the segregated free-grave system. When Frederick Davidson, a Citizen alderman, proposed beautifying the free burial area, Farmer declared that he was against a free section, beautified or not, because it represented discrimination against one class. To this, Davidson and Alexander Leonard questioned if anyone would want to be buried in a cemetery that had neglected graves scattered throughout. But Farmer held firm, and by October, the city decided to revamp its free grave system. No longer would free graves be segregated in one section of Brookside Cemetery, they would be mixed throughout. Even if Winnipeg's poor could not avoid class divisions while alive, they could at least do so when they were dead.

Farmer also continued to use council rulings to shape council debates. Just as he had used this power during debates over the Parker scheme in 1923, he continued to raise Citizen hackles for employing his powers as chair. In December 1923, for example, Alderman Herbert Jones of the ILP was asked to withdraw remarks he had made about a Citizen alderman. After doing so, Alderman Leonard complained that council had not had quorum and so the withdrawal should be repeated. Farmer refused, saying that the matter was now closed and that council had to move on to other issues. At this, two Citizen aldermen staged a walkout, angering Farmer, as protocol insisted that they request permission from the chair before leaving the council chamber. Alderman John Sullivan, one of those walking out, commented that "when you have been giving such rulings as you have been for the last couple of terms, I don't feel any necessity to wait for permission."⁵² To calm the situation, Alderman Jones apologized again, which Leonard accepted.

Just over a month later, Farmer was accused by Citizen aldermen of being discriminatory in his rulings. Alderman Thomas Boyd, in particular, was annoyed at his treatment in the council chamber. He accused Farmer of cutting him off during debates and picking on him. Referring to the December walkout, he commented, "I've been on council for three years and have never heard one member leaving the council chamber ask permission to go yet one night you called me back and asked that I request that permission."⁵³ Despite an inability to control the direction of the city, Farmer could shape council discussions using the power of the mayor's chair in a way that frequently infuriated his opponents.

It seemed that no one expected the raucous election campaign of 1924 that would ultimately result in the defeat of S.J. Farmer. In October, many ILP leaders thought that Farmer might even be acclaimed, letting them focus on pushing for two more labour aldermen to give him a majority to work with.⁵⁴ It would not be until well into November that an opposing candidate, Ralph Webb, would come forward, with Farmer saying as late as November 18, ten days before the election, that there were no real issues in the campaign and that he did not really feel that he even had an opponent. His opponent, Farmer said, had a platform that could be summarized in a single world: "Boost."⁵⁵

When Ralph Webb finally made his first election campaign appearance nine days before the election, he immediately shook up the campaign. Large gatherings formed to see the decorated, one-legged soldier who had come to Winnipeg only twenty months earlier. Webb was carried by his tremendous ability as a public speaker, winning crowds over with his sharp, off-the-cuff quips and pointed attacks on Farmer and the ILP. As city solicitor Jules Preud'homme recalled, Webb's "ideas would flow forth, in the proper sequence, at the most effective moment."⁵⁶

Webb was much more successful than either Sparling or Jacob had been at denouncing the ILP. For example, Webb denounced Farmer for "representing only a small portion of the honest labour in the city; 97 percent of the people in Winnipeg are 'labour' and, thank the Lord, most of them are sane. A few Communists have got the community buffaloed. Hit 'em in the right spot and they'll come back among the decent citizens."⁵⁷ Webb appealed to Winnipeggers, quipping, "when you get out the vote, no 'ism' can rule in an Anglo-Saxon country."⁵⁸ In substance these attacks were not dissimilar to those of Sparling or Jacob in the previous two years, but Webb's barbs seemed to stick in a way that neither Sparling's nor Jacob's had. Webb had a reputation of being able to connect with working-class voters, something that recent Citizen candidates had had little success with.

Webb's military credentials played a significant role in the campaign. As the *North Ender* pointed out, Webb "lost a leg fighting for which Mayor Farmer did not lose a hair on his head."[59] Webb, after all, was a decorated soldier who had won the DSO, MC, and Croix de Guerre, whereas Farmer had opposed the war altogether. In the past two elections, the *Manitoba Free Press* had shown some indifference to the result of the mayoral election, and even subtly suggested that a labour victory might not be such a bad thing in 1923. In this campaign it played an active role in supporting Webb by featuring daily letters on the front page from Webb's military contacts across the country attesting to his leadership, patriotism, and business savvy.

The campaign would become one of personality, with Farmer, an "effective and dignified debater,"[60] quickly swept aside in favour of the easily quotable, populist Webb. Farmer tried to refocus the campaign on his strong suit, the public ownership of utilities. It would be the council in 1925 that would have the final say over the extension of the WEC's franchise in 1927. He suggested that Webb was not being honest when he said that he was in favour of public utilities, arguing that only he had the track record of defending public utilities in the city. Webb, however, had learned the lesson of previous Citizen candidates. Rather than tacking to the right on the public utilities issue, he essentially took the issue off the table by adopting Farmer's platform on the issue, with both candidates arguing that the street railway question was one for the electorate. Indeed, promising a referendum enabled Webb to appeal to a broader swath of the electorate without losing his base.

The quiet debate over the public street railway would be the closest that Winnipeg voters would get to hearing a policy discussion in the 1924 election. The campaign quickly became personal. Webb accused Farmer of "not being big enough for the job" and told voters that "the present mayor does as he's told by the ILP, and cannot do much more."[61] The insult fit well with Webb's portrayal of himself as the candidate in control. Farmer was dismissed as weak: he had not fought in the war; he was supposedly under the control of party or class interests; he could not motivate the city.

Farmer could see the campaign that he had taken for granted slipping from his grasp. In the final days of the campaign, he desperately attacked Webb, accusing him of "insufferable ignorance" of civic affairs. The campaign, he declared, was not a serious election campaign. After all, Webb had lived in the city for only twenty months—how could he expect to be mayor? Instead, Farmer announced, Webb's campaign was "one of the best advertising schemes I have ever seen for an individual's business (the Marlborough Hotel)." He expanded from there: "it is amazing that we can for one minute tolerate a man, who has been in the city for only twenty months and also consents to run for mayor of the city, and lend himself to such a campaign of vilification in order to satisfy his inordinate vanity and advertise the business he is engaged in."[62]

On 27 November 1924, Ralph Webb told his supporters in a radio address, "get out to vote and let's tell the world—like Britain and the USA—that Winnipeg is solid for progress."[63] His message was embraced by Winnipegers. The election that was supposed to be a cakewalk for Farmer ended in a stunning defeat to a candidate who was new to politics and who had campaigned for all of nine days. Webb carried 22,014 votes, with a winning margin of nearly 5,000. The result was not good for labour in other ways, with both Ward Two and Ward Three headed by non-labour candidates. Webb would go on to have a prominent mayoral career built on his winning recipe of jingoistic boosterism. Always a strong proponent of the city's capitalist status quo, he described his victory as a "staggering blow" to the "ambitions of the Red element of Winnipeg."[64] He will continue to be a presence throughout this book, particularly in his fights with local communists.

At Farmer's last city council meeting, two long-time opponents, Dan McLean and John McKerchar, brought forward a motion that was unanimously accepted by council congratulating the mayor for his years of service. Farmer, the motion read, "has upheld with dignity the highest honor the people of Winnipeg can give any of its citizens and has rendered the city efficient and faithful service."[65] Praise was also to be found in the editorial page of the *Manitoba Free Press*, which told its readers that Farmer's defeat "should not be interpreted as any condemnation of [his] two years' occupancy" and that Farmer "has been a creditable chief magistrate."[66]

In terms of changing the city, Farmer had actually been able to do very little. He left office with the street railway in private hands, civic workers governed by the Slave Pact, and conditions for the unemployed much as they had been two years earlier. The mayoralty was largely a symbolic role, particularly with a hostile majority on city council. Farmer could participate in public debate, lending credibility to an alternative view of the city, but could do very little to actually achieve it. This should not be seen as a failure of Farmer's, however, but a recognition of the limitations of the mayoralty.

Speaking to a group of supporters shortly after his defeat, Farmer said that while he was a defeated candidate, he was "a member of an organization which could not be defeated."[67] There would be some tough years for the ILP in municipal politics as they struggled to recapture the heights of the early 1920s. Citizen candidates used what the ILP described as "steamroller tactics," denying ILP aldermen any committee chair positions and any place on the important police commission.[68] A story from the *Weekly News* described the frustration of ILP aldermen in council: "Practically no discussion took place as to the merits or demerits of the proposed increases [to taxes]. The majority of the Aldermen voted steadily against any increase. The labour aldermen steadily supported the increases and a very few managed to get through."[69] In such a polarized environment there was little that labour could do on council without a majority of the seats.

It would take another decade for an ILP candidate to be elected as mayor. But the next time a labour candidate would be elected as mayor it would be along with nine candidates sympathetic to labour, enough for a slim majority. That would take another decade to develop. Meanwhile, a new force was about to enter the political arena in Winnipeg, opening up a new front for the ILP, which now had to ward off attacks from within its working-class base.

CHAPTER 3

THE REVOLUTIONARY PARTY ON THE PARLIAMENTARY MAP

Winnipeg's May Day celebrations during the 1920s and 1930s were an impressive sight. Ten thousand workers marched the streets in an orderly procession, taking forty-five minutes to pass any given point, with red revolutionary banners flitting in the breeze above them. Placards with slogans such as "Against Hunger, War, and Fascism" and "Workers of the World Unite" were hoisted proudly on the shoulders of marchers. At the head of the parade, 600 children sang songs glorifying proletarian revolution and the working class. As the Federation of Russian Canadians marched, wearing black jackets and open white shirts, their deep bass voices sang the national anthem of the Soviet Union. Gradually, the procession would make its way into Market Square, just outside City Hall. Workers and curious onlookers gathered in the Square as local communist leaders denounced capitalist war preparations and declared that the overthrow of the capitalist system was necessary to end the suffering of the working class. Before they dispersed into the cool spring evening, the crowd joined in a rousing rendition of "The Internationale."[1]

After the defeat of S.J. Farmer in the 1924 mayoralty race, the political left and the Citizens entered somewhat of a holding pattern for the next decade, with Citizen candidates winning approximately two-thirds of council seats and the mayoral election. It would be another decade before the left was in a position to challenge the governing power of the Citizens. However, there was much happening within the left itself during the mid-1920s that would shift Winnipeg's political landscape for decades to come. It was after the defeat of Farmer as mayor that the Communist Party of Canada, which participated in municipal elections under a variety of names, emerged as a small but significant force within local politics, a force that would challenge the ILP from the left for aldermanic seats and political legitimacy in Winnipeg's North End.

Two years after Farmer's defeat at the hands of Ralph Webb it appeared that there would be nothing particularly interesting in the results of the November 1926 election. Mayor Webb was re-elected with a convincing 61 percent of the vote, and after the first-place votes had been counted in the transferrable ballot system, the *Manitoba Free Press* predicted that all incumbent aldermen would be re-elected and the balance of power in the council chambers would remain the same: eleven Citizens and seven ILP members. As second-place ballots were counted, however, things began to change. Much to the surprise of many, William Kolisnyk (1887–1967), the Communist Party candidate, edged ILP incumbent Robert Durward for the final council spot in Ward Three. The Communist Party had come close before. Matthew Popovich had come within seventy-nine votes of a council seat a year earlier. But this was a historic first for the Communist Party: Winnipeg was declared to be the first place in North America to elect a communist to office.

As far away as New York, communist newspapers reported the victory of William Kolisnyk.[2] Yet while press from far-flung destinations trumpeted the news, the win went almost without notice in Winnipeg's mainstream press. The only mention of it was a small editorial in the *Free Press,* which said, "Mr. Kolisnyk is linked to the staff headquarters in Moscow; he is the local officer of the Bolshevist army which marches under the red banner." It went on to say that, "Bolshevist Russia has now established a definite outpost in the healthy heart of Canada."[3]

Despite limited press coverage, the result would have key ramifications for the political left in Winnipeg. No longer could the ILP count on a united labour vote in Ward Three; vote splitting was now a reality. Kolisnyk's win had not come at the expense of a Citizen candidate. Rather, it was a loss for the ILP. The defeated candidate, Robert Durward, was known for his fine labour credentials, having been blacklisted and losing his job for his role as assistant secretary to the Strike Committee in 1919. Kolisnyk's win, therefore, marked a new era in Winnipeg municipal politics in two ways. First, it marked the beginning of a communist presence on city council that would last, almost uninterrupted, for nearly sixty years. Second, it also indicated the rise of the conflict within the political left, illustrating the sharp division and rivalry that would develop between the ILP and the CPC, particularly in north Winnipeg.

Kolisnyk would serve on council for only four years but his life in public office illuminates several intriguing aspects of communist history. First, since his term was split roughly in half by the introduction of Third Period ideology to the Communist Party, his career demonstrates practical shifts that resulted from a change in international party policy. Meanwhile, Kolisnyk's career also reveals pragmatic political decision making and an attention to grassroots issues not always associated with Third Period communism. Second, the seemingly conflict-prone Kolisnyk highlighted ethnic divisions within the party and the role of ethnicity in the relationship between communists and other parties on the left. Finally, Kolisnyk's election (and his re-election in 1928) demonstrates the tremendous effort that communists in Winnipeg put into municipal politics.

Winnipeg was the first but would not be the only Canadian municipality in which communists participated successfully in local electoral politics. Estimates given by *The Worker* and internal party reports to the Communist International indicate that the number of elected communist aldermen and school board trustees ranged between twenty-five and ninety by the early 1930s.[4] Many of these were elected in small villages and towns such as Maillardville, British Columbia and Headley, Alberta, each of which elected a communist alderman. Closer to Winnipeg, Lac du Bonnet, Manitoba elected two communist aldermen and a communist reeve. But perhaps the communists' best known foray into municipal politics occurred in another small community, the mining town of Blairmore, Alberta, where the party would win control of town council, famously renaming Main Street as "Tim Buck Boulevard," after the national CPC leader.[5] More importantly for the miners who had elected communists, the council "brought about changes big and small to favour the hitherto disadvantaged."[6] Although CPC candidates had less success in other large western centres, they elected an alderman in Regina in 1935. In Brandon, Manitoba communists polled over 1,000 votes in an unsuccessful aldermanic campaign in 1934.[7]

The Communist Party also enjoyed some electoral success in eastern Canada, particularly in Ontario. The city of East Windsor elected several communist aldermen, while communists were also occasionally elected as aldermen in communities such as Stratford.[8] Even in cities where communists did not win seats on local councils, they increased their share of the vote throughout the early 1930s. In 1931, for example, the CPC bragged that it had doubled its vote total in Toronto and increased it six-fold in Hamilton.[9] Over a decade after winning a seat in Winnipeg, the CPC would eventually elect a communist alderman in Toronto, when Stewart Smith was elected on 1 January 1937. Communists delighted in these electoral victories as signs that their party was gaining popularity. This, they believed, suggested that workers were becoming increasingly confident in the party's program of revolution and that the working-class base of the party was growing.[10]

Across Canada, therefore, the CPC viewed municipal government as an important front on which to wage its revolutionary struggle. The CPC recognized that the "realm of municipal government embraces those things which affect the everyday lives of the masses more directly than do even the national politicies [sic] of the capitalist class."[11] Municipal politics involved more than debates over sidewalks and spite fences. Unemployment relief, police intimidation of striking workers, public transportation, and property taxation, to name a few, were issues that communists could address through activism on a municipal level. These issues also helped make communism real (and popular) for some of the working class. Whereas national policies and international relations were distant to everyday life in Winnipeg's North End, shifts in municipal policy could have an immediate impact on the living conditions of the working class.

When Kolisnyk was elected in November 1926 he could not possibly have imagined the changes that were in store for communist strategy in the coming years. In 1928, two years after Kolisnyk's election, communists around the world accepted a radical shift in their political outlook known as the "Third Period." This change originated from the Comintern, or Communist International, the body of Communist parties from around the world. While the Comintern was an international organization, the Soviet Union played a special role within it. In part this was because the Soviet Union was the first successful communist revolution, giving it special status within the communist world. Pragmatically, as well, the Soviet Union provided the Comintern with financial resources and hosted representatives from around the world. Interestingly, much of what we know about communism in Canada during the 1920s and 1930s is from reports back from the CPC to the Comintern, sharing in great detail what was occurring in Canada.

The "Third Period" was based on an interpretation of communism advocated by Nikolai Bukharin and Joseph Stalin. The capitalist system, they declared, was on the brink of a catastrophic crisis as it buckled under the weight of its internal contradictions. The name for this time of crisis, the "Third Period," was derived from an understanding of history that divided capitalist development after the First World War into three periods. The first period was marked by worker uprisings around the world and lasted until 1923. Capitalism, Bukharin and Stalin argued, then took the offensive and stabilized itself. The result of this "Second Period," however, was that the internal contradictions of capitalism became increasingly apparent. The ability of capitalist nations to produce goods was growing, while their markets were not. This, Third Period theorists proposed, would inevitably mean that capitalist nations would wage wars against each other to gain new markets for their products. Additionally, as capitalist nations increased their productivity, unemployment would ensue, thus making workers increasingly dissatisfied with their oppression. The outcome of this frustration would be the overthrow of the capitalist system by the working class under the leadership of a communist party. To prepare for this moment, communist parties around the world were instructed to "Bolshevize" themselves in order to properly lead the workers.[12]

The Worker noted that the Third Period represented "a turning point in the history of our party in bringing to a close a period of tolerance and conciliation towards right, opportunist tendencies, and outlining a policy of decisive struggle against such tendency in our Party."[13] One practical result of the Third Period was that the Communist Party was instructed to cease cooperating with social democratic parties and mainstream trade unions, who were dismissed as "social fascists" in order that they could "lead the masses to a frontal assault on the bourgeois state."[14] Criticism of others on the left was certainly not entirely new for the communists. Lenin had used derogatory phrases such as "social patriots" and "social chauvinists" to describe reform-minded opponents on the left.[15] Nevertheless, this marked a sharp shift for the CPC. No longer would they endorse ILP candidates like John Queen for office. Instead, these so-called "social fascists," communists declared, "restrained the workers from revolutionary action against the capitalist offensive and growing fascism, [played] the part of a screen behind which the fascists [were] able to organize their forces, and [built] the road for fascist dictatorship."[16]

The Third Period was adopted wholeheartedly by the CPC. Members who did not fervently accept Third Period ideology were expelled. District and national conventions adopted the "correct Leninist line," which they believed would lead to the creation of a truly revolutionary party.[17] In Winnipeg, communists pledged themselves to "energetically strive to build and consolidate our Party on a Marxist-Leninist revolutionary theory, that it may be a worthy section of the fighting Communist International."[18]

Ian Angus strenuously condemns Third Period communism in Canada as a time when the CPC isolated itself from the masses more than ever.[19] He argues that the party's disdain for all possible allies and its "go-it-alone" policy led to massive defeats.[20] Bryan Palmer comes to a similar conclusion, arguing that although there are positives to be found in the communist work among the unemployed, "these were years that set the stage for the acceptance of the irrational, for blind faith in the 'line,' however far removed from Canadian reality it might have been."[21]

John Manley, conversely, has proposed that despite the "indigestibly provocative" style of the Third Period, the Workers' Unity League was "unexpectedly responsive to its context and the moods and needs of its constituency."[22] Communist unionists, Manley argues, placed flexibility above doctrinal purity and studied the local working class as much as any Comintern directive.[23] The result was that while Communist Party membership fell significantly in the first eighteen months of the Third Period, it reached record heights by the end of the

Third Period. Clearly something about this intransigent style appealed in a time of economic desperation.

The Third Period is also a pivotal moment in the study of communist parties around the world, particularly relating to the relationship between national communist parties and the Soviet Union. Historians have largely divided into two schools in a debate so intense that it has been remarked that, "although the Cold War was over...it continued among historians of American [and, one could likely add, Canadian] communism."[24] Traditionalists stress centralized, Soviet domination or influence over party structures around the world, arguing that the direction of the Third Period was decided in Moscow and parties around the world had little agency in the implementation of the party line.[25] Revisionists, conversely, have argued that the grassroots had far more autonomy than the traditionalists have credited them with. A revisionist would argue that while the party line came from Moscow or national party offices, how this line was implemented was shaped by the communities in which communists lived, worked, and organized.[26]

Consequently, traditionalists have charged revisionists with, among other things, being "strong on the periphery and weak at the core,"[27] essentially saying that while histories of grassroots communists might be interesting, they miss the key power dynamic at play within the party. Revisionists, meanwhile, argue that traditionalists miss understanding how actual communists lived and worked, how communism was experienced at the grassroots.

Others have tried to hold a middle ground. Andrew Thorpe, in his study of British communism, suggested a third interpretation, "post-revisionism," to incorporate the strengths of both traditionalist and revisionist scholarship. This scholarship suggests that communism was shaped both by "local factors, personal experiences, and contingencies as well as by global events and international politics."[28] As Mark Solomon has suggested, communists were "neither mindless dupes of the Soviet-dominated Comintern nor the new historians' wily, independent radicals clearly sidestepping external directives."[29] "Post-revisionism" too has been critiqued, primarily for seeking to "construct and demolish a straw man" by simplifying the complexities of the other two arguments.[30]

The post-revisionist model is in many ways reflective of William Kolisnyk's career. Just as Kolisnyk's career points to the way that the Third Period created a radically different Communist Party in Winnipeg, it also points to local variances in how this new line was implemented. As Nancy Butler has written, "counsel received from the Comintern was anything but idle advice." But, as Butler says, local circumstances required a "complexity of strategy and tactics" that are lost in a monolithic interpretation of communist activity. There were wrinkles in its adoption shaped by the unique circumstances and people within the Party, perhaps no more so than Kolisnyk himself.[31]

William Kolisnyk, or Wasyl Kolisnyk in Ukrainian, was born in western Ukraine in 1887 and immigrated to Canada in 1898. His first experience with labour activism, claimed a CPC tribute, came as the spokesperson for a group of soft-drink bottling workers at the age of fourteen.[32] He would later be instrumental in the establishment of a branch of the Social Democratic Party in Portage la Prairie, Manitoba before moving to Winnipeg in 1910, where he quickly became involved in the Ukrainian radical community. Kolisnyk was also involved in the creation of North America's first Ukrainian workers' paper, *The Scarlet Banner*.[33]

Kolisnyk's rise in the local structure of the CPC came as a result of his work amongst the Ukrainian community. In 1917, he undertook a fundraising tour in eastern Canada for the Ukrainian Labour-Farmer Temple Association. He also played a prominent role in organizing a General and Building Trades Union, which represented primarily immigrant workers (Ukrainian, Polish, Russian, Italian, and Icelandic) in the construction trades in 1917.[34] His organizing activities drew the attention of the police. In 1917, Kolisnyk was arrested for organizing for the Social Democratic Party in Creighton Mine, Ontario and ordered to return to Winnipeg.[35] RCMP records on Kolisnyk date back to speeches made by Kolisnyk for Ukrainian Labour Temple events in 1921, although given his involvement in radical politics it is likely that police were aware of his activities earlier than that.[36]

It is not clear when Kolisnyk became a party member, but he must have done it shortly after the CPC was founded in 1921, as by 1922 he ran for the Workers' Party of Canada (the name for the legal wing of the party) in the District of St. Clement's, Manitoba, where he finished a distant third out of four candidates. Two years later he was the Secretary of the Communist Party Ukrainian Branch in Winnipeg.[37] As the RCMP reported in 1927, "Kolisnyk has been very active recently in giving his time and advice to Ukrainian workers who have asked for some, in this way thinking to acquire some degree of popularity."[38] He was a frequent speaker at communist gatherings, and was described as one of the "community's best orators."[39] He also was a member of the National Ukrainian Party Fraction Bureau and visited numerous camps, mines, and communities across Manitoba in that capacity.[40] Through these connections, Kolisnyk developed a natural constituency for his political career and remained tremendously influential among Ukrainian communists until the mid-1930s. It was to be this

9. The May Day march in 1936. William Kolisnyk is second from right in the first row. (AUUC-WBA Archives)

popularity in the Ukrainian community that would lead to his selection as the Communist Party candidate in place of Matthew Popovich in the 1926 election.

Kolisnyk earned a living by operating a bicycle shop in a large store on Main Street, which, according to the RCMP, was "quite prosperous."[41] Some party members, it was said, resented the fact that Kolisnyk was a small business owner rather than a worker. Yet, despite Kolisnyk's business background, James Mochoruk has described him as a man with "impeccable radical credentials."[42] Kolisnyk would use his business experience to found and manage the Workers' and Farmers' Cooperative Association, an important North End institution, in 1928.[43] Kolisnyk argued that a cooperative would help workers struggle against "unmerciful capitalism" while providing a vital service to meet the needs of the North End community.[44] The organization quickly became a success, selling $20,000 of fuel in its first year alone. The Cooperative eventually branched out into dairy operations. Under Kolisnyk's management, the Cooperative achieved a substantial membership, including many non-communists, and was known within the community for its fair business practices and quality products.[45]

In one of the very few descriptions of Kolisnyk that exist in secondary literature, Lita-Rose Betcherman describes him as a "little man with runny eyes, he was a Chaplinesque figure among the solid burghers of City Council."[46] She goes on to say that Kolisnyk would have been content to live a life of obscurity, a minor party member running a bicycle repair shop. Kolisnyk's electoral career, she claims, was thrust upon him when Matthew Popovich decided not to run for city council in 1926. This characterization, however, does not seem to align with much of Kolisnyk's biography. He had run for elected office long before 1926 and had previously served as a leading force in other socialist movements in Manitoba. Additionally, he played a significant role in the Workers' and Farmers' Cooperative and the Ukrainian communist community. Even after he was defeated in 1930, he continued his political career, running for political office in 1932 and considering further election campaigns as late as 1934. This would not appear to be a reluctant candidate who shied away from the spotlight.

William Kolisnyk was elected on a nine-point platform summarized by the slogan "Shall the Workers or Bankers Rule?"[47] The program focused on restoring the right of civic employees to organize in unions, full-time work for all unemployed workers or the equivalent in relief, municipal ownership of all public utilities, the removal of tax exemptions for corporations, the establishment of universal franchise (rather than a property-based voting system) for municipal elections and referendums, and a reduction in the tax rate for working-class houses.[48] On the surface, these policies, although radical, were certainly not revolutionary. As the *OBU Bulletin* sarcastically observed a year later, the most "revolutionary" CPC policy in the election was a five-cent street-car fare.[49]

The campaign to get Kolisnyk elected involved much of the CPC's membership. Young Pioneers, a communist youth group, contributed by distributing campaign bulletins throughout the North End. According to *The Worker*, over 12,000 flyers were distributed in English, while leaflets were also published in several other languages to attract support from the numerous ethnic groups in the ward. The immigrant population of the North End played a significant role in the CPC's election strategy. Jewish, Polish, German, and Ukrainian sub-committees were formed to carry out election work among the major language groups.[50] The RCMP noted that Kolisnyk's election campaign was being handled in a "very systematic and businesslike manner," as he was the only candidate to appeal to foreigners in their own language.[51] Unlike the Citizens or the ILP, the CPC was not dominated by people of British descent and was able to appeal primarily to the North End's numerous immigrant communities.

Despite the intense rivalry that would grow between the ILP and CPC, communist election materials actually encouraged voters to support ILP mayoral candidates and to give their second-choice aldermanic votes to ILP candidates. In 1927, for example, a campaign newspaper explained that the "main thing is the defeat of bourgeois candidates" and that voters should support a "solid labour ticket," albeit with communist candidates ranked first.[52] In the mayoral race that year, the paper advised that "it is the duty of the workers to oust [Dan] McLean (the Citizen candidate), smash the united efforts of the Liberals and Conservatives to defeat Labour and elect [John] Queen as mayor over the heads of the reactionary capitalist parties."[53] Defeating Citizens was important, and if there were no communists to vote for, ILP candidates would do. This type of endorsement, typical of the CPC's political activity in the mid-1920s, would be considered heretical in the Communist Party when the Third Period would be adopted later that decade.

The ILP had a different impression of communist electoral tactics. During the same election highlighted above, for example, supporters of communist aldermanic candidate Leslie Morris had given more of their second choice votes to J.F. Palmer, the Citizen candidate, than to J.A. Cherniak of the ILP, ensuring Palmer's election. It is not clear why communists were instructed to support one ILP candidate, but seemed to contribute to the defeat of another. The ILP's *Weekly News* declared that "this so-called Simon pure working-class party who prate no truck or truckle with the boss, have a lot of explaining to do as a result of the transfers of the ballot."[54] Additionally, the ILP was annoyed with the communists' tendency to only focus on the ILP rather than their Citizen opponents. The *OBU Bulletin* described how after the communists elected Kolisnyk, "the message went out to the world that the Communist Party had defeated the Independent Labour Party in Winnipeg. They did not say a word about defeating a capitalist opponent."[55] The ILP, naturally, was concerned about the competition for working-class affiliation from a party whose ideology it so despised. Their rivalry with the communists certainly involved ideology, but the rivalry in part was based on simple mathematics: if communists were elected, ILPers were not.

The ILP and their supporters vehemently opposed communist participation in municipal elections, particularly denouncing the appeal the communists held among Eastern European immigrants. The *OBU Bulletin* wrote that the communists were "opportunists of the first water" who were "exploiting the sentiment of two or three nationalist groups."[56] They suggested that communists had "no knowledge of Canadian conditions, Canadian problems, or the working class movement in this country."[57] Thus, the communists were cast by their labour opponents as foreigners unfamiliar with local conditions who could only appeal to the nationalistic tendencies of immigrants.

Not surprisingly, the ILP's newspaper, the *Weekly News*, minimized the significance of the communist victory. It suggested that "the number of North Winnipeg voters who understand the communist philosophy and desire to see the communist platform carried out in Winnipeg, or Western Canada, are [*sic*] negligible."[58] Furthermore, the paper declared, "everybody is saying that Mr. Kolisnyk was elected to the City Council not by a communist vote, but by a nationalist vote."[59] An RCMP investigator came to a similar conclusion, reporting that campaign literature published by the Ukrainian Sub-election Committee of the CPC emphasized the importance of electing a Ukrainian worker to council, although it should be noted that both the ILP and RCMP were opponents of the communists and had an interest in portraying them as foreign.[60]

Communists dismissed allegations of nationalist voting and countered that Kolisnyk's election demonstrated that the workers were tired of the ILP's reformist approach and desired a more radical alternative. *The Worker* commended the Winnipeg comrades for placing "the revolutionary party on the parliamentary map."[61] Although they had spent much of their campaign attempting to reach out to immigrant voters, communists did not believe that Kolisnyk's nationality was the reason for his victory. Instead, the CPC argued that the victory of Kolisnyk demonstrated that their message was reaching the working class. Moreover, the CPC appealed to the legacy of the General Strike, arguing that "over two thousand Winnipeg workers showed that they had not forgotten the lessons of 1919 by voting for a true Communist programme of immediate demands."[62] No longer on the margins of municipal politics, communists were now able to play a more significant role, both in elections and on council.

The issue of ethnicity continued to be a point of tension between the ILP and the communists after Kolisnyk's election. While the ILP and its allies accused the communists of merely appealing to nationalistic sympathies in their 1926 election victory, communists later suggested that the ILP was itself engaging in such activities. In 1927, the CPC accused the ILP of using an "old electioneering trick of the bosses" when they ran Stanley Bobiwski as an aldermanic candidate in Ward Three. The communists suggested that this merely served to split the Ukrainian vote and to "play on the national feelings of the Ukrainian workers." They called upon "the class-conscious workers of Ward Three to vote for our men, not as members of any race but as Communist Party candidates voicing the Communist Party program."[63] Yet by making the accusation that the ILP was targeting the Ukrainian vote, the communists perhaps demonstrated that they were hoping to benefit from national sentiments by running their own Ukrainian candidates. The fact that communists recognized that a second Ukrainian candidate would split the Ukrainian vote suggests that they had counted on it as their own.

If the ILP's plan was indeed to capture enough Ukrainian votes to win an aldermanic seat, the plan failed miserably, as Bobiwski won only 9.6 percent of the first count vote (1,244 votes). If the purpose, however, was to split enough Ukrainian votes away from the communist candidate, Matthew Popovich, to ensure the election of the two other ILP candidates, the strategy succeeded, with Popovich missing out on election by approximately 500 votes. This incident demonstrates the intersection of ethnicity with politics in Winnipeg's North End. While it is impossible to determine the relative importance of each category in the mind of Winnipeg voters, local politicians believed that ethnicity was a significant factor in the political decision making of the immigrant community.[64]

Although the CPC often fretted over the lack of Anglo-Saxon members in its midst, they attacked the relationship between the ILP and Eastern European ethnic groups. They condemned the ILP for being Anglo-centric and ignoring the needs of the immigrants who made up much of the North End's population. In 1929, for example, the CPC's election newspaper declared: "The ILP, professedly internationalist, but having a PATRONIZING attitude to foreign-born workers, has one member within its ranks who speaks for the chauvinist 'superiority' of the nobly-born Anglo-Saxon. Recently a session of the Improvements Committee of the City Council was held to investigate the discharge of some workers and charges against one of the city foremen. Alderman Flye made the statement at this meeting that "THE SOONER THEY FIRE THESE FOREIGNERS THE BETTER IT WILL BE!"[65] Despite the importance that the CPC placed on the recruitment of Anglo-Saxon workers and its attempts to expand their organization beyond the confines of North Winnipeg's immigrant communities, the CPC also attempted to position itself as the natural home of radicalism among Eastern Europeans and as the protector of immigrants. It is important to note that this inflamed rhetoric was a sign of the Third Period in action.

Ethnic division was not only a wedge issue between the ILP and the communists but also within the CPC itself. In particular, there were regular disagreements between the Ukrainian and Jewish branches of the party. There was a long history of Ukrainian-Jewish political division on the left in Winnipeg, dating back to as early as 1911, and throughout that decade "the unfriendliness of the Jewish-Ukrainian political competition brought to the surface hatred and fear."[66] In 1924, the RCMP reported that the Jewish branch had "taken a disinterested view on Party activities" after Matthew Popovich was chosen as the CPC's municipal candidate that year.[67] After Kolisnyk's victory, an RCMP informant reported, "the victory of Kolisnyk is all the more pleasing to the radical Ukrainian element at the Ukrainian Labour Temple by reason that his candidature was opposed by the Jewish section of the Communist Party."[68] Thus, even though there were many close connections between radical Jews and Ukrainians in Winnipeg (for example, the Ukrainian Matthew Popovich's wife was Jewish), there was tension between the two groups within the CPC for years to come.[69]

There were also tensions between Ukrainian communists in Winnipeg and the CPC leadership. The Ukrainian leadership, and the organizations they controlled (the Ukrainian Farmer Labour Temple Association and the Workers' Benevolent Association), were too independent-minded for party leadership. Particularly during the Third Period it was seen as important to bring all aspects of the party under centralized control. In an attempt to gain control of the local party apparatus from the Ukrainians, Leslie Morris was sent to Winnipeg in 1926. In the November 1927 municipal elections Morris sought the party's nomination by getting the City Committee rather than a general meeting (which could be dominated by the Ukrainian majority) to nominate him. After Popovic threatened that Ukrainian party members would not support Morris as a candidate, the CPC national committee declared that a full member meeting would be held.[70] Morris would eventually be confirmed as a candidate in a special by-election held alongside the election that year, but Popovich would be the communist standard bearer for Ward Three in 1927. Unlike Kolisnyk a year before and a year after, both were unsuccessful in the municipal election.

A year later, Thomas Ewen fought Kolisnyk for the party's nomination, even though Kolisnyk was a sitting alderman. Ewen nearly defeated the incumbent, who won by a slim majority of eleven votes to ten. Kolisnyk's support came from the local Ukrainian community. Many non-Ukrainian members felt that Kolisnyk had been "outwitted by the ILP" and were concerned that he was a businessman rather than a worker.[71] Dan Holmes went as far as to suggest that "with such a representative on the City Council, the 'Party' is being discredited on every move [Kolisnyk] makes."[72] He complained that, "for all we tried to remedy the situation, we were always confronted with the groups of Ukrainian comrades."[73] Conversely, Ukrainian communists saw the attempt to block Kolisnyk's renomination as another attack on Ukrainians by the CPC leadership.[74] Additionally, while Kolisnyk was being portrayed as a blundering fool by non-Ukrainian communists, the *Ukrainian Labour News* regularly published letters to the editor highlighting how Kolisnyk had assisted local workers. According to one, sent by D. Havrylenko, "Alderman Kolisnyk is a true and sincere helper in working men's matters."[75] There was seemingly a significant difference of opinion, split along ethnic lines, regarding Kolisnyk's effectiveness in his position.

The debate within the party in Winnipeg grew to the point that the national Central Executive Committee (CEC) of the CPC intervened to end the turmoil. After Kolisnyk was narrowly nominated over Ewen, the CEC reviewed the events that had transpired in Winnipeg. It was explained that "considerable internal Party dissent" had arisen out of the nomination process. On one side, Ukrainian communists claimed that no candidate other than Kolisnyk would stand a chance of winning. It was also suggested that withdrawing Kolisnyk would strengthen anti-communist Ukrainians in Winnipeg. Meanwhile, non-Ukrainians argued that Kolisnyk was not the most able communist to hold the post of alderman. The CEC sided with the Ukrainians of Winnipeg, supporting the nomination of Kolisnyk by a vote of seven to one. They proceeded to condemn those who had suggested that they would not support Kolisnyk fully during the election campaign. This, the CEC explained, "must be combated and condemned. It could not be tolerated in the Party."[76]

It is not clear what to make of the rivalries between the ethnic groups in the CPC. It was not, after all, supposed to be a federal party, but rather one that practised democratic centralism, particularly during the Third Period. However, powerful ethnic-based federations played prominent roles in the CPC, particularly since much of its membership was not of British descent.[77] In a city whose communist community was dominated by a tight-knit group from a particular ethnicity, and which had experienced some electoral success, it was only natural that jealousies and tensions should arise. At the very least, this demonstrates that there was significant tension between the various ethnic groups in the party in Winnipeg. It also indicates that some groups in the city were willing to disobey the decisions of the CPC regarding their municipal candidate. Some party members appear to have been more interested in internal squabbles than carrying out the party's decisions. Nevertheless, these inner-party divisions were kept carefully hidden from the outside world, so Kolisnyk appeared to most of the city to be the uncontested communist candidate.[78] Yet, the issue of ethnicity continued to plague the party for many years. In 1934, the Ukrainian Labour Farmer Temple Association (ULFTA) wanted to put forward Kolisnyk or another leading member of their organization as the communist candidate, but it was felt that this candidate would have lost "owing to nationalistic jealousy."[79]

The Ukrainian community was also deeply divided politically during this period between those who supported Ukrainian nationalism and the Ukrainian Catholic Church and those who supported radical left-wing politics. Based on their experience with Soviet communism, Ukrainian nationalists denounced Winnipeg's communist leaders, warning Ukrainians that "what happened in Russia, in Mexico and in Spain can happen in Canada." If communists succeeded in Canada, they declared, it would only be a matter of time before priests, nuns, and nationalists who did not submit would be put to death.[80]

Ukrainian nationalists referred to leaders such as Popovich and Kolisnyk as "men of Ukrainian origin," suggesting that their politics made them no longer Ukrainian. Furthermore, Ukrainian nationalists would attack Ukrainian communist leaders as "adherents," "hirelings," and "agents" of the "Jewish-Muscovite clique."[81] Nationalist leaders, by comparison, were supportive of conservative politics. Fourteen of twenty-six signatories to Robert Jacob's Citizen mayoral campaign against Farmer were from the Ukrainian nationalist community. Some Ukrainians went as far as to espouse fascist politics, often using anti-communism to attract Ukrainian members. These politics were frequently anti-Semitic, such as one meeting in 1936, where a Dr. Mihychuk described Jews as "the curse of mankind."[82] While it is unclear how many Ukrainians fell on either side of the nationalist-communist divide, polarizing politics were a reality of the Ukrainian community in Winnipeg during this period.

With a representative on city council, were communists now in danger of falling into the "trap of parliamentarism" that they so despised? Communists argued that municipal council was not a place for merely debating trivial local issues, but was part of the broader class struggle. J. Naviziwsky, the manager of the Ukrainian Labour-Farmer Publishing Association, argued that the CPC was "not sending its representatives to city council because it wanted a new sidewalk, but for the definite purpose of class fighting." Kolisnyk added, "we use the civic election campaigns for propaganda."[83] Elections offered a venue for communists to access the media, gain the attention of working-class voters throughout the city, and were seen as an opportunity to "draw native elements into the Party," thus solving one of the CPC's greatest perceived problems: the lack of "Canadian" members.[84]

Clearly the proletarian revolution could not come about through municipal reforms. Yet at the same time, immediate reforms were not altogether ignored. A year after Kolisnyk's defeat the CPC acknowledged that it was proper that the "Communist Party program in these elections is composed of the immediate and pressing demands of the masses" even if the ultimate goal was the "abolition of capitalism and the rule of the workers."[85] Immediate and practical reforms were an important component of Kolisnyk's activity, along with more revolutionary stances. Therefore, communist campaigns cannot merely be dismissed as a propaganda exercise. While the election of aldermen was not the desired revolution, communists seemed willing to seek out immediate solutions along the way.

Once they had succeeded in electing an alderman, communists had to determine what his role would be. *The Worker* proposed that Kolisnyk had the double task of "exposing the reformist tactics of the ILP and fighting the bosses' aldermen."[86] It was further suggested that Kolisnyk was to vote with the ILP while providing a "Communist interpretation" in council debates.[87] The latter was obviously written before the Third Period, as it publicly endorsed cooperation on council between the ILP and the communists. Kolisnyk was the visible representative of the CPC and was supposed to carry out the party line. As a member of the CPC, his role on council was linked to the revolutionary struggles of the CPC outside the council chamber, working alongside mass organizations, and bringing their causes before city council.

An interview with Kolisnyk shortly after his election suggests that he had a different interpretation from that of the rest of the party as to what his role on council was to be. He declared that he was "in the council as an alderman. I have the interests of the city at heart as much as anyone, and I will do my best for the city as a whole." He went on to say, "it is senseless to suppose I would ignore the general affairs of the city and narrow my activities to the particular demands of the working class only. I have friends in all classes and get along very well with people directly opposed to me politically and economically." Kolisnyk also explained that the CPC did not believe in the use of force to bring about revolution and denied that the Soviet Union controlled or financed the CPC.[88] Rather than being the unequivocal voice of the working class, Kolisnyk identified himself as a representative of numerous interests within the city.

This interview was not received well by fellow communists. The RCMP reported that Kolisnyk was immediately ordered to appear before a CPC committee composed of John Navis, Leslie Morris, John Esselwein, and Dan Holmes. Leslie Morris visited the *Free Press* reporter, who showed him the longhand and shorthand notes from the interview to verify his account. Morris reported to Esselwein that the incident "must be kept mum" and that "in the future, we will have to guard [Kolisnyk] closely from taking such false steps in this direction."[89] Kolisnyk was commanded to immediately retract his interview and was reminded of his role as the party's representative.[90] Interestingly, Esselwein would turn out to be an undercover RCMP investigator who infiltrated the CPC between its founding and 1928. Indeed, several of the reports in Kolisynk's RCMP file were written by Esselwein, who would also testify as a key witness against party leader Tim Buck and seven other prominent communists in 1931.[91]

As the public face of the CPC in Winnipeg, Kolisnyk was expected to be a close adherent to the party line, not an independent spokesperson. Party discipline was a fact of life in the CPC, and one that would not be changed by an electoral victory. Indeed, a year into Kolisnyk's first term as alderman, the CPC's election bulletin explained, "he was responsible to the Party all through. He reported regularly upon his activities therein. He was not a free-lance but a party member sent to the Council in the name of over two thousand workers."[92] It would seem, according to this report at least, that Kolisnyk had learned his lesson and was properly carrying out the party line. In an article written by Kolisnyk that appeared in the *Workers Election Bulletin*, he made it clear that "most...matters taken up by the city council are of a class character."[93]

A second scandal erupted after Kolisnyk backed away from a promise to give 40 percent of his aldermanic salary to the CPC. He claimed that he needed the money to pay off his debts and could not afford to turn it over.[94] After significant debate, Kolisnyk successfully convinced members that he should be able to retain his entire salary. Nevertheless, the combination of a controversial interview and the question of Kolisnyk's pay raised questions in the minds of many communists even before Kolisnyk was able to officially take office.

Interestingly, the ILP was also forced to deal with similar issues when they had aldermen elected to city council. Many members of the ILP requested that anyone elected on an ILP ticket give 10 percent of their salary back to the party, a suggestion that met stiff resistance from the elected representatives. In 1921, significant discussion was held on this point. The proponents of the plan thought it was in the best interest of the party and did not think that individuals should be benefiting when it was the party that had got them elected. Meanwhile, opponents pointed to the small salaries that aldermen received. Alderman John Blumberg contended that he was losing money by sitting as an alderman so he should not have to pay additional amounts to the party. After extensive debate, the ILP decided not to mandate donations from its elected officials.[95]

How, then, did William Kolisnyk advance communist policies as an alderman for Ward Three? What kinds of issues would this revolutionary "Bolshevist" bring to the fore? How did the seismic shift in communist strategy affect its lone representative on Winnipeg City Council? It is possible to centre Kolisnyk's career on city council around three main themes: transportation, labour rights, and unemployment relief. These topics were at the forefront of his politics both before and after the introduction of the Third Period. These were matters that were tremendously important in the daily lives of people in the North End. Rather than those of an isolated ultra-revolutionary, Kolisnyk's efforts on municipal council were primarily based on the needs of the North End's working-class community. Furthermore, issues of ethnic relations, personality conflicts, and local political concerns played important roles in shaping the successes and challenges of Kolisnyk's career as much as, and likely more than, any outside influences. Despite this, while Kolisnyk would frequently demonstrate an independent spirit (much to the chagrin of some of his fellow communists), he was still operating within the framework and guidance of broader party structures.

Kolisnyk regularly brought transportation issues to the attention of council. The affordability and accessibility of transportation was important for North End residents because they relied on streetcars and buses to travel to work in the downtown core. The ILP and Kolisnyk often cooperated on efforts to reduce streetcar fares to five cents per ride.[96] This effort failed, as they were outnumbered by Citizen aldermen who opposed the plan. Kolisnyk also regularly brought forward motions throughout his time on council asking that the city engineer investigate streetcar service in the North End or to request that the WEC (which had a monopoly on streetcars and buses in the city) open new bus routes through his ward. Additionally, numerous requests were made for infrastructure programs on North End streets. This was by no means a revolutionary activity, but rather an attempt to ensure that working-class people received proper transportation services.

A second topic that Kolisnyk frequently discussed on council, both before and during the Third Period, was working conditions for labourers. He used his platform as an alderman to bring forward the plight of workers, including those outside the city. Kolisnyk used his position to question the fate of agricultural labourers imported from Great Britain or those working in bush and mining camps.[97] Most of Kolisnyk's efforts on labour issues were on behalf of the city's own workers. After the General Strike, municipal employees had been prohibited from unionizing. Kolisnyk demanded that municipal workers be allowed to unionize and took up their cause for increased wages and improved working conditions. He put forward several motions demanding increases in wages and increased holiday time for municipal employees. In 1927, Kolisnyk held a meeting attended by approximately 250 civic employees to determine what should be done to increase wages, which was seen as the first step towards the recreation of a civic employees union.[98] In an article in the *Marxist Review* many years later, Kolisnyk claimed to have encouraged workers to organize the Federation of Civic Employees (FCE).[99] *The Worker* was quick to claim credit for the lifting of the "Slave Pact" in 1930, when a Citizen alderman put forward a motion to allow unionization. *The Worker* took credit, claiming that this action was the result of pressure that the communists had exerted on the issue for a long time, most notably through their representative on council.[100]

It is interesting to note that the communist policy on municipal employees was not significantly different from that of the ILP. Both parties worked on many of the same issues in regards to working conditions and the right to organize, and both demanded the end of the Slave Pact. Cooperation on these issues did not change with the onset of the Third Period. That communists such as Kolisnyk were willing to work on behalf of the organization of municipal employees shows remarkable flexibility for the Third Period, considering that the FCE worked closely with the OBU, enemies of the communists at the time. At a time when the communists were promoting the radical version of unionism offered by the Workers' Unity League, the decision to support an OBU-backed union for civic employees demonstrates an openness to making pragmatic decisions.

Kolisnyk also used his position on council to support labour unions, both locally and internationally. In doing so, he demonstrated how communist aldermen could be involved with much broader labour struggles. For example, Kolisnyk seconded a motion put forward by ILP Alderman Durward that the city should show sympathy with Local 122 of the Machinists' Union.[101] Similarly, Kolisnyk put forward a motion (seconded by Durward) calling on the city to boycott American La France and Foamite Corporation until a strike at that company had ended to the satisfaction of the strikers.[102] Despite the inability to pass motions on labour issues because of the large Citizen presence on council, this demonstrates that communists did not conceive municipal politics as isolated from their other areas of activism. Rather, a council seat was but one tool to further the communist program and advance the cause of organized labour.

Kolisnyk often used his position as an alderman to complain about municipal expenditure on items that did not assist the working class. For example, he voted against motions to provide a luncheon for a visiting group of lawn bowlers from New Zealand and to give grants to the Manitoba Curling Association.[103] On one occasion, when Kolisnyk voted against a grant to the Curling Association for its annual bonspiel, he explained that the city should not be giving money to curling clubs while claiming that there was not enough money available to support the unemployed.[104] In a similar move, Kolisnyk attempted to have the money spent on receiving distinguished visitors transferred to unemployment relief. While the sum of money itself was not large, only $4,000, it was indicative of Kolisnyk's attempts to re-orient city politics toward workers and away from the bourgeoisie.

With the collapse of Winnipeg's economy at the onset of the Great Depression, unemployment became an increasingly important issue on city council, and Kolisnyk and the CPC played a pivotal role in this debate. With the possible exception of transportation, unemployment was the topic most frequently addressed by Kolisnyk on city council. He repeatedly put forward motions requesting that relief provisions be extended to more people and to have conditions improved for those already on it. ILP aldermen tended to be relatively reliable allies of the CPC on the issue of unemployment prior to the introduction of the Third Period. As late as 1928, the OBU, often a close ally of the ILP, coordinated a public meeting with the CPC on the issue of unemployment that was attended by 3,000 people (according to communist estimates) and sent a delegation, led by Kolisnyk, to meet with the Unemployment Committee of city council.[105] A few weeks later, another joint rally was held. Marchers paraded from Market Square to the legislative building and were addressed by Tim Buck and William Kolisnyk from the CPC and John Queen and William Ivens from the ILP.[106]

Less than a year after holding the joint rally with the OBU, though, the introduction of Third Period ideology led to a dramatic shift in how the communists' unemployment policy was implemented. Communists became outspoken critics of the unemployment system, both inside and outside the council chamber, castigating the ILP for failing to protect the interests of the unemployed. In the summer of 1930, for example, a group of unemployed communists harassed ILP aldermen John Blumberg and Thomas Flye at city hall.[107] Whereas Kolisnyk had once worked with ILP aldermen to put forward motions on unemployment, he now found that no ILP aldermen would second his motions on relief rates.[108]

The problem of unemployment and its effect on the relationship between the ILP and the communists devolved into an ugly dispute in May 1930. During a mass meeting in Market Square, Kolisnyk declared that James Simpkin, an ILP alderman and the chair of the Unemployment Relief Committee, was "instrumental and responsible for [the] unemployed being sent to the city wood yard as a relief measure."[109] Kolisnyk disliked the wood yard because he said it was a means test in disguise and was unfair to the unemployed. Simpkin and the ILP vehemently denied the charge. Simpkin claimed that Kolisnyk was "misrepresenting and he knew it! He was deliberately heroizing before his friends."[110] He suggested that Kolisnyk himself had supported the wood yard in committee and so was being hypocritical by denouncing it.[111] Citizen aldermen also rallied to Simpkin's defence. They reminded Kolisnyk that since Simpkin had been the chair of the committee, he would not have voted on the establishment of the wood yard as the chairman only voted in case of a tie.[112]

ILP aldermen had heard enough communist attacks. They had endured numerous verbal assaults from their revolutionary opponents, who had ceaselessly accused them of failing to assist the unemployed and bowing to the wishes of the bourgeoisie. The *Weekly News* explained that the incident marked "an important point in the campaign of gross and deliberate misrepresentation of the ILP aldermen which for several years has been almost the stock-in-trade of local communists."[113] John Blumberg, an ILP alderman who was often outspoken on

78 | WE'RE GOING TO RUN THIS CITY

10. Protests by unemployed Winnipeggers were common throughout the 1930s in response to low levels of unemployment relief. (AUUC-WBA Archives)

11. Winnipeg's city council in 1930 led by Mayor Ralph Webb. This was also William Kolisnyk's final year on city council. (Archives of Manitoba, N686)

his dislike of communism, said that "it is not the first time that he [Kolisnyk] and his Communist friends have done this sort of thing. Kolisnyk also stated that the Labour members of council were behind the police force using clubs at the parade last month. That was a lie."[114] The ILP, with the support of the Citizen aldermen, demanded that Kolisnyk apologize to the council for his statement. Since Kolisnyk refused to do so, the council passed a motion that he should withdraw from the chamber. When he declined to leave voluntarily, Kolisnyk was escorted out by a constable.[115]

The saga did not end there. At the next council meeting Kolisnyk took up his regular seat but was asked once again to apologize to Simpkin. John Blumberg called the CPC the "most autocratic" organization in existence and proposed that council should not be blamed for expelling Kolisnyk since the Communist Party had done much the same to Leon Trotsky.[116] A few Citizen aldermen tried to negotiate a truce between their warring colleagues, but the effort was to no avail. Since Kolisnyk continued to refuse to retract his statement or apologize to Simpkin, he was again ordered to leave the council chambers. When he did not leave, the constable was asked to remove him. This time Kolisnyk resisted, informing the constable that he would only go with him "if you're stronger than I am." The constable jerked Kolisnyk out of his seat and hauled him out of the council chamber.[117]

This incident marked, one could argue, the coming of age of the Third Period in Winnipeg. Kolisnyk, who had once cooperated with the ILP on unemployment issues, had now accused them of betraying the interests of the unemployed. Communists linked this incident on council to their broader efforts. According to *The Worker*, over 1,000 unemployed workers met in Market Square with the express purpose of protesting Kolisnyk's removal.[118] Kolisnyk also used the incident as fodder for a May Day speech shortly after his expulsion. He declared that his ejection was a scheme of Ralph Webb and the "labour fakirs" to eliminate the communist voice on council.[119] For the communists, the expulsion of their alderman served as a "clear verification" that the ILP were truly "social fascists."[120]

Such denunciations, an integral part of Third Period communism, were nothing new to Winnipeg communists. In 1927, communist aldermanic candidates had referred to the ILP as "politically degenerate" and "continually bankrupt."[121] During the Third Period, these comments escalated even further as communist speakers frequently attacked the ILP with great ferocity. An RCMP informant at the International Unemployment Demonstration in 1930 commented that Kolisnyk spent his speech "venting most of his spleen on the social democrats and ILP and especially the local members of the latter party, who he described as labour fakirs and capitalist lick-spittles."[122] Meanwhile, Tom Ewen, another Winnipeg communist, described the ILP as "lackeys and agents of the ruling class and deserters of the true Labor movement and traitors to the workers' cause."[123] This aspect of Third Period ideology was eagerly accepted by Winnipeg communists who, seemingly, were more than happy to denounce their ILP opponents.

Interestingly, the General Strike played a role in the new tone used by the CPC, who accused the ILP of living off the legacy of the strike. *The Worker* declared that the ILP "can't live forever on the traditions of the Winnipeg strike. Their activity now denies the whole dynamics of that historic event in Canadian working history." In their defence, the ILP's *Weekly News* asked if there was a single member of the CPC who had played a prominent role in the Strike.[124] A decade after the General Strike occurred, it still was a moment so key that it was worth fighting over.

Conflict was now commonplace between the CPC and the ILP. In one election race, the ILP was not amused when the communists ran Saul Simkin in the same ward as the ILP's James Simpkin. The resulting confusion increased the communists' vote by nearly four-fold.[125] The ILP also tired of the frequent assaults against them made by Kolisnyk or other communists. The *Weekly News* suggested, "no line of attack was too dastardly for these saviours of society to launch. No slander was too base for them to circulate."[126] Descriptions of communists in the ILP's *Weekly News* dripped with sarcasm. In one instance the paper derided "the idea that when such a day comes persons like Kolisnyk and [Leslie] Morris shall rise as supermen out of the wreckage, establish a dictatorship, and tell us one and all just where we get off at. A pleasing prospect!"[127] Marcus Hyman, a frequent mayoral candidate for the ILP, warned against both the demagogues of the CPC and the reactionaries of the business community, suggesting that communists "carelessly and sometimes even maliciously throw sparks in all directions in material all too inflammable" while the reactionaries created the conditions for such behaviour.[128] Whereas the *Weekly News* had once treated the communists as an inconsequential pest, they were now singled out as important enemies of the ILP who had to be fought at all costs.

One practical result of this was a dramatic decline in the number of motions forwarded or seconded by Kolisnyk. This is significant because, since there was only one communist on council, a member of another group always had to agree to second his motions if they were to be put before council. In 1930, Kolisnyk managed to put forward only two motions, one on streetcar service and the other on rent assistance for those on relief. Compared to his other years on council, this marked a dramatic drop-off. In 1927, Kolisnyk had put forward six motions, fourteen in 1928, and six in 1929.[129] He was no longer able to find the support he had once had to put his motions forward. At his last council meeting, Kolisnyk remarked that he hoped "if he was ever in council again [that] he would find someone willing to second his motions."[130]

William Kolisnyk was defeated in the municipal election of November 1930 after serving two terms on city council. Communists interpreted Kolisnyk's defeat as the result of an unprecedented effort by the "social fascist" ILP to remove him from office because of his increased attacks against their "deception of the workers." *The Worker* accused the ILP of turning "openly fascist and leading the movement against the party."[131] The ILP, meanwhile, celebrated the defeat of their communist rival, arguing that workers were simply tired of the "unfair tactics" utilized by the communists.[132] They argued that communists had spent too much time attacking the ILP and were not interested in practical solutions to the unemployment problem.[133]

Interestingly, the platform that Kolisnyk ran on when he was defeated was essentially the same as it had been in 1926, despite the introduction of the Third Period. Unemployment was the focus of the campaign, particularly increases in unemployment relief. Other prominent platform planks included a minimum wage for municipal employees, a five-cent streetcar fare, and the right of free speech for demonstrations.[134] Considering the dramatic shift in communist politics that had taken place between 1926 and 1930, it is intriguing that there was very little change in the municipal party platform as it continued to be dominated by fairly reformist measures rather than revolutionary demands.

Upon his defeat in 1930, Kolisnyk continued in his role as a manager at the Workers' and Farmers' Cooperative Creamery and maintained his other business ventures in bicycle and automobile repair.[135] He continued to attract controversy after his defeat. He was accused of not properly following the party line during the Workers' Benevolent Association executive election because he supported a slate of candidates that included non-party members.[136] Thus, when he considered running for office again in 1931, a group of communists signed a letter to announce to the City Central Committee that they would not support Kolisnyk's campaign "materially or morally."[137] This disunity likely also contributed to his defeat. Kolisnyk did not disappear from municipal politics, however. In 1934 his name resurfaced as a potential communist mayoral candidate, although eventually the CPC decided not to run a candidate.[138]

Two years after leaving council, Kolisnyk and Harry Sydor (another manager at the Workers' and Farmers' Cooperative) were accused of personally profiting off the 1929 purchase of a lumberyard by the Cooperative. A member named J. Kozlowski brought documents to the 1932 annual meeting claiming that the agents who bought the land for the Cooperative had purchased it for $8,800 before reselling it to the Cooperative for $12,000. Someone had profited at the Cooperative's expense. Scandal erupted within the Ukrainian community in the North End. Such humiliating gossip was the perfect excuse for anti-communist Ukrainians to attack their political opponents, and the result was a bitter fight between pro- and anti-communist Ukrainians. A five-member board of inquiry was formed to investigate the accusation and, eventually, Kolisnyk and Sydor were cleared of all charges. Despite being cleared by the board, Kolisnyk resigned from his post, although he retained his party membership.[139]

This was not the last controversy for Kolisnyk. In 1935, an RCMP informer reported that Kolisnyk had committed "acts of malfeasance and scandalous manipulation" in his role as creamery manager. He stood accused of manipulating the sale of cream and covering it up by pouring milk into the sewer. Kolisnyk, it was suggested, was literally skimming the cream off the top. No independent sources, however, supported the claim of this informant. Given the hostile atmosphere surrounding the Cooperative at the time, it is possible that the informant was relying on rumours that were undoubtedly rampant in the Ukrainian community over the issue. Presumably, if Kolisnyk had committed such an egregious offence against a CPC-run organization he would have been quickly expelled from the party. No disciplinary action was taken and the issue seemed to fade away.[140]

On 6 July 1940, Kolisnyk's home was searched and, according to the RCMP, subversive literature was seized. Given its prevalence in Kolisnyk's RCMP file, the police were seemingly fixated on a comment he had made in 1931 that "we must copy the example given us by our comrades in Soviet Russia, and we will fight and win a Soviet Canada."[141] Along with several other local communists, Kolisnyk was interned as part of the war effort. Kolisnyk, who had a history of severe illness (he had spent two months in hospital in 1928 with inflammation of the brain), did not take well to detention.[142] He lost his sight while incarcerated and was eventually released on medical grounds. He spent the rest of his life in British Columbia where he worked on behalf of the Canadian National Institute for the Blind.[143] Kolisnyk died in Vancouver on 4 November 1967.

If the leadership of the CPC had had their say, Kolisnyk likely would not have been their first elected standard bearer. He was often controversial, and not for the reasons that party leadership would have appreciated. He, like many of Winnipeg's communists, was Ukrainian, not an upstanding Anglo-Saxon to appeal to the masses. He wasn't notably charismatic or a particularly great speaker.

Yet Kolisnyk managed to achieve something that had never happened before, a historic moment not only for the CPC but the communist movement internationally; it was Kolisnyk who would figure out what it meant to be an elected communist official in a parliamentary system seeking revolutionary changes; and it was Kolisnyk who was carrying the communist banner in elected politics at a time of profound change within the party structure.

Taken in isolation, Kolisnyk's career gives little reason to seriously challenge the interpretation that emphasizes the influence and power of centralized decisions within the CPC. Nevertheless, his career also demonstrates the significance of ethnicity, personality, and local communities, which, while not necessarily opposed to traditionalist models, does highlight the importance of studying communists at the local level. For example, while the CPC was supposed to be a centralized unit with no room for internal divisions, the ethnic politics played out in Winnipeg demonstrate the difficulties of bringing numerous conflicting ethnic groups within the party together to work for a common candidate. Similarly, while Kolisnyk was supposed to act as the public voice of the CPC on council, he often, according to other communists, misspoke. Finally, at a time when communist publications and speakers were fervently using revolutionary rhetoric to attract support for their causes, it appears that communists in Winnipeg continued to mobilize for election campaigns based primarily on ameliorating the working class's immediate concerns. Thus, while recognizing the importance of international and national decisions on the career of a local politician such as Kolisnyk, it is also necessary to recognize and acknowledge the importance of the communities in which communist politics were played out. It would be another few years before communists would return to Winnipeg City Council, and when they returned they would remain there for decades to come.

CHAPTER 4

A VICTORY FOR THOSE ENGAGED IN THE STRUGGLE FOR BETTER CONDITIONS

Despite the controversial end to William Kolisnyk's career, communists would soon return to city council. In November 1933, Jacob Penner was elected, followed a year later by Martin Forkin (1899–1962). Both men served on city council for decades, beginning a period of uninterrupted communist presence on city council that would last for nearly fifty years. This chapter will focus on the earliest years of those terms, exploring how these communist representatives engaged their community, the ILP, and their Citizen opponents. Communists were uniquely positioned within the North End community. They were frequently the most vocal advocates for the neighbourhood's unemployed. For many North End residents, Communist aldermen became the people to turn to in order to solve problems with local government—tireless advocates who could achieve results.

The election of Penner and Forkin, however, occurred during the last years of the Third Period, the period in communist history that had begun midway through Kolisnyk's aldermanic career. The CPC was still vigorously and publicly attacking the ILP with every opportunity. There were frequently public hostilities between the two parties, as both fought for support from North End residents, each claiming to be the appropriate voice for labour. Yet this hostility would not be the defining feature of Penner's and Forkin's careers on council. There were moments of intransigence, to be sure, but Penner and Forkin would prove to be remarkably adaptable, putting local needs above a purely revolutionary struggle.

Jacob Penner and Martin Forkin acted on council similarly to how John Manley has described the Workers' Unity League (WUL)—an organization of communist unions—during the Third Period. He described the WUL as both "indigestibly provocative" in style but "unexpectedly responsive to its context and the moods and needs of its constituency."[1] To paraphrase Manley, CPC aldermen in Winnipeg made "good aldermen" rather than "good Bolsheviks."[2] Their communism was neither obscure nor isolationist. While there were unsavoury aspects to Communist activities during this period, the primary concern of the CPC's elected representatives was meeting the immediate needs of the working class and the unemployed. As a result, despite the CPC's efforts to distinguish itself from the ILP and its use of revolutionary rhetoric, the communists pursued similar policies at the municipal level to their supposed enemies on the political left.

YEAR	CANDIDATE	1ST PLACE VOTES	PERCENTAGE
1925	Matthew Popovich	1,945	17.5%
1926	William Kolisnyk	1,874	18.2% (elected)
1927	Matthew Popovich Leslie Morris	2,443 2,936	18.9% 25.2% (special by-election)
1928	William Kolisnyk	2,342	19.7% (elected)
1929	Tom Ewen	1,701	13.3%
1930	William Kolisnyk	2,332	15.5%
1931	William Kolisnyk	2,762	16.5%
1932	Leslie Morris Dionys Moysiuk	3,056 175	19.0% 1.1%
1933	Jacob Penner	3,990	22.3% (elected)
1934	M. J. Forkin	4,429	23.8% (elected)
1935	Jacob Penner	4,604	25.0% (elected)

Table 1. Communist Votes in Ward Three (1925–1935)
Source: Information compiled from *Municipal Manuals*, 1926–1936.

Communists invested their municipal electoral efforts in Ward Three, the only ward in the city that they stood a chance of winning. Ward Three, however, was also the ILP's most fertile electoral ground, and the resulting clash would frequently play out in public meetings and election campaigns. Stories abound of rowdy election meetings. Joseph Zuken (1912–1986), who later would be elected as a communist alderman, recalled, "in the old Talmud Torah you had maybe John Queen or John Blumberg speaking at an ILP meeting. The Communists would be holding their meeting at the Hebrew Sick Benefit Hall, which is perhaps two or three minutes away. You would have a courier who would run and tell you what the competitor was saying—and then there would be an instant reply."[3] Gloria Queen-Hughes, an ILP school board trustee and daughter of John Queen, recollected how the communists would, allegedly, send numerous cadres to ILP meetings. They would leave one at a time, making a large noise on the way out to disrupt the proceedings.[4] Hecklers also frequented their opponents' meetings. For example, when Jacob Penner condemned Section 98 during a 1932 municipal debate, a woman began heckling him from the floor, concluding with the question: "What did you do to Trotsky?"[5] Conversely, the RCMP reported that several communists planned to attend a meeting held by Alderman Thomas Flye of the ILP in 1931 to ask "questions which could not be answered" in an attempt to spoil the meeting.[6] The ILP and the communists were frequent opponents, not only in the council chambers, but also in the streets of the North End, where election campaigns were won and lost.

Communist election campaigns, however, were far more than good opportunities to heckle their ILP opponents. Winnipeg communists took municipal election campaigns seriously. The rigorous preparations made for municipal election campaigns in Winnipeg were highlighted by the CPC as an example for other cities to follow.[7] In 1932, *The Worker* reported that the Winnipeg branch had distributed 30,000 election bulletins in English and an additional 7,000 in Ukrainian for the municipal election.[8] A central election committee was established and ward committees formed to support the candidates in each ward. In Ward Three the halls of numerous sympathetic organizations were used as campaign offices, while in Wards One and Two, the houses and stores of supporters were "appropriately decorated" with communist paraphernalia.[9] Finally, it was stressed that the CPC needed to have enough scrutineers on election day to monitor every poll, lest bourgeois election officials invalidate legitimate communist votes.[10]

Public meetings played a significant role in communist election campaigns. In 1932 it was reported that the CPC had held over forty meetings over the course of the two-week campaign.[11] Candidates used these events to expound communist doctrine and the CPC platform. By 1933, communists had learned that radio speeches were of "great value" and decided to utilize them in the future.[12] As for other party, canvassing was also important for a communist election campaign. The Central Agit-Prop Department of the CPC declared, "the importance of house to house canvassing, which must commence IMMEDIATELY AND NOT AFTER NOMINATION DAY, cannot be stressed too much."[13] It was the goal of the CPC to visit every house in Ward Three. Wards One and Two were lower priorities, given the low likelihood of success in those districts and the small working-class population.[14]

Just as they had in the 1920s, communist election campaigns also focused on the ethnic groups from which they received much of their support. Communists were often the only party to prepare election materials in multiple languages. In a 1935 publication, the *North Winnipeg Elector*, instructions on how to vote were given in five languages: English, German, Ukrainian, Polish, and Hebrew.[15] Communists also spent time appealing to ethnic organizations. For example, during the 1933 mayoralty campaign, the *Winnipeg Free Press* reported on a day in the life of communist mayoral candidate Martin Forkin. On one typical day, Forkin visited the Russian Workers Club in the morning and then went to the Polish Labour Temple where he "for two hours listened to a Polish speaker, not understanding one word."[16]

The communist municipal platform combined the fight for the immediate needs of workers with the broader aims of the Communist Party. In 1931, the CPC produced a national municipal election platform, but stated that each municipality should adopt the platform to suit local conditions as "the very essence of municipal elections...[is the] direct relationship to [the] immediate living problems of the masses."[17] A few years later, the Winnipeg Communist Election Conference adopted a platform that they argued gave "expression to the urgent, pressing needs of the working people of Winnipeg."[18] Communists believed that they enjoyed the most electoral success when "the speeches made during the campaign...dealt with the [local problems] and raised questions of mutual interest to the workers."[19]

What were the local problems that the CPC claimed to be addressing? In 1931, for example, unemployment relief and the battle for a non-contributory unemployment insurance bill were the main points of the communist municipal platform. The program went on to discuss other positions of significance to the CPC: a prohibition on the importation of strike breakers from outside the municipality; improved working conditions and hours for municipal workers; the unconditional right of free speech including an end to Section 98; increased taxes for the rich and lower taxes for workers; a program of house building to replace slum dwellings; a five-cent fare on streetcar and bus systems; free hospital treatment for the needy; and the granting of universal suffrage in municipal elections.[20] This platform remained relatively unchanged throughout the Third Period. Indeed, the 1934 election program was almost identical to its 1931 counterpart.[21]

On the surface, this platform appears to support reformist measures that would not have differed significantly from the program of the ILP. In 1934, the ILP election platform called for the Dominion government to pay the whole cost of unemployment relief and to provide a higher standard of assistance, that efforts should be taken to eliminate slum conditions, that there should be a shorter work week with no reduction in pay, a sewage disposal scheme should be funded with the help of federal and provincial governments, that the city should provide public health services, that the WEC should be municipalized, and that the city should only buy from firms that respected fair wage rules.[22] The main planks of the platform may have differed slightly from those put forward by the communists, but, on the surface at least, both parties appeared to advance rather reformist solutions to the city's problems. Was the CPC falling into the "trap of parliamentarism" that it so despised?

Despite the reforms outlined in their municipal program, the CPC argued that they had not become a parliamentary party, or at least not one in the sense that the ILP was. In *Socialism and the CCF*, Stewart Smith wrote about a "revolutionary Communist parliamentarism" that differed from the "parliamentary deception" of the CCF (or the ILP).[23] How, then, did local communists conceptualize this difference? Municipal council was not seen as a place merely for debating local issues, but part of the broader class struggle conceptualized by communists. The communist election platform in 1931, for example, recognized that while the "Communist Party program in these elections is composed of the immediate and pressing demands of the masses...only the abolition of capitalism and the rule of the workers...can solve the problem of the masses."[24] Immediate reforms were important but such reforms could not achieve the CPC's goal, the abolition of capitalism.

Communists also saw value in contesting elections beyond winning seats. Elections could be a propaganda tool for spreading the communist message. William Kolisnyk stated, "we use the civic election campaigns for propaganda" while Forkin proposed, "whatever the result of the election campaign, it has been a victory for those engaged in the struggle for better conditions, because it has forced other people to come out and acknowledge the conditions under which many of the workers labour."[25] Communist candidates used the platform provided to them by the campaign to link issues such as unemployment relief with wider condemnations of the capitalist system.[26] While doing so, election campaigns gave candidates a unique opportunity to address a broader audience, providing an opportunity to "draw native elements into the Party."[27] Election campaigns, therefore, served as a means to propagandize among workers outside the CPC's regular circles.

The Worker proposed that there was an organic connection between the elected city councillors inside the halls of power being supported by, and supporting, the whole militant movement on the outside. Elected communists were successful because they were "exposing the class nature of city government, and using their positions to further the militancy of the workers."[28] Forkin declared that the communist role was both to "assist the organized fight for the immediate betterment of workers' conditions and also to show the working class that they cannot win their emancipation from capitalism through the city councils and parliaments."[29] These sentiments were echoed by a local document that stated, "Penner will have to become a public figure in the sense of leading and supporting the actual struggles of the Winnipeg workers and will have to be supported in same by the whole movement."[30] It may be a matter of semantics, but the document emphasizes "the actual struggles of the Winnipeg workers" rather than the interests of the Comintern or the larger party structure.

Penner demonstrated that he would not be a "normal" alderman early in his career when, a month into his first term, he refused to stand to honour the death of Thomas Hooper, the chief of the city's water works department. As the other aldermen rose around him to offer condolences to the family, Penner remained firmly planted in his chair. He explained to the shocked aldermen, "if a working man meets his death on the city's streets in an accident we do not pass a vote in his memory. Or if a miner is killed in a mine accident we do not rise. Does this council not think it worthwhile to respect the memory of working people?"[31] This episode would repeat itself two weeks later when he refused to stand to honour the death of a prominent fire fighter. Penner was clearly going to be a very different sort of alderman.[32]

Jacob Penner was born in Russia in 1880. He would first experience radical politics through conversations with an elderly peasant. After finishing school he attended teacher's college, but learned quickly that he could not keep discipline in the classroom because he was only seventeen years old and younger than many of his students. Penner returned to school to study to become a land surveyor. While there, he witnessed the beating of metal workers at the hands of Cossacks and came to the conclusion that private factories were immoral. Deciding he needed to learn more, Penner joined a student study group reading Marx's *Das Kapital*.

12. Communist alderman Jacob Penner, pictured during the 1933 municipal election campaign. (Archives of Manitoba, N8915)

As he became increasingly involved in the Russian Social Democratic Party, his parents worried that he would be arrested and decided to immigrate to Canada.[33]

The family first settled in Altona, Manitoba, but Penner disliked rural life and wanted to be closer to other political radicals. He moved to Winnipeg and found employment at The Rosery florist shop where he became the florist for several of Winnipeg's elite. Soon after moving to Winnipeg, Penner became involved in leftist circles, was one of the founding members of the Socialist Party of Canada local in Winnipeg in 1906, co-wrote the platform of the Social Democratic Party, taught at socialist classes and served on the Sub-Committee on Political Action during the General Strike. Fired from his job as a florist in 1917 because of his opposition to conscription, Penner worked as a candy salesman before joining the Workers' Cooperative, where he became a bookkeeper.

After arriving in Winnipeg, Penner met his future wife Rose Shapack. Shapack was born in Odessa, Ukraine in 1888 and was involved in the famous Odessa General Strike in 1904 that would be commemorated in Sergei Eisenstein's film *Battleship Potemkin*. She would eventually flee Ukraine, arriving in Winnipeg in 1907. Shapack, a radical in her own right, and Penner met at a reception for internationally known anarchist Emma Goldman. One example of the radical nature of this couple was their "marriage." In 1912, they invited friends to the announcement that they were now husband and wife with neither a civil nor religious ceremony. Marriage, they thought, was a bourgeois institution that was best avoided. It would not be till 1931 that they were legally married, in a ceremony performed by William Ivens, and even then it was only "for the sake of the children."[34] It was through Shapack that Penner became connected with the North End's radical Jewish community, and the two were frequently involved in many of the Jewish fraternal organizations that dotted the North End.

According to his son Roland, Penner was present in Guelph, Ontario in 1921 when the CPC was founded.[35] He would quickly take on roles in the new party, becoming its western literary agent and the chief organizer for the CPC in the Manitoba district.[36] He would also become involved in numerous radical community organizations. For example, Penner taught lessons at the predominantly communist Russian Children's School at the Liberty Temple on Saturday afternoons and led educational meetings for the CPC on the main tenets of communism.

Penner was known for his clean living and honest manner. He was frequently portrayed as a serious man who, according to the *Weekly News*'s tongue-in-cheek council reporter, had "forgotten how to smile."[37] A frustrated RCMP investigator reported, "while intemperate in his political thought, [Penner] is temperate in his habits, and might be classed as a 'domestic fellow.' He is not an immoral man nor a drinking man and he smokes little. He is strongly opposed to gambling.... He never has been mixed up with any scandal."[38] He dressed conservatively and spent his Saturday afternoons listening to *Saturday at the Opera* on the radio from Bismarck, North Dakota.[39] As the RCMP would report, "it is impossible to get something on the man as far as his personal daily life is concerned." Another RCMP report suggested that Penner appeared to be "very smooth, intelligent in his manners, shrewd, careful, and well educated."[40] Despite this intelligence, Penner was also described by the RCMP as a "poor speaker, having very bad pronunciation, and extremely hard to understand."[41] Yet, even those on the opposite side of the political spectrum had some respect for Penner. Charles Simonite, a Citizen alderman, described him as a "gentleman" who "wasn't a bad fellow," albeit one with some "peculiar ideas."[42] Unlike the controversy-prone Kolisnyk, Penner seemed to earn the grudging respect of his opponents on council, even if they vigorously disagreed with his politics.

In November 1934, Penner was joined on city council by a second communist alderman, Martin Joseph Forkin. Forkin was described by the RCMP as a "neat quiet dresser" with a slight build, dark brown hair, brown eyes, and a sallow complexion.[43] Forkin was of Irish and English descent, his father, also Martin, having been born in Ireland before moving to England. The family came to Brandon just prior to the First World War, where the family lived an essentially hand-to-mouth existence and Martin Forkin Sr. found work as a boiler washer's helper on the Canadian Pacific Railway. At the age of sixteen, Martin Joseph would enlist in the Canadian army and head to war. When his age was discovered he was sent home, only to promptly re-enlist. He would serve for three years in the Canadian Expeditionary Force, receiving a shrapnel wound in his knee.[44] He would also spend a year after the First World War as a member of the RCMP.

Martin Forkin Sr. was a devout Catholic, but his children did not have any interest in following him in the church. Upon returning home, Forkin worked briefly for the RCMP but his real passion was radical politics. Indeed, six of seven Forkin siblings would join the CPC, and by the early 1930s were scattered across the country in a variety of organizing roles. These radical politics were informed by their impoverished upbringing and their awareness of the tremendous challenges facing the working class and unemployed in postwar Canada.

Martin Joseph Forkin gained prominence in the OBU before joining the Workers' Party of Canada. Forkin was employed for a while at the General Hospital in Brandon but, after losing his job, became the secretary of the Brandon Unemployed Association. He was an active labour organizer and served as the secretary of the WUL in the Winnipeg District. In this role, he is particularly known for his leadership role in a miners' strike at Bienfait, Saskatchewan, where he was dubbed the "generalissimo of the strikers" by the local press.[45] Stephen Endicott suggests that while Forkin may not have been the greatest orator, he had a keen political sense and could be highly persuasive.[46] Forkin was charged for his role in the Bienfait strike but the case against him was dismissed.[47] Later, he would be sentenced to four months in prison for Unlawful Assembly for his activities at the Parkhill Bedding Plant strike in Winnipeg, a conviction that was later overturned. Forkin served on city council until his death in 1962.

The CPC was actively involved in the fight for free speech, largely because it was tightly circumscribed under the provisions of Section 98 of the Criminal Code, which outlawed numerous radical political groups. Section 98 had its roots in the Winnipeg General Strike, when it was brought in by a federal order-in-council to make such strikes illegal. It read:

> Any association, organization, society, or corporation, whose professed purpose or one of whose purposes is to bring about any governmental, industrial or economic change within Canada by use of force, violence, terrorism, or physical injury...shall be an unlawful association. Any person who acts or professes to act as an officer of such unlawful association and who shall sell, speak, write, or publish anything as the representative or professed representative of any such unlawful association, or become and continue to be a member thereof, or wear, carry, or cause to be displayed upon or about his person or elsewhere any badge, insignia, emblem, banner, motto, pennant, card, button or other device whatsoever, indicating or intended to show or suggest that he is a member of or in anywise associated with any such unlawful association, or who shall contribute anything as dues or otherwise to it or anyone for it, or who shall solicit subscriptions or contributions for it, shall be guilty of an offence and liable to imprisonment for not more than twenty years."[48]

For the CPC, these sweeping terms meant that even membership in the party could be considered illegal, putting the fight against it at the forefront of their activity, particularly after party leader Tim Buck and seven other party members were found guilty of sedition under Section 98.

The struggle for legality was described as "the very essence of the Party campaign."[49] Local election campaign materials described how "workers in Winnipeg are jailed and clubbed if they dare to assemble in mass to protest present conditions. Workers who strike against wage cuts are met with police batons [sic].

Only recently Winnipeg workers were almost blinded by tear gas simply because they assembled en-masse to protest against the jobless being refused medical and hospital treatment."[50] The CPC warned its supporters that, although repression was less severe in Winnipeg than in other centres, the "rule of terror" found in Toronto would soon move westward. Increased media coverage during election campaigns allowed communists to spread this anti-persecution message broadly.

Since Section 98 was a piece of federal legislation, however, there was little that communists could do about it in city council. Instead, the CPC's aldermen focused their efforts on local affronts to free speech. For example, Penner vigorously attempted to have the Police Commission reverse a decision to ban the performance of *Eight Men Speak*. The Progressive Arts Club had intended to perform the play, which depicted the trial and imprisonment of Tim Buck and seven other prominent communists. Penner put forward three motions on the subject, the first two of which were ruled out of order by Mayor Webb. Penner argued that the Police Commission's decision was an "infringement on freedom of expression and the rights of the legitimate stage."[51] When his motion was finally put to a vote, it was defeated by nine votes to seven, with all ILP aldermen except John Blumberg siding with the communist.

This incident highlights two key aspects of Penner's term on council. Despite communist propaganda to the opposite effect, ILP aldermen were largely in agreement with the communists on the issue of free speech, as six of their seven aldermen supported the motion. Thomas Flye, an ILP alderman, said that he supported the Penner motion because it was an issue of free speech and that he would not condemn people before they were proven guilty. Blumberg, meanwhile, defended his vote with the argument that the free speech that communists believed in fostered hatred. Even though communists frequently attacked the ILP for defeating their motions in council, it was often only one or two ILP aldermen who sided with the Citizens.

The *Eight Men Speak* incident was also an example of a role that communist aldermen were supposed to play: supporting the CPC's wider activities with their work on council. Just as Penner did in this instance, communist aldermen frequently demanded to know why their or other organizations' meetings had been prevented by the police. Council was, therefore, seen as a valuable forum for demanding free speech within the city. Indeed, the publicity received from the banned play and the fight to have this reversed was probably more significant to the CPC than actually performing the play. As Fred Harvey, a member of the Progressive Arts Club, remembered, the dispute led to "more discussion and sympathy for us than we could possibly have achieved with a play that was written, with the best intentions, by a committee, and acted by a group of under-rehearsed amateurs."[52]

Communist aldermen also used their platform in city council to denounce another threat to communism: fascism. Winnipeg was home to a local variant of fascism, the Canadian Nationalist Party. The Nationalists paraded through Winnipeg streets wearing Nazi brown shirts that bore the insignia of a swastika and a beaver, and spread anti-Semitic and anti-immigrant propaganda throughout the city.[53] Communists frequently battled the Nationalists in the North End, filling meeting halls to ensure that Nationalist meetings could not take place and spreading anti-fascist propaganda. They were assisted on city council by Penner, who pressured Mayor Webb, albeit to no avail, to prevent Nationalist meetings with as much zeal as he obstructed communist ones. Penner proclaimed before council that the greatest danger of the day was fascism, but Webb told him to sit down, as, he claimed, the other aldermen did not want to hear such an ideological speech.[54] Nevertheless, by denouncing fascism in the city council, Penner was taking the broader fight against fascism into the halls of municipal government.

On 5 June 1934, a riot broke out between communists and Nationalists in Market Square just outside the City Hall. The *Winnipeg Free Press* described the riot in fantastical terms: "battling in self-defence, the Nationalists, about fifty of whom were clad in the brown shirt uniform of that organization, drew batons from their pockets and fought furiously for their lives. Knives flashed in the fast waning sunlight, heavy clubs crashed against cap-protected skulls, and huge slabs of wood were torn from the stalls of market gardeners and used as battering rams against the tightly pressing wall of snarling humanity."[55] With the sounds of the fighting filtering into the council chambers, Citizen Alderman James Barry described Penner as a "snake in the grass" and accused him of fomenting "race hatred."[56] The ILP's newspaper, the *Weekly News*, an avid opponent of fascism itself, denounced Penner for demanding free speech for some while denying it to the fascists.[57] Despite the hostility, Penner continued to defend the actions taken by communists against the fascists and was consistent in his demand that city council, the mayor, and the Police Commission take the fascist threat seriously.

While the city could do little about Section 98, it controlled access to Market Square, a common site for protests and speakers. This access would also become an issue over which there was significantly less agreement between the communists and the ILP. Market Square, located just outside City Hall, was a popular meeting place for both communists and other organizations. Tom McEwen remembered how communists, the Salvation Army, OBU, Rationalist Society, and other political and social groups would set up their platforms around the Square and compete for listeners every Sunday afternoon.[58] Often these meetings were quite large, drawing hundreds and even thousands of people.

As its name suggested, however, Market Square was also used as a farmers' market. The Market Gardeners' Association said that communist meetings in the Square damaged the stands where they sold their produce and interfered with business. Not surprisingly, Mayor Webb eagerly denounced those who used the Square to "stir up trouble and strife." In 1931, city council voted to prohibit meetings in the Square during business hours. Although some ILP aldermen voted for the ban, others remained opposed. W.B. Simpson, for example, declared to council that closing the Square to meetings would be "the biggest mistake of your lives."[59] Nevertheless, the motion passed, with the support of several ILP aldermen. Communists could no longer hold daytime meetings in Market Square.

The Market Square issue did not end there, as communists made access to the Square a central component of future municipal platforms, particularly after Martin Forkin was elected to council. In February of 1935, Forkin and Penner put forward and seconded a motion to rescind the limitations on the use of the Square.[60] The motion was sent to committee, where it was studied closely. Market gardeners and Citizen politicians remained opposed to daytime communist demonstrations. A suggestion was put forward that a vacant lot on Princess Street could be an alternate site for public meetings. Penner, however, described the lot as a "mud hole" and an "insult to the working class." Forkin was equally dismissive of the proposal, proclaiming that it was an attempt to "gag public expression."[61] In the end, however, some members of the ILP remained reluctant to permit daytime demonstrations and the motion failed.

The fight for free speech extended beyond dramatic productions or public gatherings. During the Great Depression, Winnipeg communists faced the threat of deportation either for being on relief or for their political ideology. Under the terms of the 1907 Immigration Act, municipalities were allowed to request the deportation of any immigrant who became a public charge. Winnipeg used this provision with great regularity to deport immigrants who requested relief and occasionally used this power to rid itself of political radicals.[62] Deportations became so common in the city that the consuls of numerous European countries inquired into why so many of their citizens were being deported from Winnipeg.[63]

Prior to Penner's election in 1933, the ILP protested deportation on numerous occasions. ILP Alderman Thomas Flye, for example, claimed that his office was "besieged" with people who had been threatened with deportation.[64] In 1932, ILP aldermen brought forward the case of three communists (Dan

Holmes, Orton Wade, and Conrad Cessinger) who had been smuggled out of the city for deportation, arguing that this was a violation of British democracy.[65] *The Worker* described ILP protestations against deportation as "fake protest" and the *Workers' Vanguard* accused the ILP of "acquiescing" to the practice, but in reality the CPC and ILP had similar deportation policies.

When Penner was elected to council, he worked with the ILP to have the practice ended.[66] Shortly after his election, Penner, along with Flye, Morris Gray, and John Blumberg, inquired in the city council about the attitude of the Dominion government towards the deportation of people on relief. The sustained pressure of these aldermen revealed that the City of Winnipeg was using its deportation powers excessively and, by 1934, they had revealed enough evidence of the scope of these activities that even Citizen aldermen began to second-guess the practice. These aldermen, who had supported automatic deportation for economic reasons, were convinced through the "apparent betrayal of British principles of fair play and justice."[67] With municipal opinion turned so decidedly against the deportation of immigrants on relief, city council decided in 1934 that it would no longer report cases of public charges for deportation due to unemployment.[68] Penner, and his ILP counterparts, had won a major victory for the working class in Winnipeg.

This was a significant accomplishment because many CPC members, and other immigrants residing in Winnipeg, had previously faced deportation for requesting relief. The termination of this practice relieved the immigrant community of a significant source of fear. It serves as an example of practical cooperation between the ILP and the CPC on an issue that was important for both parties. At a time when CPC policy denounced the ILP and demanded that there be no cooperation with them, Penner worked with his ILP counterparts on the issue of deportation because it was an important issue for his constituents.

Despite agreement between the CPC and the ILP over some issues, there remained a large gulf between the two parties. A small but symbolic example came during preparations for King George V's Jubilee in 1935. Most ILP aldermen were British and, despite their left-wing politics, remained loyal to the British monarchy. The CPC, conversely, had no time for monarchy, and used the planning process to express their antipathy towards monarchy in general, a move that sparked considerable discontent within the council chambers. The *Free Press* remarked that there was "considerable patriotic murmuring when Alderman Forkin was expressing his views, which became more articulate when Ald. Penner went into a verbal voodoo dance about potentates and kings."[69] In a public meeting shortly thereafter, Forkin criticized "ex-working class leaders" for accepting decorations from the King to mark the occasion, saying that a communist leader would "not accept any decorations, even from the King personally."[70] The debate over royalty both revealed the ethnic divide between the ILP and the CPC, and demonstrated a difference between the ILP, with its deep British roots, and the revolutionary perspective of the CPC.

The debate over Jubilee celebrations was insignificant compared to the CPC's ongoing attacks against the ILP for their unemployment policy. The CPC accused the ILP of following a policy of "peaceful waiting and quiet starvation."[71] The communist press was filled with stories of how ILP aldermen had failed to assist unemployed constituents. In one example, the newspaper for the WUL described how Alderman John Blumberg had refused to help an unemployed worker who had had his light, rent, and water cut off by the city.[72] It is unclear, however, what the ILP could have done differently about unemployment relief given their minority status on city council for much of the 1930s.

In a city where nearly one in five wage earners was out of work, and in which expenditures on relief doubled between 1931 and 1935, unemployment was a contentious issue.[73] The approach of the Citizen aldermen towards the unemployed remained largely unchanged during this period. It was firmly rooted in the fear that granting too much to those on relief would make recipients dependent on the state and that the financial well-being of the city was a higher priority than unemployment relief. Citizens, therefore, passed regulations that made it difficult for Winnipeggers to get on relief and maintained low relief rates.[74]

Given that Citizen aldermen made up the majority of city council, there was often little that either the CPC or the ILP could do to change the treatment of the unemployed. That being said, in the early 1930s, the ILP did not put forward an unemployment strategy that differed significantly from that of the Citizens. The *Weekly News* explained, "there is a genuine effort being made to extend relief as far as possible. All this, we fully admit, is of a palliative character, but in an imperfect world, it is at least something. It is at least better than fine-spun theories of cure-alls and dictatorships."[75] The ILP's willingness to accept the status quo was frequently critiqued by the CPC, who portrayed their opponents as traitors to the unemployed who followed a policy of "peaceful waiting and quiet starvation."[76]

As the Depression worsened, the ILP became more critical of the city's relief apparatus and its Citizen supporters. The ILP's 1934 election campaign focused on attacking the treatment of the unemployed by the previous municipal government. It proposed to humanize conditions for those on relief. "Common humanity," declared John Queen, "demands that all their requirements be met."[77] Instead of conceiving of the unemployed as a drain on resources, the ILP re-interpreted them as formerly contributing members of society who needed assistance due to a situation beyond their control. As such, the ILP put forward a platform that offered medical and dental services to the unemployed, established relief depots throughout the city, and increased relief rates.

Unemployment was a central issue for communist parties throughout the world. The CPC took its cue from the Comintern to fight for the unemployed and launched extensive organizing efforts among the unemployed population. Through organizations such as the National Unemployed Workers' Association (NUWA) and its neighbourhood associations, the CPC reached out to unemployed people nationwide. Since municipal governments were responsible for unemployment relief, it was at the local level that changes could be made for the unemployed. As the economic crisis worsened, the CPC leaders in Winnipeg focused increasingly on unemployment as the central feature of municipal campaigns. Although there was top-down direction on the issue of unemployment, local communists also recognized the necessity of working alongside and organizing their unemployed neighbours.

CPC unemployment policy in Winnipeg had two main points. The first was the nationwide campaign for non-contributory unemployment insurance. This was not strictly a municipal policy, as the CPC demanded that the Dominion government pay for the program, but it was through their representatives at the municipal level that it was fought for. One of Forkin's first actions after he took office in January 1935 was to put forward a motion, seconded by Penner, calling for the city to endorse a non-contributory plan. He argued that the burden to pay for unemployment should be on those who were able to pay. The motion was first allowed to stand and was later accepted by city council.[78] The campaign for the national non-contributory insurance scheme demonstrates how Penner and Forkin worked as part of a broader agenda dictated by the CPC. Thus, although local people were important for the CPC's unemployment policy, significant aspects of the unemployment program were developed outside of the city.

Municipal support for legislation that required federal approval, however, was not a particularly practicable solution for the immediate problems faced by the unemployed. The CPC was frequently an advocate for increasing relief provisions. Penner, in his victorious election campaign, declared that the first goal of a CPC alderman would be to increase food and rent allowances.[79] When elected, Penner, and later Forkin, put forward numerous motions calling for increases in food vouchers, rent provisions, and medical care for the unemployed. Forkin, who had been an NUWA organizer, was very familiar with the plight of Winnipeg's unemployed as well as CPC national unemployment policy. These actions both fulfilled the requirements of national policy but also gained the CPC aldermen a tremendous following in the North End. In a 1935 article reflecting on his first term on city council, Penner wrote that the CPC had achieved practical results to better the lives of the unemployed: household utensils were now included in relief support; lien notices that the unemployed were compelled to sign had been cancelled; and compulsory work for relief was abolished.[80] While it is true that the CPC played a key role in keeping unemployment on the radar of municipal policy makers, Penner failed to mention in his article that all of these accomplishments could have only come with support from ILP aldermen. Any changes to unemployment relief had to be a combined effort between the ILP and the CPC, given the avowed opposition of nearly all Citizen representatives.

When Penner was elected in 1933, he quit his job at the Workers' and Farmers' Cooperative to become a full-time alderman, much to the disappointment of his wife, Rose, who now had to manage the home with considerably less income. His son, Roland Penner, writes that Penner had been earning twenty-five dollars per week prior to becoming an alderman and, as an alderman, made the paltry sum of thirty dollars per month. His action was abnormal. Since aldermen received very little compensation for their municipal role, it was assumed that aldermen would continue working in their previous jobs. Penner, however, decided to dedicate his attention to the needs of his constituents, and particularly their needs when it came to unemployment relief, telling his wife, "I was elected to serve the people and I cannot do that part-time!"[81]

The Worker reported that although Penner was not on the Municipal Relief Committee, he attended every meeting and regularly brought a long list of individual relief cases for the committee to address.[82] The Penner home became "virtually a drop-in centre" as anyone with a problem would come by for assistance.[83] Michael Harris recalled that Penner "never refused a single [person]: a request to him to do something in the City Council when they had a problem whether it was their homes or their jobs or anything like that that needed City Hall assistance." Regardless of their political allegiance, Penner helped Winnipeg's unemployed navigate the hostile channels of the municipal relief department. Even the local Conservatives knew that, if they had a problem, Penner was the man who would solve it.[84]

Communists were not only particularly attuned to the interests of the unemployed but also to workers and organized labour. When the *Winnipeg Free Press* reported on the daily activities of mayoral candidates in 1933, they discovered that Forkin spent most of his time meeting with union officials.[85] Similarly, the communist election press bragged, "the only two aldermen on the City Council who have been on a picket line during the past two years, and more, are Penner and Forkin."[86] CPC aldermen regularly behaved as an extension of the labour movement through the motions they put forward on council.

During a lengthy strike at the Western Packing Company, Penner raised the plight of the strikers at the council table and put forward a motion (seconded by the ILP's James Simpkin) to condemn sweatshop conditions at the company.[87] Penner twice put forward motions to protect strikers from police intimidation while picketing. In 1935, during a strike by the typographical unions at the *Winnipeg Free Press* and the *Winnipeg Tribune*, Penner and Forkin requested that the council cease from doing any business with the newspapers that was not required by law. This motion passed with the support of the ILP aldermen and elicited praise from the unionists who, while admitting that they did not always agree with the communists, still appreciated their consistent support on city council.[88] As Penner wrote in 1935, "whenever such strike struggles took place we brought out the workers' side of the dispute on the floor of council."[89] Communist aldermen advanced the cause of organized labour, even if in doing so they were assisting mainstream unions opposed by the communist-organized WUL. This demonstrates a degree of flexibility within the CPC, which, in 1935, was transitioning away from Third Period sectarianism and towards the Popular Front period, where they tried to work with other parties and groups on the left.

Consequently, support for communist aldermen was rooted in their commitment to the issues that directly affected the lives of their working-class constituents. As Michael Harris remembered, "the Communist candidates had a big vote because the Communists helped them. They were devoted to the working peoples' welfare." He recalled how people would vote for Penner because "he was their friend; he helps them. Not anybody else."[90] The communist press had a similar interpretation of the CPC's success. The *Voice of Labour*, a communist newspaper published for a few months in 1934, declared, "these workers and hard pressed members of the lower middle class who voted communist did so not only because they had before them the example of Alderman Penner's record in City Council, but also because the communists have shown, through their policy in the City Council and their day-to-day work outside the council, that they have fought for the everyday interests of Winnipeg workers."[91] In addressing these immediate needs, Penner and Forkin often demonstrated flexibility in being able to work with and for numerous types of people, including those specifically condemned by Third Period ideology. Undoubtedly, they also remained tied to national and international policy decisions. Yet, contrary to CPC instructions that the program of communists must be "contrasted sharply with those of Labour parties,"[92] Penner and Forkin demonstrated a willingness, at times, to adapt to local conditions in their engagement with non-communist unions or the ILP.

Despite agreement on policy and similar voting records on particular issues, the CPC was still very much in the Third Period, and denunciations of the ILP as "social fascists" remained the status quo. National CPC leaders such as Stewart Smith energetically followed the Comintern line and equated "social fascism" with fascism, arguing, as late as 1934, that the two represented the "ideological superstructures of decaying monopoly capitalism."[93] Winnipeg CPC members eagerly followed the party line, and focused much attention on a "concerted offensive against the social fascist leaders...to draw [the workers] into the revolutionary movement."[94] Both at the national and the local level, social democrats and labourite politicians, represented in Winnipeg by the ILP, were a target for communist attacks.

Winnipeg CPC members believed that the ILP regularly demonstrated social fascist tendencies, citing occasional cooperation between the ILP and the conservative, but widely popular, Mayor Webb. In 1930, Kolisnyk declared that he had learned of the friendship between the ILP and Webb when he heard Webb refer to Alderman William Simpson of the ILP by his first name, while Simpson replied by referring to Webb as "Ralph."[95] While an exchange of polite pleasantries is not compelling evidence of ILP collaboration with Webb, communists interpreted the ILP's decision a year later not to run a mayoral candidate as an endorsement of Webb. This is somewhat hard to believe. Although Webb's populist politics were quite popular with working-class Winnipeggers, the ILP frequently criticized Webb's mayoralty in their publications and at party meetings. Nevertheless, the alleged support of a labour party for a conservative mayor not only infuriated communists—it also gave them something to talk about on the campaign trail. An excited communist organizer wrote to Sam Carr, announcing, "ILP Alderman [Thomas] Flye has stated in the press that his party is satisfied with Mayor Webb. Think how we can play that up!"[96]

CPC municipal candidates often spent their entire campaign attacking the ILP, not even mentioning their Citizen opponent. Forkin's mayoralty campaign in 1933 is an excellent example of this. He confined his remarks in election debates to challenging the ILP's positions on city council, without criticizing his other opponent, the notorious Webb. Forkin explained to the audience that it would be merely a side issue to attack bourgeois politicians, as communists "make no pretence of appealing to the whole of society." The CPC argued that they were a class-based party that sought votes from the working class. In a direct attack on the leadership of the ILP, Forkin explained that he was "for a labour movement led by workers and not by ex-clergymen."[97] After the election, the CPC celebrated their perceived victory over the ILP, and emphasized that the votes they had won had been taken away from ILP candidates. Gaining votes at the expense of their labour opponents seemed to be as significant an accomplishment to the communists as actually winning a seat on council.[98]

The ILP responded to these attacks in two ways. First, it argued that the CPC merely split the labour vote and allowed bourgeois candidates to win. The ILP also denounced the CPC for purportedly advocating dictatorship. The *Weekly News*, for example, posited that "communism is simply a new form of a very ancient evil, namely the evil of dictatorship."[99] Attacking communists served multiple purposes. First, the ILP believed that it was the more effective representative of Winnipeg workers. Second, it hoped to win seats in Wards One and Two. The ILP was concerned that, if associated too closely with communists, they would forgo any chance of electoral success in those wards.

The relationship between the two parties gradually thawed despite the ongoing exchange of insults. As Norman Penner remarked, the ILP and CPC emphasized similar issues and developed similar solutions to them.[100] Even though the 1933 campaign highlighted previously was focused almost exclusively on the ILP, the *Weekly News* noted that Forkin's mayoralty campaign "kept away from [the] abusive attacks on the ILP which have characterized communist campaigns in recent years." The paper also assumed that, despite attacks by the CPC on the ILP, Penner (who was elected that same year) would "as spokesman for a section of the working-class...be bound to fall into line [with the ILP] on a great many issues of immediate concern, regardless of the fundamental differences in philosophy, political theory, and tactics."[101] At the council table, the CPC were also described in terms that minimized their anti-ILP rhetoric. The *Winnipeg Free Press*, in depicting Penner's first council meeting, said he "left his soap-box oratory outside the council chamber and his moderate utterances held the attention of the other aldermen. [He] voted as a member of the 'leftist' group."[102]

Cooperation with the ILP, as far as the CPC were concerned, could have reached its apex in 1934, when they offered their support to the ILP's mayoral candidate, John Queen. This could be understood as the first significant move by the CPC in Winnipeg away from the Third Period and toward the next period in Communist Party history, the Popular Front. The shift to the Popular Front meant that communist parties around the world were no longer to be isolated from others on the left, but instead to reverse course from sectarianism and establish broad alliances with all anti-fascist parties. While the shift towards the Popular Front began in 1934 (to be fully adopted in 1935 at the seventh World Congress of the Communist International), this move in Winnipeg remains somewhat remarkable given that Stewart Smith, a key leader in the Canadian national party, published a pamphlet entitled *Socialism and the CCF*, which viciously attacked the CCF as an obstacle to revolution that very year.[103]

The CPC provided the ILP with a list of six demands on which to build a common platform. They requested that Queen pledge to struggle against fascism in Winnipeg, fight cuts in relief and provide adequate relief for all the unemployed, repeal the decision to cut off family relief vouchers for single men over the age of eighteen, end the deportation of the unemployed, oppose the Bradshaw Report,[104] and provide the same medical care to war veterans as was given to the unemployed.[105] The CPC agreed that, were Queen to accept this minimum platform, they would actively campaign on his behalf in the mayoralty race against Citizen candidate John McKerchar.

The ILP viewed the coalition offer quite differently. Queen replied to the CPC that he was "at a loss to understand your actions" and questioned why a unity offer would be made after a communist newspaper had allegedly provided encouragement to his bourgeois opponent and when the CPC was running Saul Simkin against the ILP's James Simpkin, allegedly to confuse voters.[106] Looking back, historians Harry and Mildred Gutkin described the offer as nothing more than a "publicity stunt for the extremists."[107] To the ILP, the offer was incomprehensible after years of hostile attacks. As the *Labour Leader* newspaper put it, "after fourteen years of defaming and denouncing every labour organization both political and economic—except their own...as the betrayers of the working class, one would think it was about time they were getting wise to their own stupidity."[108] For Queen, the victim of vicious verbal assaults for years at the hands of communists, there was to be no unity.

Winnipeg CPC members, in turn, reacted angrily to the rejection of their offer. They proposed that Queen feared losing middle-class votes by accepting a coalition and that his refusal meant that the ILP had "exposed themselves not as champions of unity, but as splitters in the ranks of Labour."[109] In sharp contrast to a 1927 proclamation that communists should vote for Queen in the mayoralty race of that year, the CPC declared that both Queen and the Citizen candidate, John McKerchar, represented bourgeois interests. Members were advised to spoil their mayoralty ballot by writing "COMMUNIST" across it. Forkin went further, saying that if communists really wanted to vote for one or the other, "they might as well vote for McKerchar rather than for that Labor demagogue," ironic, given the denunciation of the ILP's relatively quiet support of Webb only a few years earlier.[110] Formal cooperation with the ILP, which had briefly appeared a possibility, albeit on the CPC's terms, was now completely off the table. The two parties would remain rivals on council for years to come.

The coalition offer did, however, confirm in the minds of many Citizens that the ILP was linked to the CPC, likely another reason why the ILP might have been so reticent about accepting the offer. Looking back on municipal politics a year after losing the mayoralty election to Queen, McKerchar remarked, "Winnipeg is now at the mercy of communists. There is no particular difference between the ILP and the [Communist] party. They all get their inspiration from Moscow."[111] Despite the vast ideological gulf that separated the two parties on the left at times, they were lumped together by their rightist opponents.

Communist aldermen on Winnipeg City Council, and CPC efforts to elect and support these aldermen, demonstrated the powerful connection that the party could have with a working-class neighbourhood. North End Winnipeg would continue to elect communists to council until 1983,[112] particularly remarkable given the anti-communist Cold War rhetoric that dominated political dialogue for most of those years. Although the Communist Party in Winnipeg towed close to the rhetoric and ideology of the Third Period until 1935, especially through its verbal attacks on the ILP, its members in places such as Winnipeg demonstrated a willingness to adapt the party line to local conditions and work with significant flexibility within a local setting.

The CPC's relationship with the other party on the political left, the ILP, was complex. Despite frequent antagonism and distrust, aldermen from the two parties managed to work together on issues of common interest. The two parties frequently found themselves voting together on issues such as unemployment, deportation, and public transportation, issues that were vitally important to the everyday needs of working-class Winnipeggers. This is not to say that there were not disagreements. The CPC frequently accused their ILP opponents of betraying the working class, while the ILP accused the CPC of dictatorial tendencies. Nevertheless, despite the public rhetoric, the two parties appear to have shared, in some ways, a similar vision for Winnipeg's municipal government, a vision that stood in profound opposition to the policies of their collective opponents on the political right.

When the Protection and Community Services Committee of Winnipeg City Council met in early May of 2000, the city's communist history was up for discussion. A proposal had come before the committee to name a park in the city's West End after Jacob Penner. Councillor Garth Steek declared, "my grandparents came to this country from Russia to escape communist oppression. So did a lot of people and it's objectionable to name a park after someone who represented that way of thinking." Dan Vandal retorted, "the Cold War is over. He [Penner] dedicated his life to the community."[113] In the end, Steek was the only vote opposed to the renamed park. Jacob Penner Park now occupies the southern block of Notre Dame Avenue between Victor and McGee, a testament to the legacy of this revolutionary figure in Winnipeg's municipal life.

CHAPTER 5

FOR FREEDOM'S CAUSE, YOUR BAYONET'S BRIGHT

In the early light of a July morning in 1931, a crack squad of well-trained and well-armed Bolshevik revolutionaries stocked with machine guns provided by the Communist Party USA stormed downtown Winnipeg's Bank of Montreal at Portage and Main, in the process seizing cash and positioning machine gun posts over the pivotal intersection. A few kilometres to the west, another squad of communists was in the process of seizing the Minto Barracks, where additional arms were captured and distributed to trained machine gunners. From these bases, the invasion continued, as communists seized the means of communication—radio stations, the post office, and telephone operating hubs—and transportation networks. Prisons were emptied and prisoners armed, each urged to join the new revolution. Money from the Bank of Montreal and banks seized later in the day was quickly squirrelled away throughout the city, hidden in case of failure.[1] By mid-day, the insurrection was complete and Winnipeg was a new Red outpost in the Canadian West.

These events never happened, and likely were never seriously contemplated, let alone planned. But precisely this plan appeared in files of Manitoba's Attorney General, quite possibly the product of the overactive imagination of an ambitious police informant, perhaps one who took some comradely dreaming a little too seriously. In a tribute to the nervous mood of the time, it was taken seriously despite the fact that no evidence was ever found to support these claims, no cache of machine guns located, nor was any of the documentation you might expect to find of an imminent invasion.

While armed communists never did storm Portage and Main, the Attorney General's files reveal a few key issues related to the political left in Winnipeg in the 1920s and 1930s. First, it demonstrates the level of paranoia within the political and police establishment about the perceived threat of revolutionary communism. Despite a membership numbering in the hundreds, many in the city's political and business elite were concerned about the radical threat. This would have consequences for others on the left, such as the ILP. Citizens regularly accused the ILP of secretly supporting the revolutionary ambitions of the CPC, painting both parties as being controlled by Moscow for socialist revolution. Often, in doing so, Citizens directly or implicitly linked the ILP back to an earlier perceived attempt to seize the city, the 1919 Strike.

Secondly, the police surveillance that led to the creation of these files demonstrated a reality that Communist politicians lived with throughout the 1920s and 1930s. The party and its members were watched closely. In turn, this directed much of their activity on city council as the CPC sought to reduce restrictions on political freedom, increase freedom of speech, and address the threat of prosecution (and often deportation) for party members.

Finally, these files demonstrate a point of tension within the CPC itself. It was an avowedly revolutionary party. What would this mean in the Winnipeg (or broader Canadian) context? Did local communists imagine a Bolshevik-style armed revolution storming the local banks, barracks, and prisons? Or was revolution to be achieved in the staid halls of city council? While many of their opponents, both Citizens and the ILP, have suggested that there was a sinister hidden agenda to the aldermanic careers of William Kolisnyk, Jacob Penner, and Martin Forkin, it would seem that for these communist leaders, revolution looked much more like the latter than the former, something that was a long-term proposition to be achieved through a lengthy process of political involvement.

Throughout the 1920s and 1930s, the RCMP kept a close eye on CPC activities across Canada. Threats of proletarian revolution were monitored, even if the CPC seemed to have little capacity to actually carry out its threats, which tended to be more rhetorical flourishes than actual possibilities. Well over 1,000 pages of RCMP surveillance files were kept on CPC activities in Winnipeg alone, with dossiers stretching into hundreds of pages for key leaders. These included everything from descriptions of character traits to records of speeches and publicity campaigns, a historian's dream but likely a nightmare for those constantly being watched and followed. The RCMP were also successful in planting informants within the local CPC apparatus, with surveillance files frequently referring to comments made at internal party meetings. Many of these reports, however, are not particularly reliable. At times it seems that jocular dreaming was recorded as fact, or perhaps eager informants sought to increase the value of their services by magnifying the stories that they heard.

Police did not have to work too hard to find examples of avowedly revolutionary language being employed by communists both nationally and locally. The Seventh National Convention of the CPC in 1934 proclaimed, "there is no way out except the way of revolutionary mass struggle against capitalism and the final overthrow of capitalism."[2] This type of rhetoric was particularly indicative of the Third Period, as communists separated themselves from reformers on the political left to focus on revolutionary aims. At a national level, the CPC was home to such leaders as Stewart Smith, who declared, "little do [people] realize that in a very short time the streets of Toronto will be running with blood."[3] Communists expected that the crisis in capitalism created by the Great Depression would inevitably result in a proletarian revolution and their candidates did not shy away from revolutionary rhetoric. This, they thought, could be their moment for a true proletarian revolution in Canada.

Winnipeg communists also declared themselves to be fervent believers in revolution, particularly during the Third Period. *The Worker* reported that Winnipeg CPC members pledged in 1929 to "energetically strive to build and consolidate our Party on a Marxist-Leninist revolutionary theory, that it may be a worthy section of the fighting Communist International."[4] Interestingly, this pledge focused on contributing not just to revolution, but a fighting one, and an international one. Revolution was not just to be a local affair, it was something that was to happen across the nation and, indeed, around the world.

Even as election promises and aldermanic careers often focused on the immediate needs of Winnipeg's working class, municipal candidates for the CPC did not forget that their ultimate objective was revolution. During municipal election campaigns and regular speeches in Market Square, communists were consistent in articulating that revolutionary action was the only way to end the economic troubles of the Great Depression. As he opened his 1932 mayoralty campaign, Penner declared, "capitalism has reached a stage of development where, like a man afflicted with a deadly disease, it cannot recuperate or bring back prosperity."[5] It was the role of the CPC, Penner believed, to fight an "uncompromising struggle to unseat the dictatorship of the bourgeoisie."[6] This fight was necessary, he believed, because it was only by overthrowing the capitalist system that a more just system could be created. In the 1950s, Penner wrote to his son Norman that "a Marxist-Leninist Party is a Party of sharp, uncompromising struggle to unseat the dictatorship of the bourgeoisie, bring to power the dictatorship of the working-class, expropriate the expropriators and thus abolish the exploitation of the working-class. There is no other way of accomplishing this historical task."[7] Participation in municipal politics could achieve this, Tom Ewen explained, because if the CPC was elected to power at the municipal or provincial level, it could use this position to overthrow the capitalist system.[8]

Despite the emphasis on the necessity of revolution to cure the perceived evils of capitalism, and the rhetoric of the Third Period that suggested that the crisis of capitalism was forthcoming, communist politicians in Winnipeg never imagined an imminent revolution. According to his son Roland, Penner never thought of the revolution as a "rush to the barricades." Penner was not planning stealthy dawn invasions. Instead, he envisioned a long-standing war of position that focused on increasing working-class consciousness.[9] As Roland Penner recalled, when he asked his father when the revolution was coming, he would always be told, "in twenty years."[10] Another prominent communist, Andrew Bilecki, who was elected to the school board in 1933, compared the proletarian revolution to the process of abolishing slavery. It would take hundreds of years, he argued, to change enough minds to bring about the moment of revolution.[11] Despite CPC policy that focused on immediate contradictions in capitalism, municipal politicians did not interpret the revolution as something that was going to happen in the near future. Rather, they were content to fight for the immediate needs of the workers, and included little explicit talk of revolution in their efforts on city council.

One possible illustration of the attitude of Winnipeg's municipal communists towards the revolution comes from the writings of a German journalist, A.E. Johann, who travelled through western Canada in 1931 and 1932. His writings describe a prominent communist politician in Winnipeg named "Comrade Wacher." There is no record that an actual Comrade Wacher existed in Winnipeg, but the description is remarkably evocative of Penner. The physical appearance, ethnicity, character, and occupation would all seem to suggest that Wacher and Penner were the same person. Johann quotes Wacher as saying that "neither of us will live to experience [a Communist revolution in Canada].... That day seems to be further away in this land than anywhere else." While it is impossible to conclusively determine that Wacher was indeed Penner, this does match what other sources have described as Penner's attitude toward revolution.[12]

RCMP surveillance records do suggest that there were communists in Winnipeg who were less philosophical about future revolution. Orton Wade, who served as the muncipal campaign manager for the CPC in 1935 and would eventually be deported by the federal government, was alleged by the RCMP to have suggested at a CPC meeting in Market Square that members should frequently attend moving picture shows that involved weapons handling in order to instruct themselves for the impending revolution. Wade allegedly went on to suggest that setting fires would be the best way to relieve pressure from machine gun fire and declared that communists would have barrels of gas under high pressure on every street corner so they could "simultaneously set the whole of Portage Avenue on fire. It would not take long to destroy the whole thing, barricades could be constructed during the excitement and machine guns set up."[13]

Wade was not the only communist to allegedly call for violence. Aubrey Brock, who ran as a school board candidate for the CPC, is quoted as saying "you cannot fight with empty hands, so take what you can, you know yourselves what I mean, I cannot tell you more." He apparently would also add, "if the police start to shoot at you, you have a perfect right to shoot back."[14] Another anonymous communist in 1931 reportedly declared, "if in 1914 you could volunteer to die in the defence of the capitalists and went to kill our brothers in Germany, then now go and defend the rights of the workers.... Who is ready to die in the fight with the dogs of policemen?"[15]

Violent rhetoric also made its way into municipal political activity, in part through song. A song sheet provided for a Penner campaign rally included lyrics such as "Our bombs are ready, our machine guns rattle, against the world's imperialistic greed" and "For freedom's cause, your bayonet's bright / For workers' Russia, for Soviet Canada, get ready for the last fierce fight."[16] Incorporating a more municipal theme, a popular song amongst the Young Communist League in Winnipeg included the lyrics, "let's hang Mayor Webb from the sour apple tree." Sung to the tune of "John Brown's Body," a common protest song during the period, this song and others were not a sign of intention to do violence. However, they do represent examples of how insurrectionary, violent language was incorporated into municipal campaigns.

Given all this revolutionary rhetoric, it is not surprising that some saw an imminent threat. While it is not clear how widespread this fear was, the self-proclaimed Vigilante Committee of Winnipeg wrote to Premier John Bracken to inform him that "the ambition of the Communist Party is that they may involve our country in Civil War and bloodshed."[17] In 1931, the same year that "Comrade Wacher" thought that the revolution was a lifetime away, the Manitoba Provincial Police (MPP) and the RCMP suspected that a communist plot was afoot to capture the city. As depicted earlier in this chapter, an MPP informant claimed that the CPC was divided into two units, one of which was composed of artillerists, machine gunners, and bombers. The intelligence indicated that the CPC had access to thirty machine guns in the city and were planning to launch a surprise attack on the Bank of Montreal at Portage and Main, seize machine guns stored at the Minto Street Barracks, and then capture other important infrastructure.[18]

Local police anticipated several other plots endangering the city and its leadership. The RCMP seemed equally convinced of a CPC plot but were less certain as to the number of weapons in their possession. They suggested that the CPC possibly had three machine guns and 2,500 shells hidden in Winnipeg that had been delivered to the city by agents from the United States.[19] Furthermore, an RCMP informant said that the CPC had ordered 100 instructional books on how to conduct battle during revolution that were to be delivered from

Moscow. At the provincial level, H.J. Martin of the provincial police wrote to the Attorney General warning that while no mention had been made of bombing the legislative buildings, an attack was possible on Winnipeg City Hall. The Attorney General files revealed that police had been informed of a perceived communist plot to get "Mayor Webb alone some place and attack him."[20] Other plots were also anticipated. Premier Bracken was warned in 1932 by Inspector J.A. Browne of the provincial police that the CPC was "secretly preparing the organization of a fighting group with the purpose to obtain funds...these groups will have to rob banks and stores."[21]

There is no evidence to support the findings of the provincial police or RCMP. Despite several police raids on communist headquarters and halls, no guns were ever found nor were any revolutionary plans. It is highly unlikely that communists flooded movie theatres to learn marksmanship from action heroes. This is not to say that communists did not employ the language of, or believe in, insurrectionary revolution. Communists, by definition, believed in proletarian revolution, although there was a wide variety of ideas on how to achieve it.

There are many reasons to question evidence provided by federal and provincial informants. First, informants were paid to produce information about communist revolutionary activities. It would not have taken much to record bravado as fact or even completely fabricate revolutionary tales for a gullible audience. Doing so could advance the career of an informant and prove their value to the police force. Additionally, in many cases informants demonstrated that they were not aware of the subtlety of relationships or rhetoric within the party, so they could have completely misunderstood what they were talking about. And third, it is entirely possible that a small portion of the party membership could have been seeking a more immediate revolution than what leaders like Penner were imagining. Some party members were talking the language of immediate insurrectionary revolution, although they had precious little capacity to bring it about.

Talk of revolution also served a valuable purpose for the CPC's opponents. It allowed them to play off the existing fears of radicalism and revolution, a fear that was linked to the class divisions within the city. This had two effects. Notably, it reinforced fear among many middle- and upper-class residents that the ILP, with a much larger electoral presence, was also insurrectionary and was working alongside the CPC. Both, it was assumed, were taking revolutionary marching orders from Moscow. Nothing could have been further from the truth. The ILP frequently denounced the idea of Bolshevik revolution in the clearest of terms. Nevertheless, Citizens were effective at lumping the ILP and CPC together as co-revolutionaries, both with a hidden agenda to bring a Red revolution to the city.

Warning people of radical revolution was a tactic long used by Winnipeg's political establishment against the political left, an approach that dated back to the General Strike. Warnings of imminent revolution were frequent during the General Strike of 1919 to discredit the Strike and its leadership. Reflecting on the Strike, *The Globe* in Toronto wrote, "the 'Reds' who acted as leaders were interested only in fostering a spirit of revolt and in getting more power into their own hands. Their newspaper at the outset of the strike let the cat out of the bag by proclaiming a Soviet Government in Winnipeg."[22] Within Winnipeg the *Winnipeg Citizen* declared, "rioting on the streets of Winnipeg was the effort of the Reds to commit all strikers to revolution."[23] Indeed, the Citizens Committee of 1000 sought a royal commission into the threat of Bolshevik revolution.[24] Talk of revolution would continue to be an effective way to ensure public support for anti-communist policies to limit free speech and crack down on communist leadership.

The most significant consequence of this focus on revolution was police intimidation. This occurred in a variety of ways—direct confrontation with police forces, police surveillance, raids on communist offices and venues, and intimidation of individual members. The early 1930s were a time of severe repression against the CPC and others involved in radical politics across Canada. The trial of Tim Buck and seven other communist leaders attracted the most headlines, but in 1932 alone, internal CPC documents claimed that 839 members had been arrested, resulting in 111 years of jail time and 59 deportations.[25] Intimidation was such that Winnipeg communists remarked, "Canada is being made to resemble Russia under the tsar."[26] The "iron heel of ruthlessness," to use a phrase from Canadian Prime Minister R.B. Bennett, the crackdown on the CPC that resulted in these arrests, was a significant threat to the CPC and its membership.[27] The 1930s were a dangerous time to be a communist in Canada.

On 6 March 1930, for example, an impromptu procession of unemployed communists was charged by forty police officers. After a frenzied speech in which William Kolisnyk denounced the exploitation of labour, he urged the crowd to form a procession. When it had assembled and began marching to Main Street, the police charged. The *Winnipeg Free Press* described how police came "charging across the market place, beneath the shadow of the old city hall building, the police swept the demonstrators before them, batons swinging and fists pounding, until the solid mass was shattered into a melee of fleeing people, leaving the street covered with hats and coats, rubbers, [and] overshoes." It went on to say, "police used their 'billies' generously; sent obstinate Communists to the pavement with punches and thrusts and hustled the leaders from the forefront away down the side-streets."[28]

The *Free Press* said little about violence committed by communists, likely because there was little, focusing instead on the batons and billy clubs of the police. The images of violence in the article were not those committed by unruly hordes. This is not to say that the *Free Press* in any way supported the communist protestors, arguing that the police were justified in their actions because the communists had failed to apply for a march permit. Therefore, the article suggested, there was no similarity between the police charge and crackdowns on communists in other Canadian centres. Communists in Winnipeg, stated a *Winnipeg Free Press* editorial, continued to have freedom of speech, and only when they incited the police, as they had allegedly done on 6 March, was there any response from the police.[29]

Interestingly, Kolisnyk, who had had a seat on city council until not long before this march, played a prominent role in this incident, leading the march and shouting encouraging words to his comrades before being dragged away by two large police officers. He has even been described as the "hero" of the demonstration.[30] Kolisnyk was also able to use his prominent municipal role to offer a rebuttal to the editorial line taken by the *Winnipeg Free Press*. While acknowledging that the proper permits had not been sought, he suggested that the CPC had not applied for them, as they knew that their application would never be approved.[31] Kolisnyk would later accuse the ILP of encouraging the police crackdown, an accusation that ILP Alderman John Blumberg dismissed as "a lie."[32]

Communists used their public election meetings to publicize police tactics, such as when Saul Simkin declared that the municipal administration sympathized with the "terroristic methods of [the] police."[33] The CPC warned its supporters that, although repression was less severe in Winnipeg than in centres such as Toronto, the "rule of terror" found in Toronto would soon move westward. Indeed, communists accused Citizen aldermen of openly supporting the tactics of the Red Squad and Police Chief Dennis Draper of Toronto.[34] The CPC also accused the ILP of supporting "repression either through silence or open incitation" by accepting rulings of the police commission or failing to assist communists fight perceived injustices.[35] Workers were reminded of the General Strike's "Bloody Sunday," and the CPC suggested that police tactics made another such event imminent.[36] Unlike any other time of the year, an election campaign gave the CPC the potential to reach the masses through the mainstream press. To this greatly increased audience, the communists were able to spread their demand for an end to the oppression of their party.

While it is perhaps true that Winnipeg communists faced less pernicious persecution than those in some other parts of Canada, Mayor Ralph Webb was described by the communists as a "would-be Hitler," and was known for his vehement anti-communist stance, referred to by some as a Western version of Toronto's notorious police chief, Dennis Draper.[37] In 1930, Webb launched a one-man coast-to-coast campaign to whip up anti-communist enthusiasm, a campaign that would embarrass even the ardently anti-communist *Winnipeg Free Press*, saying that his activities reflected poorly on the city.[38]

Webb lobbied the federal government to deport communist agitators and even provided the Minister of Immigration with the names of Winnipeg communists who had travelled to Moscow. In a letter to Prime Minister Bennett, Webb asked him to "deal with these agitators in the way they should be dealt with, and that is—to speak roughly—send them back to Russia, the country of their dreams."[39] He also suggested that "the Dominion ought to maintain a secret service expressly for combating the Bolshevik menace…and the ring-leaders, instead of being hauled up in the ordinary law courts and allowed to hire high-priced counsel, ought to be spirited out of the country and back to where they came from."[40] According to Norman Penner, Webb once declared that he hoped to deport all communists or, if that was not possible, he would "throw them in the Red River with Jake Penner being the first to go."[41] Communists accused Mayor Webb of using his position to encourage police intimidation of strikers or to ban communists from holding meetings. As mayor, Webb was also able to limit debate on communist motions in city council meetings or declare them to be out of order. For communists, Webb became the ultimate enemy in the city, a home-grown "fascist" who represented the suppression and intimidation that the CPC faced.

Intimidation was occasionally used against the CPC's election campaigns. Communist Party headquarters were raided just prior to the 1930 and 1931 municipal elections, and many of their election materials were seized. Police claimed to be looking for guns and ammunition, although no weapons were found. The CPC complained that it was unable to recover its election materials after the raid, thus causing serious disruption to their campaign.[42] It accused A.A. Heaps (an ILP Member of Parliament) of signing the warrant allowing the police raid on the offices of the CPC, Canadian Labour Defence League, National Unemployed Workers Association, Ukrainian Labour-Farmer Temple Association, and Young Communist League in 1931 that resulted in the seizure of their election newspapers.[43] Given the difficulties in raising funds to prepare new materials, such raids posed tremendous challenges to local campaigns. In addition to intimidation by police, opposing candidates were alleged to have warned that foreign-born workers would be fired and deported for voting communist.[44] Therefore, municipal election activity was not immune to threats or repression.

An additional consequence of this repression was that the CPC complained that they had difficulty getting their membership involved in election campaigns. Although there are a number of reasons why the membership may have been reluctant to get involved, it is not impossible that at a time when the majority of Winnipeg CPC members were both foreigners and unemployed, and when deportations of both the foreign unemployed and political radicals were common, people were hesitant to actively campaign for the CPC.[45]

Police intimidation of communists would continue throughout the 1930s and into the Second World War, when several local communists, including Kolisnyk and Penner, would be interned as potential enemies. Kolisnyk would be released due to illness, but Penner served two years in detention during the War and was only released in the summer of 1942. Many local communists likely made their way onto the Prominent Functionaries of the Communist Party (PROFUNC) list maintained by the Canadian government from the 1950s to 1980s. Police intimidation and surveillance, therefore, would continue for many decades after the first CPC aldermen were elected to Winnipeg City Council.

In response to intimidation and surveillance, CPC aldermen Kolisnyk, Penner, and Forkin called for the end of discriminatory practices and sought free speech for communist activities. It was at the municipal level that the CPC could lobby to change the practices of local police or complain of mistreatment. Often they did so in co-operation with ILP aldermen, who regularly denounced police persecution of communists even as they criticized the communists for their support of revolution. And it was through their activities in municipal politics that CPC aldermen saw themselves contributing to the revolution that they sought. Upon his retirement, Penner reflected that he hoped that his years on council would contribute to the eventual victory of socialism in Canada.[46] While he may not have been urging his comrades to the battle lines, manning a machine gun, or attending motion pictures to perfect his weapon handling techniques, Penner had, in his mind, fought for the proletarian revolution he sought. Municipal politics, he believed, could be part of the revolutionary process, not a parliamentary distraction.

CHAPTER 6

A BOMBSHELL TO MANY CITIZENS

Winnipeg's election on 23 November 1934 marked a profound shift in Winnipeg's municipal politics. In a victory described as "nothing less than a bombshell to many citizens,"[1] the political left won the mayoralty and half the aldermanic seats in the City of Winnipeg, giving them the majority of votes on Winnipeg City Council. The victory was a long time coming. Ever since the General Strike in 1919, Winnipeg's labour movement had attempted to win political control of city council. Other than the election of S.J. Farmer as mayor in November 1922, their efforts had met relatively little success and labour aldermen were usually outnumbered by a margin of two to one by their Citizen opponents. Indeed, in many ways, the election of November 1934 represented the successful climax of fifteen years of electoral campaigning.

In 1918, socialist Sam Blumenberg had declared, "we are going to run this city." The two years that followed the November 1934 election would be the closest to running the city that labour would ever come, giving the political left an opportunity to reshape municipal politics at the height of the Great Depression. This chapter will explore the policies introduced in 1935 and 1936, one of the defining moments for labour in Winnipeg politics. Second, it will explore the at times tenuous relationship that labour aldermen had with organized labour as they struggled to meet the expectations of their supporters. In doing so, it will not only illustrate the contentious politics of western Canada's second largest city in the 1930s,[2] but also demonstrate the ways that labour politicians endeavoured to reshape a city that had been dominated by business-oriented politics.

Winnipeg was not the only Canadian community to support pro-labour politicians at the municipal level during the mid-1930s. Toronto, Calgary, Edmonton, and Regina all elected pro-labour mayors or councils. Just outside Winnipeg, St. Boniface elected an ILP mayor named George Barefoot, who campaigned on the slogan "human needs before property rights,"[3] and in East Kildonan the ILP won the reeveship. Change was in the air in politics across Canada.[4] The *Manitoba Commonwealth and Weekly News* spoke optimistically about what municipal victories could mean, saying, "citizens of Canadian cities are learning either through economic pressure or through study, that the only way in which their condition and the condition of the whole community can be permanently bettered is the way in which the Socialist has indicated for decades."[5] Surely, they suggested, victories at the provincial or federal levels of government would be next.

The mayoralty and nine of the eighteen council seats were at stake in the election campaign of November 1934. The mayoralty race, which received by far the most attention in the local media, pitted the Citizens' John McKerchar, a local grocer who had spent twenty-three years on the school board and fourteen years on city council, against John Queen, a long-time ILP politician. McKerchar, who had earned the nickname "watchdog of the city treasury" during his time as chairman of the Finance Committee, ran a modest campaign in favour of maintaining the status quo.[6] In the words of a *Winnipeg Free Press* editorial, he stood for "efficient and strictly economical administration of the City's affairs."[7] His supporters declared, "a vote for McKerchar is a vote for sane government."[8] Thus, the election race for the 1935 mayoralty was drawn between a cautious, economically prudent member of Winnipeg's establishment and a reformer who was associated with the interests of the working class.

The central campaign issue in November 1934 was how the city should respond to the Bradshaw Report. This report was completed at the behest of city council by Thomas Bradshaw, the president of the North American Life Assurance Company, to investigate "the fair and proper distribution of tax liability."[9] A movement in favour of tax reform had existed among Winnipeg's business elite since at least 1932, when several notable citizens wrote to council to argue in favour of tax and civic service reductions.[10] Bradshaw suggested, "a substantial reduction in real estate taxes [is] both desirable and imperative."[11] He proposed tax cuts for businesses, warehouses, and residential property in business districts. This would be paid for with a 2 percent sales tax, a 10 percent tax on rent, and a 10 percent increase in water and hydro rates.[12] These tax increases were unpopular throughout the city. While the city's business owners and residential property owners would end up paying less tax, much of the city's working class, those who could least afford it, would have been forced to pay more for their rent and utilities.

The response to the Bradshaw Report was indicative of the divide between the ILP and the Citizens. Queen opposed the "monstrous proposals of the Bradshaw Report"[13] because, he claimed, they unfairly targeted the working class. In Queen's analysis, "as long as we have a type of mind dominant in the city council that is more concerned about protecting investments than promoting human well being we can be certain that the proposals contained in the Bradshaw Report will be acted upon."[14] In light of the public outcry, Queen was able to force McKerchar, who had supported Bradshaw, to publicly declare that he would not follow Bradshaw's recommendations.[15] Despite concerted efforts by the right-wing Home and Property Owners' Association, which launched a radio advertisement campaign in favour of Bradshaw's recommendations, the report became a defining election issue that benefited the ILP.[16]

Queen narrowly defeated McKerchar by 499 votes (26,835 votes to 26,336)[17] in a vote sharply split along class lines. In the predominantly upper-class Ward One, McKerchar won 68 percent of the vote, while in the working-class Ward Three, Queen won 62 percent. The vote also represented the highest number of votes an ILP candidate had received since the General Strike, with nearly 27,000 voters voting for Queen, and an increase of over 5,000 votes from the previous year, perhaps in part due to the fact that the CPC, who had won nearly 5,000 votes in the previous mayoral campaign, did not run a candidate in November 1934. The ILP also had success in the aldermanic races, including a surprise win in Ward One, to bring their total to six seats.

As discussed earlier, the communists had made overtures to Queen that they would support his bid for the mayoralty, an offer that was clearly rebuffed by the ILP. Yet the communists still declined to run a candidate, after having run a mayoral candidate in the two previous years. One explanation was that they decided to concentrate their energy on aldermanic races where they had a better chance of winning (in the two previous mayoral campaigns they had won 7.1 percent and 8.5 percent of the vote). The strategy might have paid off, as the 1934 election marked the first time that two communists would serve on city council together.

Most significantly, however, labour parties won enough seats (six ILP, two CPC, and one independent labourite) to hold the balance of power and, for the first time in Winnipeg's history, labour was in control of city council. This was, in the words of the *Manitoba Commonwealth*, a "labour victory." To achieve the majority, however, Winnipeg's ILP and CPC would need to work together, not necessarily a simple task given the longstanding animosity between the two groups. While the *Manitoba Commonwealth* would frequently criticize the CPC, they recognized that the ILP would need to "obtain the active co-operation of the communists" to "register such advances in the welfare of the community as will ensure still greater success next fall." The communists, it went on to say, "have as much responsibility as the others on the council and they cannot escape it by assuming the role of intransigents."[18] Would this council be able to achieve the needed co-operation? And what would this new council, Winnipeg's first with a labour majority, do? A council, no less, with a mayor who had once been jailed for his role in that key divisive moment fifteen years earlier.[19]

YEAR	ILP VOTES RECEIVED	PERCENTAGE
1919	12,514	44.4%
1920	14,360	48.4%
1921	No candidate	
1922	16,421	56.6%
1923	20,059	56.5%
1924	17,349	44.1%
1925	12,703	35.0%
1926	12,673	39.1%
1927	16,448	41.2%
1928	No candidate	
1929	13,842	31.5%
1930	16,145	37.7%
1931	No candidate	
1932	20,812	42.1%
1933	21,273	38.0%
1934	26,835	50.5%
1935	32,248	60.2%
1936	25,802	40.5%

Table 2. Votes Received by ILP Candidates in Mayoral Elections.
Source: *Winnipeg Municipal Manuals*, 1920–1937.

While the 1930s were economically challenging times across Canada, a 1937 report by Graham Towers, president of the Bank of Canada, found that Manitobans had been worse affected than most of the country.[20] This had a significant impact on Winnipeg's economy and municipal government revenue. Between 1931 and 1936, Winnipeg City Council's revenue dropped by 12 percent as the assessable value of property fell by $40 million dollars.[21] Revenue also fell because an increasing number of people could not afford to pay their property taxes. By 31 December 1936, the city was owed $12 million in tax arrears, nearly twice as much as the revenue that was actually collected in that year.[22]

Despite Citizen fear mongering that labour politicians would lead Winnipeg into economic ruin, the Queen administration prided itself in prudently administering the city's finances.[23] Winnipeg's municipal governments continued running balanced budgets, with the exception of an annual loan to cover the cost of unemployment relief.[24] A year later, during the 1935 election campaign, ILP Alderman Victor Anderson bragged that his party had provided the "most efficient" governing ever in Winnipeg's history.[25] Compared with the budgets of the early 1930s, when the City of Winnipeg did little but "live within our means,"[26] labour aldermen increased city expenditure by 11 percent. Numerous services including hospitals, social welfare, child welfare, street maintenance, libraries, and the civic pension fund received additional funding while balanced budgets were maintained.[27]

New revenue sources were required to pay for these new expenditures and labour aldermen insisted money would be obtained from the wealthy and not from the working class, demonstrating an opposite approach to that employed by Thomas Bradshaw. In 1934, Queen said, "we are going to get our revenue from those who have the wealth. We are not going into the poor homes to collect it."[28] In 1936 he reiterated that "we [the ILP] will never place taxes on poverty but we will tax wealth and...the heavier burden of taxation is going to be placed on the shoulders of the rich."[29] Instead of taxing the working class, the ILP decided to seek additional tax revenues from big business.

This represented a major departure from the Citizens' tax policy. After decades of Citizen-dominated governments, Winnipeg received by far the lowest percentage of revenue from business taxes of any major Canadian city. In 1932, for example, the business tax collected in Winnipeg was 6 percent the amount of revenue collected from residential property taxes, compared with 19 percent in Montréal, 13 percent in Toronto, and 11 percent in Ottawa and Hamilton.[30] The tax assessment on a large hotel in Winnipeg, for example, was only one-quarter larger than that of an average small home.[31] Businesses, therefore, were seen by many to be not paying their share, and the ILP and CPC both called for increased business taxes.

In March 1935 city council asked the province to approve a plan that would have generated an estimated $1.2 million annually (nearly triple the amount collected from businesses in the previous year) by allowing the city to charge taxes ranging from 5 to 45 percent of the assessed annual rental value of the property.[32] As proposed by the municipal Committee on Legislation and Reception, this meant removing the provision for a flat rate of 6.67 percent tax on business assessment and replacing it with taxation "to be determined as regards the method and rate of assessment thereof by the Council annually by bylaw on or before the first day in May in each year."[33] This legislation was intended to provide the city flexibility to charge large, profitable businesses substantially more than under the previous tax regime while reducing taxes for small businesses.

To become law, however, the motion had to be approved by the provincial legislature, where it was roundly condemned by representatives of the business community. Isaac Pitblado, representing Timothy Eaton's Company, proclaimed that the proposed tax "would throw taxation into chaos."[34] Pitblado argued that the proposed legislation would give the city an unlimited power to tax, that it discriminated between classes and between groups in each class, that Winnipeg businesses could not afford more taxation, and that payrolls and business construction would have to be reduced as a result of any tax increase. He also commented that "any legislation which sets up a rate for a department store five times greater than its competitor is most glaring discrimination."[35]

Others expressed similar concerns. C.C. Ferguson of Great West Life declared that the tax was merely "a most inequitable income tax in disguise," while others spread fear that the vagueness of the proposed legislation would allow future councils to change tax rates purely for electoral gains.[36] A representative of chain stores, John MacCaulay, claimed that the proposed tax would exceed the annual average profits of the Piggly Wiggly, Neal, and Safeway stores.[37] Numerous other business representatives appeared before the committee warning of business closures, industrial migration, staffing cuts, and price increases.

While large businesses opposed the plan, it did receive support from the small businesses that stood to benefit from a variated tax system. H.B. Scott, who represented the Retail Merchants' Association, approved of graduated taxes. He claimed that a flat tax system penalized smaller merchants, as it made independent stores pay a larger assessment per volume of goods than large department stores. Large businesses routinely got tax concessions, making it even harder for smaller businesses to compete.[38] Surprisingly, the plan received support from some Citizen aldermen. Egbert Honeyman and Cecil Gunn appeared before the provincial Law Amendments Committee to argue in favour of the legislation despite not being particularly comfortable advocating for a proposal "strongly tinctured with labour economics."[39] These Citizen aldermen may have disapproved of the idea of increased business taxes but they also recognized the city's dire financial situation.

The province denied the city's proposed business tax rates, but did grant it the right to set taxes between 5 and 15 percent of the annual rental value of business property.[40] ILP MLA H.F. Lawrence blamed the defeat on "big business in its desire to throw a monkey wrench into the machinery with which John Queen, labour mayor, was hoping to improve the condition of the people generally."[41] Most businesses ended up paying between 5 and 8 percent, although banks (15 percent), insurance companies (14 percent), and department stores (11 percent) all faced more substantial tax increases.[42] Despite providing $400,000 dollars less than the city had requested, labour aldermen had successfully generated $300,000 of additional revenue and avoided tax increases for the working class.

Labour aldermen also eyed Winnipeg's major railways as a new source of tax income. As a result of a deal with Canadian Pacific that had been signed in the 1880s, Winnipeg's railroads held nearly $7 million in tax-exempt realty, representing $450,000 in lost annual revenue.[43] Council passed motions put forward by William Lowe and Matthew Stobart of the ILP in 1935, and reintroduced in 1936 by Victor Anderson and James Simpkin (also both of the ILP) to request that the City Solicitor investigate what needed to be done to repeal all exemption agreements with the railways. This was strongly opposed by many Citizen aldermen, who argued that the city was not in the business of repudiating contracts.[44] Even though an all-party committee in the Manitoba legislature suggested that it was "opposed to the principle of granting for all time any exemption from municipal taxation," Premier Bracken and other influential legislators lobbied hard against the change. As a result, the bill was easily defeated by the legislature, with support coming almost exclusively from ILP MLAs.[45]

Unemployment and underemployment were significant challenges for Winnipeg workers throughout the 1930s. Between 1929 and 1933, the per capita income in Manitoba plunged by 49 percent.[46] Unemployment had grown significantly since the 1920s. In all of 1928, fewer than 400 men requested relief in Winnipeg, a number that fell to less than 300 in 1929. By February 1930, however, 1,306 men had already requested relief—nearly double the previous two years in the span of only two months.[47] During 1935 and 1936 unemployment hovered between 13 and 16 percent, although these statistics obscure the fact that even those with employment were earning drastically reduced wages.[48]

As unemployment was a municipal responsibility, there was much debate over how to respond to the problem of unemployment, a debate that divided largely along Citizen–labour lines.

After the November 1934 election, the *Winnipeg Free Press* reported that the "new council, with a leftist majority, will have a lot more to say about unemployment relief and relief works."[49] Unemployment had certainly played a role in the ILP's campaign in 1934. In an election debate with McKerchar, Queen said, "no good citizen can feel satisfied with the relief provided for the unemployed today. Common humanity demands that all their requirements be met."[50] The ILP believed that it was a social responsibility to help those on relief, not an inconvenience that damaged the city's credit rating. Conversely, an article prepared by the Winnipeg Board of Trade argued that direct relief "represents a huge economic loss and has resulted in a tremendous reduction of individual initiative and morale," representing the Citizen viewpoint that depicted the unemployed as corrupted and relief as a danger both to the city and to the recipient.[51]

The city's financial woes were largely attributable to the high cost of unemployment relief. This amount, which the city was forced to borrow due to lack of available funds, reached a high of over $1.8 million in 1935 and fell only slightly in 1936. Adding to the problem was that the city's share of the relief bill had increased steadily since 1931, when the city paid 36.6 percent of relief costs to a high of 50.1 percent by 1935. Not surprisingly, the city argued that the federal government should take responsibility for this expensive burden on local resources. Motions in January 1935 and August 1936 stated that the city was "in favour of non-contributory unemployment insurance which will embrace all of the present unemployed within its scope, the funds for which shall be provided by the federal government."[52] These appeals were not unique to the ILP. McKerchar, for example, in his position as Chairman of the Finance Committee in 1934, had supported requests by Premier Bracken for additional federal relief funds.[53] The difference, however, between the ILP and Citizens was that the ILP was willing to fund several municipal endeavours besides merely lobbying for increased funding.

In the election campaign of November 1936, Morris Gray, an ILP alderman, proclaimed that the ILP had successfully "humanized" the relief department.[54] The Special Committee on Unemployment Relief played an active role in the promotion of this humanitarian vision. One of its first actions was to make arrangements with the Manitoba Dental Association to provide dental services paid for by the city to those on relief. The first clinic opened on May 1, 1935 and by the summer it had been expanded to include extractions, fillings for pregnant mothers, and cases of disfiguration.[55] This agreement was later extended to include dentures and was renewed through 1936.[56] Similar arrangements were made to furnish glasses to those who needed them and had been on relief for more than six months.[57] Although these programs were not comprehensive, they did rectify some of the health problems faced by the unemployed.

Dental and optical care was beneficial but many unemployed had the more pressing problem that relief rations did not provide enough to eat. The Manitoba Conference of the Unemployed vigorously campaigned to obtain a 10 percent increase in food rations for those on relief, arguing that the rations were not enough to live on. Council voted ten to nine in favour of endorsing this effort, a vote split down labour–business lines.[58] After the province refused to fund such an increase, a second motion was passed by council, once again split along labour–business lines, ordering the Special Committee on Unemployment to increase food vouchers regardless of provincial support and to bill the city for the additional cost.[59] Winnipeg Chamber of Commerce's Civics Bureau echoed the arguments of Citizen aldermen when it recommended that an increase in the food rations was "inadvisable."[60] It argued that the city could not afford to augment rations and that such a measure would merely increase the dependency of those on relief.

Another example of how the labour council improved the lives of those on relief was its promise to establish relief depots throughout the city.[61] Previously, all the unemployed in Winnipeg had to travel to a single depot on Arlington Street, regardless of where they lived in the city. For men who lived on the outskirts of the city, the trek to receive their unemployment relief was quite a hardship, particularly in the winter. Within a month of taking office, James Simpkin and Morris Gray, two ILP aldermen, put forward a motion calling on the Special Committee on Unemployment to look at the feasibility of opening numerous depots throughout the city.[62] The resulting depots considerably eased the transportation burden for the unemployed. As a result of these policies, the Unemployed Railwaymen's Association eagerly thanked labour aldermen for the "kindly interest" shown on issues regarding unemployment and expressed hope that "the same harmonious cooperation may continue to exist."[63]

The tactic of requesting federal and provincial funds for relief works, although similar to that of earlier Citizen-dominated municipal governments, was adopted with great vigour by the ILP. City council proposed a wide range of relief work plans including a sewage disposal scheme, housing rehabilitation, bridge construction and rehabilitation, and school renovations.[64] For example, an intermunicipal sewage disposal system was developed at a cost of $4 million, provided jobs for 1,500 people for over two years, improved sanitary conditions, and restored the river (all of which were ILP campaign promises).[65] ILP Alderman Morris Gray bragged about the success of these projects, saying that the "men are working very hard and quite efficiently, indicating their anxiety to be self-supporting."[66] As a result, he said, the sewage disposal scheme had reduced the number of men on relief, providing them and their families with income and reducing the cost to the city.

Cities across Canada were seeking relief funding for work projects. In handling the unemployment issue, the emphasis was on work over charity, ensuring that the unemployed work for whatever support they received (at times with the added benefit of completing necessary infrastructure projects). Work was seen as a way of warding off the moral degeneration of idleness and dependency. In Winnipeg, the unemployed were recruited to work at the city's wood yard, and on sewers, pipelines, and quarries. Similar work happened in other cities. The unemployed in Saskatoon, for example, were used to sweep streets, shovel snow, clear brush, and repair municipal infrastructure.[67] Clearly the ILP did not oppose or end this practice. However, it did not share the view of its Citizen opponents that the unemployed were lazy or broken, as they combined their efforts for relief works with increased funding for food rations.

The actions of labour aldermen, however, did not always satisfy the unemployed. The changes that the ILP would bring in would be, as Eric Strikwerda described them, a "matter of degree rather than form."[68] The relief system that was in place may have been "humanized" but it operated in the same framework as before. A key moment of frustration was city council's handling of the On-To-Ottawa trekkers. When the Trek was still far away from the city, Queen urged Winnipeggers to be hospitable to the trekkers and said that there would be little trouble supporting them.[69] Several ILP politicians addressed a meeting of 5,000 strike supporters who identified themselves as the Relief Camp Workers' Supporting Conference.[70] When remnants of the trek arrived in Winnipeg, however, the trekkers occupied a government-run dining hall on Princess Street, demanding centralized billeting and three meals a day. The ILP rejected these demands but argued that it showed considerable restraint, preventing the rioting or police violence that had been seen in other cities. John Blumberg, who was acting mayor at the time of the occupation, declared in November 1935 that a "holocaust" had been avoided when he successfully convinced the RCMP not to intervene against the strikers and had decided not to read the Riot Act.[71] Former mayor Ralph Webb supposedly commented that "we will have to take the law into our own hands" against the trekkers, suggesting that there would have been a considerably different response had the Trek occurred a year earlier.[72] Queen later explained that it was "not in the interests of the boys that will be served by keeping them [the trekkers] here another week. The Communist

Party is keeping them here for a scheme of its own."[73] In response, representatives of the trekkers expressed notable frustration with ILP officials. A Mrs. E. Johnston summed up this frustration when she said, "you are not the John Queen I knew three years ago, when I looked up to you as a real leader in the labour movement."[74]

Labour aldermen also had mixed success appeasing their labour supporters. One of the contributions that labour aldermen made, with the support of some of their Citizen counterparts, was a motion that city departments should not sign contracts for goods or services from firms "who do not regularly pay fair wages or who refuse their employees the right to collective action."[75] The fair-wages motion mandated both the pay (ranging from 37.5 cents per hour for an unskilled labourer to one dollar per hour for bricklayers, plasterers, and stone masons) and maximum weekly working hours (ranging from forty-four to fifty-four) for any company seeking city contracts.[76] Despite some Citizen support for the fair-wage bylaw, labour aldermen were the only council members willing to invoke it. When the *Winnipeg Free Press* and the *Winnipeg Tribune* refused to acknowledge the Winnipeg Typographical Union No. 191, the council voted on strictly labour–Citizen lines to not place any ads in either paper unless required to do so by the city charter until the conflict was resolved.[77] Their efforts on behalf of labour brought praise from several unions, including the International Brotherhood of Boilermakers and Helpers and the needle trades union, both of which congratulated the ILP for their support of workers' rights.[78]

ILP aldermen used their position on council to endorse a recommendation by the Winnipeg Trades and Labour Council to the provincial legislature, calling for the enactment of legislation giving workers the undisputed right to unionize for collective bargaining.[79] Additionally, a motion put forward by Simpkin and Victor Anderson was carried that requested that "all employers recognize this elementary right of employees to organize and deal collectively with their employers."[80] Two labour disputes allowed council to put these policies into action. First, a strike by the International Fur Workers Union was cautiously supported by the labour aldermen who, while calling on the strikers to remain peaceful, insisted on the right of the workers to engage in collective bargaining. Later, in September 1936, when 312 CPR employees were laid off, the council passed a motion calling on the mayor to appoint a committee to attempt to have the workers reinstated.[81] The actions of council gained the sincere support from at least some of Winnipeg's labour community. A.B. Stuart, the Secretary of Lodge No. 126 of the International Brotherhood of Boiler Makers and Helpers, wrote, "[I want to] convey to you the sincere appreciation of the Boilermakers and Helpers of this Local for your efforts on behalf of the organized fur workers in Winnipeg. Your action in introducing and passing the Resolution condemning the actions of certain employers and supporting the rank and file in their battle is to be commended."[82] Other labour groups, such as the needle trades unions, continued to unanimously back the ILP, particularly after their support of the fur workers.[83]

Despite successes in supporting the rights of organized labour throughout the city, the ILP struggled to placate their own municipal workers. The first major dispute between the Federation of Civic Employees (FCE) and the city council originated over the issue of restoring the wages of civic employees who had been forced to take a 10 percent wage cut in 1933. Upon the election of a pro-labour council the *Labor Leader* reported that "in view of the fact that labour has a majority on the city council, coupled with the fact that the restoration of the employees' wage reductions was an outstanding plank in the labour aldermen's platform during the last civic elections, they [FCE leaders] expect no difficulty in procuring the restoration of their 1932 wage scales."[84] In his inaugural address as mayor, Queen commented in regards to civil service cuts that "we must have learnt by now that this kind of thing does not get us anywhere."[85] The labour aldermen, however, were forced to reckon with the city's financial difficulties and opposition to wage increases from Premier Bracken, who questioned the city's proposal to increase wages while collecting more than $1 million annually for unemployment relief from the province, and conservative groups such as the Home and Property Owners' Association, who threatened a tax strike if wages were increased.[86]

After considering a pay increase as high as 8.33 percent, the Committee of Finance eventually settled on a partial wage increase of 3.33 percent, only one third of the initial promise.[87] Only the CPC aldermen, Penner and Forkin, continued to advocate for an 8.33 percent restoration. Not surprisingly, the FCE was angered and wrote to council saying that its members were "very dissatisfied with the delay and the unsatisfactory development that has taken place this year in dealing with the agreements governing wages."[88] They saw the pay increase as a betrayal of the support they had granted the ILP during several municipal elections.

The 1935 controversy over wage restoration paled in comparison with a vicious battle over civic pensions in 1936. A report studying the plan's financial situation found that the municipal pension fund's liabilities were $7.4 million, while it had only $6 million in assets. The $1.4 million deficit was a marked increase from the $800,000 deficit the fund recorded in a similar survey in 1929, a trend that was forecasted to continue unless reforms were implemented.[89] According to Jules Preud'homme, the fund was in such a position because it paid out too many disability pensions, mandated compulsory retirement at the age of sixty-five, too many employees were hired at an advanced age, salaries had been reduced without a reduction in the pension, and the fund had failed to make normal gains through employees leaving the service.[90]

On the advice of a Professor M.A. Mackenzie, the city passed Bylaw 14813, which increased payments made by the employees, reduced benefits, and forced workers to work longer to receive benefits.[91] The city also established a fund of $323,000 of which it would pay 4 percent annually into the pension fund in addition to its regular contributions. Payouts to pensioners were immediately reduced by 10 percent, while future pensioners would be paid a minimum of $480 annually, a reduction from $720.[92] The bylaw also established a Pension Board to manage the fund in the future, composed of the Chairman of the Committee of Finance, the City Treasurer, one member of the Committee of Finance, and two representatives elected by the contributors. By reducing payouts and increasing contributions, it was hoped that the fund could recover the losses of the previous years and remain solvent in the future.

These reforms incensed the FCE, who had not been consulted and who saw the changes as a breach of contract and launched a vigorous fight at both the municipal and provincial levels against the bylaw. They argued that since they contributed equally to the fund they should be treated as equal partners. Additionally, they suggested that the fund was losing substantially less than the city claimed.[93] R.B. Russell, the secretary of the OBU in Winnipeg, claimed that the city could restore the fund's solvency by simply investing $629,000 over fifteen years.[94] The FCE was also concerned for the financial state of older employees. In a letter to Premier Bracken, the Federation's lawyer, Hugh Phillipps, wrote, "an old employee can now be looked in the face, after years of service and compulsory contributing to the fund, and told that the promised pension of $60 a month is to be cut to $40."[95] The FCE fought adamantly against these reforms, which from its perspective were unnecessary, harmful to their membership, and had happened without consultation.

When the city sought approval of the bylaw from the province, it made three main arguments. First, it pointed out that in 1920 it had guaranteed the solvency of the fund and so, it believed, it had the right to pass legislation to maintain it. Second, it dismissed the FCE's argument that it was an equal contributor to the fund. Jules Preud'homme, the City Solicitor, produced numbers showing that the city had actually contributed 69 percent of the fund's value.[96] The city also claimed that the impact on pensioners would be far less catastrophic than the FCE had suggested. The reduction in the minimum pension from $720 to $480, for example, seemed drastic but would not affect those who had spent their whole working lives as city employees and, claimed Preud'homme, the $720 was extraordinarily high in the first place. Finally, city council claimed that it had no choice but to reform the pension plan. Bylaw 14813 may have breached the contract with the employees, but it was better that than to let the fund fail, they argued.[97] The bylaw was passed conditionally for one year, subject to the city negotiating with employees to minimize their objections to the proposed changes.

The animosity created by this controversy was exacerbated when it was reported that "many members, including Labour aldermen, are in favour" of firing all 1,569 civic employees and dissolving their pension because of their reluctance to accept Bylaw 14813.[98] It is not clear how many ILP aldermen supported such a drastic move, and the threat was never carried out, but the fact that it had even been considered prompted R.B. Russell to comment that "the labour council was doing something worse than a non-labour council dared to attempt."[99] He questioned how the council could "press for reconciliation of union rights for other labour organizations when they are denying them to their own men?"[100] Numerous FCE leaders reported that they had been intimidated by council. One man, Fred Martin, claimed to have been "warned five or six times I should lose my job if I did not discontinue attacking the Council."[101] The FCE even called for the defeat of labour aldermen and rejected an ILP request for funds for the November 1936 election because, according to Secretary George W. Boorman, "we have received worse treatment from the ILP representatives than we would tolerate at the hands of a non-labour aldermanic body."[102]

The ILP, in turn, said that they were "actuated by a sincere desire to serve the best interest of employees" and to let the matter go unsolved would have meant financial disaster for civic employees in the future.[103] Furthermore, they accused the FCE of "intimidation of the worst kind,"[104] claiming R.B. Russell was frustrated because he had continually failed to win election nominations under the ILP banner. Others accused Russell of seeking power for himself. One columnist in the *Manitoba Commonwealth* described Russell as wanting to be "a Mussolini or Hitler and [as] using the civic employees as a means to gain his ends." The columnist went on to suggest that the civic employees would be in for a shock if the election went against labour.[105]

These incidents represented a major threat to the ILP's reputation as a labour-friendly party and likely negatively affected their election campaign in November 1936. It demonstrates the challenge of managing the diverse interests of a city in a time of economic crisis and so, while labour aldermen may have been successful in some of their attempts to improve the status of organized labour in the city, they were also limited by the city's fiscal challenges. In trying to balance the practical realities of the city with the aspirations of their supporters, labour aldermen did not always succeed in delivering the results that organized labour sought.

One of the first priorities for labour aldermen in 1935 was to democratize Winnipeg's electoral system. At the time, only those who owned over $100 in property or rented over $200 in property were allowed to vote and, if they held property in multiple wards, they were allowed to vote in each ward in which they held property. Additionally, absentee property owners were also afforded the right to vote. This clearly benefited the upper classes and the Citizens as much of the working class was ineligible to vote, while the wealthiest Winnipeggers often held multiple votes.

Winnipeg's electoral system that allowed for multiple votes had been put in place in 1890. While it is unclear how many people were voting multiple times in the 1920s and 1930s, Alan Artibise found that in 1910 there were 6,000 repeated names on the civic voters list. As Artibise concluded, these property qualifications were one way for the commercial elite to maintain their control of the city, and they reduced the ability of lower-income groups, particularly unskilled immigrant labourers, to vote in municipal elections.[106] As early as the mid-1920s, the ILP's *Weekly News* had published several articles pointing out the practice of multiple voting.[107] The threat of multiple voting, voting which worked in favour of Citizen candidates, had been a key concern of the ILP for a long time.

Municipal taxation and government was founded on the principle that those who owned part of the city should have a stake in its services. As Michèle Dagenais has written, "the territorialisation of state power at the local level was grounded in landed property."[108] Opponents of electoral reform argued that someone should have a financial stake in the city before gaining the municipal franchise. The Winnipeg Real Estate Board defended the rights of non-residents to vote if they owned property in the city.[109] It would be unfair, they argued, for someone without property to vote for representatives who could impose taxes on those with property. The right to vote was not inherent in being a citizen but rather in owning a physical stake in the city.

Proponents of universal suffrage argued that it was unjust to deny large segments of the population the right to vote simply because they did not own property. Similarly, they argued, it was undemocratic to allow some individuals multiple votes, giving them greater say over the operation of the city and allowing them to choose representatives for wards in which they did not live. This represented a different conception of what access to the city and its services meant. Was the city to be only for those who owned part of it, or for all of its residents?

Labour aldermen attempted twice to introduce universal adult suffrage for council and school board elections. This would have enfranchised approximately 30,000 people, an increase of 33 percent.[110] In 1935 and 1936 motions were passed by city council in favour of this change, with the vote largely breaking down on labour–Citizen lines. A CPC motion, also supported by the ILP but not by independent labourite Thomas Flye, was defeated by a single vote. This motion would have extended universal suffrage for fiscal referendums as well.[111]

After being passed by the city, with the support exclusively of labour aldermen, the legislation hit a roadblock in the Law Amendments Committee of the Provincial Legislature, where MLAs reported that many briefs had been presented against the proposal, while none had been given in favour of it.[112] The Winnipeg Chamber of Commerce, for example, insisted that the "one man–one vote" principle was "an attack on property rights."[113] W. Sanford Evans, the leader of the provincial Conservative Party, suggested that universal franchise would be a mistake under present circumstances (in other words, during a time that would benefit the ILP) while N.V. Bachynsky, a provincial MLA for Fisher, said that events in the last Winnipeg civic election (the election of labour politicians) convinced him that it would be a mistake to extend the franchise.[114] As a result, the electoral reform legislation proposed by labour aldermen was unsuccessful and was defeated in committee by eight votes to three. The property qualification would only be dropped in 1942.[115]

One of the key issues that city council faced during the 1930s was housing. Housing was hard to come by before the Great Depression, but with the construction industry nearly shut down for much of the 1930s, adequate housing became a major concern. Interestingly, while council was often divided along traditional left–Citizen lines, there were times in housing debates where Citizen and ILP aldermen co-operated and where middle-class reformers joined with labour leaders in calling for the housing issue to be addressed.

Housing was first recognized by municipal leaders as a problem late in 1933, when Mayor Webb commented, "I have been in many cities of the world and some of the slum conditions I have seen in Winnipeg are about as bad as can be found anywhere."[116] A municipal survey of 673 slum houses that year found eighty-three families living in single rooms, ninety-four families living in two-room suites, and seventy-one families living in three-room suites.[117] The housing shortage meant that Winnipeggers were paying the highest proportion of their income on rent in the country despite the large amount of low-quality housing in the city.[118]

In response, city council approved a $1.5 million self-liquidating plan to provide units to be rented out for between twenty and thirty-five dollars per month.[119] The site, which encompassed two full city blocks, was located one and a half miles from downtown and was near industrial areas, thus providing easy

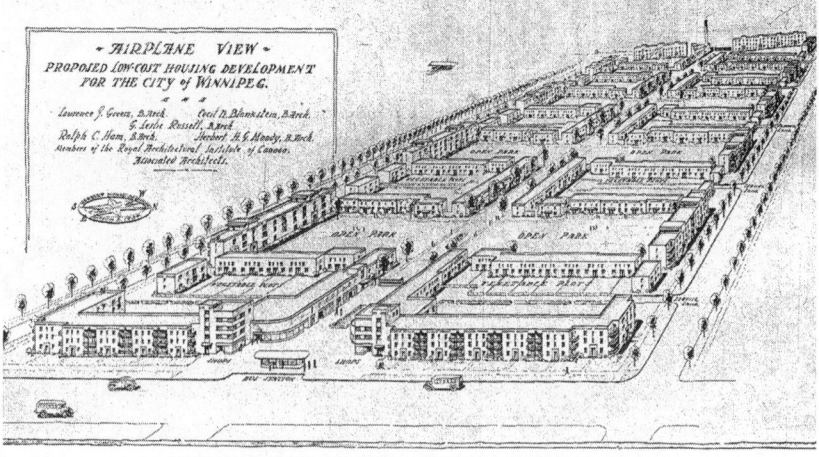

PROPOSED LOW-COST HOUSING DEVELOPMENT FOR THE CITY OF WINNIPEG

A plan for public housing in Winnipeg from 1934. The plan was the first of many plans for housing in Winnipeg during the 1930s that were not implemented.
Source: *Journal of the Royal Architectural Institute of Canada* (July–August 1934): 111.

access to employment. Architects Lawrence Green, Cecil Blankstein, G. Leslie Russell, Ralph Ham, and Herbert Moody proposed building a ring of three-storey apartment buildings around the perimeter of the site with two-storey row houses grouped around service drives in the middle, accommodating up to 588 families. The rest of the grounds, 7.5 acres of the total 16.75, was set aside for parks and vegetable plots. A shopping area stood at the main entrance and office space for doctors, dentists, and other professionals was included to provide amenities for the residents, with the revenue earned by the stores to be used to sponsor a community hall and day nursery.[120]

Despite support from local politicians and national organizations such as the Royal Architectural Institute of Canada, the plan was never carried out due to significant opposition from within the city. The North Winnipeg Taxpayers Association, for example, wrote to council to protest the decision to build houses because, they argued, there were already numerous vacant houses in the city.[121] Although city council voted to support the $1.5 million proposal, it had no money to spend on this, or any, housing development.[122] Thus, it was left to wait for the support of the federal government, which had yet to show significant interest in the field of housing.[123] Federal refusal to assist the project was not based solely on national policy, however. Prime Minister R.B. Bennett explained that he had considered supporting the city's request but had been petitioned by local residents not to assist the municipal plan because it might interfere with property rentals.[124] He explained that the "lack of support from Winnipeg made it impossible to proceed with [the] project."[125] Those who owned property were not interested in competing with the municipal government for tenants. Thus, the proposal died when the Bennett government refused to provide the necessary funding.

Housing remained an important political issue in Winnipeg in 1935. Upon his election to the mayoralty, John Queen declared, "there is undoubtedly a strong case for a housing scheme."[126] By March, a proposal was in place to borrow $2 million from the Dominion government to build dwellings on city land in the Norquay Park district of the city, between Granville and Disraeli Streets near downtown. Importantly, the committee believed that the money should be spent without a municipal referendum.[127] The city hoped that since the federal government was considering funding housing, the project might be able to start that summer.[128]

The plan was not without controversy. Alderman Cecil Rice-Jones condemned it as "an absolute outrage" that would "break one-third of the taxpayers!"[129] Other Citizen aldermen were equally critical of the plan. James Barry worried that building affordable rental units would depreciate the value of nearby better housing. Frederick Davidson argued that it was outside of the city's jurisdiction to build houses to sell or rent. Additionally, he declared, the type of people who would live in such houses would just ruin them anyway.[130] Opposition to the $2-million plan, therefore, was centred on financial concerns, whether for the city, the taxpayers, or the surrounding property owners.

The city, however, could not borrow money without a referendum of ratepayers. To avoid such a referendum, provincial approval was required. The provincial government in Manitoba had a reputation for being "cautious, reasonable, and pragmatic" and its overwhelmingly rural membership was not keen to support what they deemed to be extravagant urban spending.[131] Thus, when Bill 98, which sought to authorize the city to create a debt for the purpose of house construction without a referendum, was defeated in its second reading by the Manitoba legislature, the plan died.[132]

The demise of the $2-million plan did not mean the end of the housing debate in the city in 1935. In the summer of that year, Alderman Margaret McWilliams released a report outlining the impact of low-quality housing on Winnipeg neighbourhoods. McWilliams, the only female alderman at the time, identified as a Liberal and received support from Citizens, although she was not nearly as rigidly pro-business as some and recognized the need for social services.[133] Her report studied two areas in poor, working-class neighbourhoods and compared that data to the city as a whole.[134] She found that rates of disease, mortality, Children's Aid cases, arrests, and delinquency were all appreciably higher in poor neighbourhoods. She concluded that the two highlighted areas cost the city $639,000 to service whereas the rest of the city cost only $612,000 despite the fact that the two areas only had one-third of the total population of the city. This provided an additional argument to campaigners for public housing: not only would the rents charged as part of a housing project make it self-liquidating, but housing would pay off in reduced medical and police costs. Furthermore, McWilliams' study quantified the link between poor housing and disease, as well as, in the minds of many Winnipeggers, between housing and delinquency.

The medical danger of overcrowded housing conditions had been widely known for a long time, but, as cited in McWilliams' report, people were also concerned about the moral consequences of living in slum conditions.[135] Consequently, social reformers believed that social and moral reform were inseparable.[136] Poor housing was blamed for a breakdown in the family and, consequently, an increase in delinquency. As the *Winnipeg Free Press* put it, slum conditions "breed, prolifically, social evils of every kind."[137] A report completed in 1934 by the Lieutenant Governor of Ontario, Herbert Bruce, was even more blunt: "Bad houses are not only a menace: they are active agents of destruction....

	AREA 1	AREA 2	CITY
Infant mortality (per 1,000 births)	58.5	52.0	42.5
Tuberculosis (per 10,000 people)	8.6	7.9	2.6
Patient days at municipal hospitals (per 1,000 people)	288	562	207
Children's Aid cases (per 1,000 children)	36.1	67.7	14.8
Arrests (per 1,000 people)	21.1	52.2	6.5

Table 3. Data from Margaret McWilliams' Report on Housing (1935) Source: Margaret McWilliams, "An Investigation into Certain Social Housing Conditions in Winnipeg," AM, File 1056 G628.

They destroy morality and family ties. They destroy the basis of society itself by their destruction of self-respect and their promotion of delinquency and crime."[138] The struggle for adequate housing was perceived as not only being about stopping the spread of physical diseases, but also addressing the supposed moral decline of the next generation.

A further problem facing Winnipeg that came to the fore in 1935 was "house farming." Individuals would rent a house and then derive income by subletting several parts of the home to different families. During his testimony before the House of Commons Special Committee on Housing, Alexander Officer, the head of the municipal health department, cited the example of an individual who rented a house for $100 and then rented out each room to a different family, collecting $227 in rent. This practice often extended to renting parts of buildings that were not suitable for habitation. People were regularly found living in poorly lit and ventilated attics and basements. These were dangerous in case of fire, insufferably hot in summer, unbearably cold in winter, provided little daylight, and had a high risk of asphyxiation from gas fumes. As the shortage of homes became more pressing, this practice intensified and more and more dwellings were "farmed."[139]

Based on the troubling findings of McWilliams' report and annual reports by the municipal health department that demonstrated the profound shortage of affordable housing in Winnipeg, labour aldermen sought to develop public solutions. Unlike most Citizen politicians who insisted that private enterprise was the only way to solve the housing crisis, labour aldermen proposed a role for the City of Winnipeg in the municipal economy. In 1935, a Special Committee on Housing investigated potential solutions to this problem and proposed issuing $500,000 in debentures to construct low-cost dwellings on city property.[140] These houses were to be four-room flats that were 360 square feet and were to be rented and heated for twenty-five dollars per month.[141] In order for the enabling legislation, Bylaw 14777, to take effect it was necessary for it to pass a referendum of ratepayers.

The ILP threw their support behind the bylaw, arguing that the construction of new housing would improve living conditions while providing much needed employment opportunities. Mayor Queen, for example, argued that the construction of social housing would actually save money by reducing the cost of hospital bills caused by low-quality, overcrowded houses.[142] ILP Alderman Matthew Stobart argued that gross overcrowding reduced the quality of life for many Winnipeggers, pointing out that there were areas of the city where 15,082 families lived in 1,819 homes.[143] The ILP was joined by the Winnipeg Building Trades Council (BTC), which pleaded with Winnipeg voters: "create better homes. Create employment for some tried building tradesmen and others."[144] In short, the ILP and its allies argued that the private sector had failed to provide for Winnipeg's housing needs and, consequently, a government-led response was required and would benefit the community in the long run.[145]

In a press release published in the *Winnipeg Tribune*, the BTC argued that although the Home and Property Owners' Association, which they said was "composed of many real estate agents and those who do the farming on overcrowded houses," declared that the housing plan "would spell ruin for Winnipeg," a housing plan would actually provide desperately needed housing. The BTC was interested in improving the construction market in the city, as they stood to benefit directly from any plan that promoted home building. They called on Winnipeg voters to, "Give your support to the bylaw in order that Winnipeg citizens get a chance to live in better quarters than at present they are domiciled in."[146] Thus, the housing plan generated support for two reasons. First, it was intended to relieve the drastic shortages in affordable housing that existed in the city. Second, many hoped that an investment in housing would provide construction jobs for Winnipeggers at a time when employment was scarce.

While some Citizen aldermen did support the bylaw, most were opposed, arguing either that rehabilitating existing housing stock (and thus benefiting the landlords who owned those houses rather than establishing competition through a public housing scheme) was a more appropriate solution or that the city had no role whatsoever to play in housing. New housing, the Winnipeg Chamber of Commerce argued, would compete with the existing housing stock and, as a result, many large one-family dwellings would cease to be revenue bearing for landlords.[147] Mayoral candidate Cecil Gunn reflected the class divide in the city, pointing out how "our own people on the south side of the river" (where most of Winnipeg's large-property owners lived) were opposed to the plan.[148] Finally, Citizen candidates and supporters played on the fear that the ILP was not an effective manager of city finances, by arguing that the plans were too vague and the money would not be well spent. One letter to the *Winnipeg Tribune*, for example, accused council of asking the voters to "endorse a blank cheque for $500,000 to build something, some place, some time."[149]

One of the leading opponents of the housing proposal was the Home and Property Owners' Association (HPOA), which described the plan as "unsound and impractical."[150] The HPOA was an association that fought on behalf of the ratepayers (property owners) of the city. Its mission was "a substantial reduction of property taxes as soon as possible."[151] It opposed any measure that could lead to tax increases, whether through housing reform, by cancelling wage rollbacks for municipal employees, or by providing additional unemployment relief. The

HPOA was the most influential organization to oppose municipal involvement in housing schemes in the 1930s and its membership, including much of the city's Citizen leadership.[152] The activity of the HPOA is indicative of the class divide in the city. While labour organizations and progressive religious groups advocated on behalf of housing reform, the business elite stood staunchly against it. Not only would a municipal housing project potentially result in a tax increase, but it would also provide competition for the numerous landlords that were members of the HPOA.[153]

Bylaw 14777 lost by an overwhelming majority, as 11,676 people voted against the debenture while only 4,674 voted in favour.[154] Property ownership requirements meant that only a small percentage of Winnipeggers were eligible to vote and only 7 percent of Winnipeg residents cast a referendum ballot. The *Manitoba Commonwealth* voiced the displeasure of the ILP, editorializing that "the defeat of this bylaw provides an excellent example of the short-sighted, anti-social and selfish attitude of many property owners in this city."[155]

Upon the defeat of the housing referendum, little would be done on housing until 1937, when a market-based solution to housing development was sought (and would ultimately fail). In 1936, city council adopted a report of the Special Committee on Housing Conditions that claimed that there was "no apparent prospect of the low-rental housing need being met through unaided private enterprise."[156] However, there was little appetite to do anything about this report. Forkin and Penner did put forward a motion in 1936 calling for a debenture of $300,000 to build public housing, but it was voted down by a margin of thirteen to three.[157] Additionally, an investigation into housing conditions had to be scrapped due to a lack of funds.[158] Thus, very little was accomplished about the need for affordable housing, despite the apparent interest from labour aldermen. Indeed, over the rest of the decade, only a single house would be built despite frequent city council debates regarding possible solutions to this municipal crisis. By the end of the decade, the city was short by over 6,600 dwellings.[159] The problem would only be solved through the eventual development of federal programs during the Second World War to address what had become a national housing crisis.[160]

The ILP's election manifesto had called for the "social ownership of the means of production, distribution, and exchange."[161] In addition to housing, ILP aldermen explored opportunities for the government to enter several economic sectors, including milk and bread production and distribution, banking, fuel delivery, and transportation. For example, city council passed a motion to seek provincial approval to "engage in the business of dealing in gasoline, oil, and all petroleum products."[162] According to Queen, private enterprise had inflated the price of fuel and five or six municipally owned fuel stations would help reduce market prices. Low-cost fuel from Romania was even identified as a possible source to supply the new fuel stations.[163] The proposal, however, was rejected by the provincial government, which opposed government intervention in the economy.

In 1922, when S.J. Farmer was elected mayor, the key issue had been the Winnipeg Electric Company. The WEC still held the franchise for street railway service in Winnipeg in 1935 and ILP aldermen explored the possibility of purchasing the WEC for $32 million. This proposal was opposed on multiple fronts. Communists argued that you could not "buy out the capitalist class."[164] The offer was also rejected by the company, which set the purchase price at $55 million, a price far too steep for a city struggling in the midst of economic depression.[165] While the proposed municipalization of a variety of services was ultimately unsuccessful, these attempts further illustrated the difference between labour aldermen, who sought a significant role for municipal government in the local economy, and the Citizens, who dismissed any municipalization as interference in private enterprise.

While there is relatively little scholarship regarding the political left in Canadian municipal politics, it is worth pausing briefly to compare what happened in Winnipeg to other similar cities in Canada at this time. Regina, for example, in many ways seemed to echo much of the Winnipeg story. Indeed, Mayor A.C. Ellison of Regina credited the election of John Queen in November 1934 and his subsequent mayoralty as a factor that "contributed considerably to our success."[166] In fall 1935, a year after Queen and the labour majority were elected in Winnipeg, labour candidates won the mayoralty and control of city council in Regina, a majority they would retain until 1939.

Unlike Winnipeg, the CCF and CPC united in Regina for the purposes of municipal campaigns under the banner of the Civic Labour League (CLL), an example of an alliance typical of the Popular Front, where communists sought to work closely with others on the left. However, like Winnipeg, Regina had experienced a key catalyzing moment for its municipal political campaigns. While labour parties had not been particularly successful prior to the mid-1930s, the On-To-Ottawa Trek brought the political left together and raised its profile.

The legislative agenda of the CLL proved quite similar to the ILP's in Winnipeg, focusing on improving conditions for those on relief, constructing housing, extending the municipal franchise, and municipalizing services.[167] The result, in many ways, was also similar. Given the economic realities of the 1930s, "with the city's treasury empty, very little in the way of significant working-class improvements at the civic level were achieved."[168] Similar to the experience of Winnipeg, many of these changes were blocked by the provincial government. Labour experienced political success in Regina till they were nearly wiped out in 1939 in the face of well-organized opponents and the patriotic fervour that accompanied the beginning of the Second World War.

In Alberta, Edmonton and Calgary both elected councils with labour majorities at various points in the 1920s and 1930s and mayors with ties to labour parties. Similar to Winnipeg, the election of labour majorities or mayors alarmed the business community. However, these elected officials had mixed records. A labour majority council in Calgary in the early 1920s, for example, failed to implement any significant changes. Elected commissioners were able to veto many of city council's decisions, labour leaders ruled with moderation to avoid accusations of radicalism, and the victory of labour resulted in a united front of business and professional leaders to win back control. Calgary also struggled with a divided labour movement, beset by internal divisions between the Dominion Labour Party and communists.[169] Veto by a higher authority, moderation in government, a united front of business interests, and a divided labour movement make the Calgary story of the 1920s very similar to the Winnipeg story of the 1920s and 1930s. However, by the mid-1930s much of Calgary's working-class support would drift to the new Social Credit movement that swept the Albertan political scene, ending the success of labour parties in Calgary municipal politics.

Edmonton had a history of electing labour-affiliated mayors and did so again in the 1930s by electing Don Knott, the Canadian Labour Party (CLP) candidate, as mayor in 1931, 1932, and 1933. He was, however, in some ways as conservative as his opponents, insisting on annual budget surpluses and fighting against labour aldermen on increasing the food allowance for the unemployed.[170] He also rejected a march permit for the communist-linked Hunger March Committee, using the same repressive force the CLP claimed to be against.[171] By 1934, Knott had lost the support of many of Edmonton's unemployed workers and labour unions, and received only 22 percent of the vote.[172] Indeed, in 1937 he would run for city council as a candidate for the Citizens' Committee.

There was much in common between Winnipeg and other cities across western Canada. The political left routinely faced united fronts from business leaders who sought to dislodge labour from places of power in the city. The left in other cities was also often divided between the ILP (or its equivalent) and communist parties, particularly in places where a strong Communist Party existed during the Third Period. Finally, the left in other cities experienced difficulty in implementing large-scale political change, blocked by budget constraints, senior levels of government, or a desire for moderation.

Nevertheless, there were some unique elements to Winnipeg's story. First, the political left in Winnipeg experienced some electoral success early in the 1920s, whereas the political left had to wait well into the 1930s before experiencing similar success in some other cities. Second, in many cities the electoral activity of the political left was more sporadic than sustained, with victories or near victories followed by periods of very little political activity. This, perhaps, was a testament to the significance of the divides between labour and business, and the size and dynamism of Winnipeg's labour movement. It was much more difficult to wipe labour parties from the political scene in Winnipeg than it was in Regina, Calgary, or Edmonton.

John Queen fought elections in 1935 and 1936 as the incumbent candidate. In his first race, he faced Cecil Gunn, a Citizen alderman. Gunn criticized ILP aldermen for overspending and warned that future labour governments would inevitably result in tax increases. Furthermore, he argued that Queen could only represent one class of society—labour—while he could represent all classes. In one campaign speech he proclaimed, "I and my father have employed as many as 35,000 men. I know their requirements and needs."[173] Gunn declared that the key issue in the campaign was the restoration of the city's credit, declaring, "we must restore confidence in ourselves and in our city, re-establish our credit which will enable us to commence the various works so urgently needed in the interest of all people."[174]

In a largely quiet election, Queen defeated Gunn by over 10,000 votes, winning over 60 percent of the vote, the largest share of the vote achieved by a labour candidate in Winnipeg during the 1930s. While Ward One remained strongly pro-Citizen and Ward Three remained strongly pro-ILP, the key change was in Ward Two. While Ward Two had been nominally pro-Queen a year earlier, it supported Queen over Gunn by a two-to-one margin. Even the *Winnipeg Free Press*, which was hostile to Queen in his 1934 campaign and would be so again in 1936, acknowledged that the result was a "recognition by the people of Winnipeg that in his first year [as mayor, Queen] served the city capably and well and sought to act in the interest of all people."[175]

A year later, five candidates were on the mayoral ballot, making for a markedly different race than the two-candidate affairs of the previous years. Pro-business candidates hammered on the theme of representation for the entire city, not merely a class or party. This was a common attack used by pro-business candidates against the ILP, which they accused of only representing labour. These business-oriented candidates seemed to conveniently forget that they usually received very few votes in the city's Ward Three and the city's working class.

Ralph Webb, who returned to municipal politics in the 1936 race, asserted that men "whose interests are in the interests of the whole city"[176] must be elected. Dr. Frederick Warriner, a long-time school board chairman and mayor of Winnipeg Beach, ran on the platform that he was the only candidate who could bring the various factions in the city together and promised to restore "city progress promotion rather than restriction of private business."[177] His campaign was boosted with an endorsement from the *Winnipeg Tribune*, which said that since both Webb (a Conservative) and Queen were serving as opposition MLAs, they were unable to effectively lobby the provincial government.[178] Unlike Webb and Queen, Warriner argued, he could make all municipal factions work together instead of antagonizing each other.[179]

The campaign, though, largely relied on familiar themes, as Citizen candidates emphasized fiscal responsibility while the ILP argued for a humanized city administration. While no issues stood out, the election really was another "pitched battle to decide whether Labor forces can or cannot be ousted from their City Hall majority."[180] Citizens were determined to end the two-year run of labour control, while the ILP was perhaps less organized and motivated than it had been in previous campaigns. In a letter to the editor of the *Manitoba Commonwealth* in 1935, J. Bellamy expressed what many ILP supporters were likely thinking. First, Bellamy acknowledged that he was "an admirer of John Queen" but went on to suggest that the labour council had not "taken one step off the beaten trail. That is, on the surface at least, the business of the city of Winnipeg has been carried on much the same as in 1934 and the years previous."[181] They may have taken control of the city, but at least for some labour supporters, it was difficult to see what difference this had made.

The result was a devastating defeat for the ILP. Victor Anderson and William Lowe lost their aldermanic seats, which swung the balance of power toward the Citizens. Queen was also defeated, losing on the fourth ballot of a transferrable ballot system.[182] After three ballots, throughout which Queen had held a comfortable lead, only Queen and Warriner remained. In the preferential ballot system, the voters who had supported the third-place Webb, however, had overwhelmingly chosen Warriner as their second choice (86 percent of Webb's redistributed votes), who was able to defeat Queen by over 1,500 votes.[183] Queen's inability to win many of Webb's voters demonstrated the polarized nature of Winnipeg politics as the supporters of pro-business candidates coalesced behind each other. The election meant that the parties of the political left were outnumbered twelve to seven on council, marking the end of the labour majority on council.

	FIRST BALLOT	AFTER 1ST REDISTRIBUTION	AFTER 2ND REDISTRIBUTION	AFTER 3RD REDISTRIBUTION
Frederick Warriner	19,517	19,545 (13%)	20,456 (32%)	29,666 (58%)
John Queen	25,802	25,853 (24%)	26,457 (21%)	27,907 (9%)
Ralph Webb	15,312	15,340 (13%)	15,834 (17%)	n/a
T.W. Kilshaw	2,803	2,838 (16%)	n/a	n/a
T.O. Woods	213	n/a	n/a	n/a
Non-Transferrable	n/a	71 (33%)	900 (29%)	6,074 (33%)

Table 4. Votes Received by Count in the November 1936 Election (Percentage of Redistributed Votes Received in Brackets) Source: *Municipal Manual*, 1937.

YEAR	VOTES FOR ILP, CPC, OR INDEPENDENT LABOUR	PERCENTAGE OF TOTAL VOTES
1933	21,042	37.2%
1934	23,958	43.3%
1935	23,905	43.0%
1936	25,643	40.7%

Table 5. Votes for the ILP, CPC, and Independent Labour as Identified by the Manitoba Commonwealth Source: *Manitoba Commonwealth*, 4 December 1936.

Despite the loss, the *Manitoba Commonwealth* pointed out, the number of people who had voted for labour aldermanic candidates was actually at an all-time high. With communist candidates and independent labourite Thomas Flye included, over 25,000 Winnipeggers had voted for an aldermanic candidate on the political left, accounting for 41 percent of the electoral vote. This was an increase of over 1,700 votes from the previous year, but the party had fallen 2 percent in the polls. While this was a small decline, the difference was enough to result in the defeat of labour candidates who had won by narrow margins in previous years. It should be noted that the *Commonwealth* decided to include the CPC in their calculations, particularly since they regularly and vigorously critiqued the CPC and denied that there was any cooperation between the ILP and the CPC.

John Queen was able to regain the mayoralty in November 1937 (taking office in 1938) and held the post until 1942. The ILP, however, was unable to regain its majority on council, and as the *Winnipeg Mid-West Clarion*, an OBU publication, pointed out in 1939, "ILP council members [do not] agree among themselves on many vital matters affecting the well-being of working people."[184] During Queen's reign as mayor from 1938 to 1942, he was concerned with many of the same issues that council debated in 1935 and 1936, except that he no longer had the support of a labour-friendly council. He focused much of his energy on housing reforms, earning praise from the *Municipal Review of Canada* for being "a reformer with a realistic mind."[185] Queen was defeated by Garnet Coulter, who remained mayor till 1954 and would defeat Queen again in 1944.[186] Queen died of a heart attack in 1946.

Perhaps John McKerchar was right when he declared that it was "absolutely impossible" under the conditions to "turn the city hall upside down, revolutionize the council, and bring about drastic changes."[187] Queen and the labour aldermen, however, did have some noticeable accomplishments that shifted municipal policy, including: tax reforms, increasing municipal spending, improving condition for people on relief, supporting organized labour, and passing motions to extend the franchise and establish a broader public vision of the city. Conversely, its treatment of the FCE and its inability to get provincial approval for electoral reform or business taxation left a record that at times seemed like "pious resolutions passed and forgotten [that] seldom accomplished anything."[188] Labour aldermen had to both manage a city that "had been built and controlled for over eighty years by men with different backgrounds and different visions"[189] and also grapple with the fiscal challenges of the Great Depression. Furthermore, because of the city's limited legislative powers, the decisions reached by city council were frequently reversed by a more conservative provincial government.

CPC Alderman Martin Forkin once observed that municipal governance was about "the problems of the people rather than simply running the city like a business."[190] While Forkin frequently disagreed with his ILP colleagues, this was an understanding he shared with the ILP. Municipal government was seen as a tool to address the burdens of the Great Depression and to humanize the economy. The policies espoused by aldermen on the political left represented a marked shift from those of the Citizens, re-envisioning a role for the city as an instrument for social responsibility to benefit all. However, the limitations of the system and economy in which they worked meant that little could be accomplished beyond "humanizing" existing systems.

CONCLUSION

After John Queen was defeated in 1936 and the political left lost its majority on city council, the status quo would return. While Queen would return to the mayoralty for two more terms, the Citizens would retain the majority of seats on city council, a council that remained sharply divided between the city's business and professional elites and the political left. As a result, it was suggested that, as late as the 1970s, "the spirit of the [Citizen] Committee of One Thousand still haunted over City Hall."[1] Even some of the leaders who had played pivotal roles in the 1920s and 1930s would remain in the coming decades, with aldermen such as John Blumberg of the ILP and Jacob Penner and Martin Forkin of the CPC serving on council into the 1960s.

The politically charged atmosphere of Winnipeg in the 1930s inspired and educated new political activists, profoundly shaping a generation of leaders and campaigners for the political left. Gloria Queen-Hughes, who sat on the Winnipeg School Board from 1933 to 1940 and was the daughter of John Queen, would become the first woman to run for mayor in Winnipeg in 1966.[2] The CPC's Joseph Zuken, who succeeded Jacob Penner as the alderman for Ward Three, learned much from the communist struggles of the 1930s as a member of the Progressive Arts Club. Zuken went on to serve on the Winnipeg School Board from 1942 to 1962 and as a city councillor from 1962 to 1983. Indeed, the political activities of the 1930s would establish a communist niche in Winnipeg, a unique presence that would last on council nearly straight through the Cold War.

Even though Winnipeg would remain a city dominated by Citizens and their descendants, many of the policies proposed by the ILP and the CPC in the 1930s were eventually enacted in Winnipeg. The idea that people should be allowed to vote whether or not they owned property struck at the foundation of what the city's elite believed it meant to have a stake in the city throughout the 1920s and 1930s, but the municipal franchise would be extended to all adult residents in 1942. The suggestion that a municipal government should have any role to play in public transportation or affordable housing seemed radical in the 1920s and 1930s, but in the postwar era the city would municipalize the services of the WEC in 1953 and the city (along with other levels of government) would also begin to address the issue of affordable housing. The shifting postwar political landscape made much possible that had been barely imaginable a decade earlier. Nevertheless, the ultimate goal—a co-operative commonwealth or proletarian dictatorship—of either party was never achieved.

This book has traced the story of how the political left engaged in municipal politics shortly after the 1919 General Strike came to a violent end. Municipal politics became a new venue for engaging in the battles that had spurred the strike. Fostered by deep divisions in Winnipeg between the business and professional elite and the working class, municipal politics became a struggle for control of the city. Only months after the Strike, Winnipeggers went to the polls to vote in the first mayoral election contested on labour–business lines. In the coming years, municipal politics continued to be shaped by the Strike's legacy: the names used for the two sides (the "Citizens" and "Labour"), the individuals who sought leadership roles in municipal politics, the language that was used to describe the threat of labour or the domination of business, the level of polarization between business and the left, and the platforms of parties in municipal politics were all shaped by that climactic moment in 1919.

Historians of the General Strike have often posited the Strike at the end of the story, and often as a tragic end. David Bercuson, for example, describes the Strike as "a complete failure in the short run" and a "mighty blow at one of trade unionism's strongest bastions."[3] According to Ian McKay, "orthodoxy requires that after the perfect storm of Winnipeg 1919, nothing but wreckage—ill feelings, smashed unions, devastated lives—remains. It can incorporate Winnipeg 1919 only by reiterating how completely the left was obliterated, how completely *over* this moment must be."[4] However, a focus on municipal politics demonstrates that the Strike was not the end, but rather the beginning of a much longer narrative. The moment was not over. While labour candidates had experienced minor success in the years leading up to 1919, it was the catalyzing moment of the Strike that would establish the left as a strong and constant presence in Winnipeg's municipal politics. Labour did not win the Strike, but the Strike did sustain "a generation of socialists and trade union militants through the reaction of the 1920s and the desperation of the 1930s."[5]

Tom Mitchell and James Naylor have written that "the counter-hegemonic challenge had not been killed that day on 21 June 1919."[6] The General Strike pointed to the possibility of an alternative to the capitalist vision celebrated by Winnipeg's business elite. Ian McKay has argued that the General Strike was "a conscious attempt to imagine what new relations of freedom would look like in the post-capitalist future."[7] The city did not need to be a space of domination for the capitalist elite; it could provide for the unemployed, the poorly housed, and the disenfranchised. The Strike was a moment where workers controlled the city, however briefly. Alternatives were possible and in the years that followed the Strike, Winnipeg's political left would seek to actualize that change through the municipal ballot box and council chambers.

Envisioning a different future and creating one are, of course, two very different things. In many ways, the story of the political left in Winnipeg after the General Strike is a sobering tale of the limited potential for change through electoral politics. The ILP and CPC chased electoral victory at the municipal level but, it could be argued, ultimately had little to show for their efforts. Most of the time they were in the minority on council, able to register their displeasure at the actions of the Citizens but only occasionally able to do something about it. When they did win a majority of council seats, it could be argued that they were still blocked by the same forces that had opposed them for the two previous decades. When they held power, labour politicians were unable to implement a radically different policy from that espoused by their Citizen opponents, as policy after policy was rejected by the province and the local business community.

This should not have come as a surprise. For fifty years, the City of Winnipeg had been run by leaders with a business-oriented view. The very structure of the city was created by those whom the political left opposed. As a result, the political and economic restrictions in which the city operated had been clearly defined for decades in a way that favoured the left's business opponents. More substantial changes required approval from the conservative province or conservative ratepayers. The result was that when the political left tried to effect serious change, it could not do so.

There were also many challenges within the political left that limited its ability to achieve the changes its constituents sought. For most of the post-Strike period, communists and the ILP were divided, often spending as much time (and at times, more time) attacking each other rather than their common Citizen opponents. Both parties were guilty of this. The CPC sought co-operation with the ILP before and after the Third Period, but between 1928 and 1934 denounced the ILP and its leadership with great vitriol. The ILP rejected CPC overtures when they were offered, frustrated with the frequent attacks and eager to ward off accusations of radicalism.

These divisions between the CPC and ILP served to split the vote in Ward Three, allowed Citizen candidates to win elections, and limited co-operation in the council chambers. Yet, while the two parties were rooted in different political theories and differed on some key issues, both had remarkably similar legislative agendas at city council. Both focused on the unemployed, affordable transportation, housing, deportations, and enfranchising Winnipeg's working-class voters. There were policy differences, but often it was a matter of degree rather than substance. However, both parties fell into a trap of fighting between "reformists" and "revolutionaries" rather than addressing those that did not want to achieve change at all.

Additionally, the reforms sought by both the ILP and the CPC in municipal politics were often not particularly transformative. S.J. Farmer, when elected mayor, did not seek a radically different vision of the city from that of his predecessors—by and large the city ran and operated exactly as it had under a Citizen mayor. After his term in office, for example, the Slave Pact for municipal employees was still in place. This key issue, one of the negative legacies of the General Strike for organized labour, went unaddressed with a labour representative as mayor. Similarly, it was difficult to see how CPC election platforms calling for cheap streetcar fares and increased unemployment relief would ultimately result in proletarian revolution.

John W. Dafoe, the editor of the *Winnipeg Free Press*, was known for his strong opposition to the 1919 General Strike and labour politicians. He once commented that incorporating labour into liberal, representative democracy was the best way to temper its radicalism. By participating in the system, he said, the left would "accept the great convention by which the British system of government lives—that their reforms, their innovations, must endure the scrutiny of parliament and receive the endorsement of a majority of people."[8] In other words, if the political left tried to transform the capitalist system on its terms, it would ultimately be swallowed up by that system. Furthermore, in engaging in British-style electoral politics, the left would also be required to expend significant energy, and moderate itself in the process, to reach enough voters to become a viable political force.

Both the ILP and CPC invested significant energy into winning votes in elections, mobilizing party members, holding large rallies, and developing and distributing promotional materials. The annual municipal election in November became a key part of the political calendar in Winnipeg. And while both parties were focused on large-scale changes to how the city was run, revolution was not in the cards, at least not in the short term. A. Ross McCormack has written that early labourite politicians "never allowed their immediate political prospect to be impaired by some theoretical commitment to co-operative commonwealth,"[9] a sentiment that could likely be extended to Winnipeg's ILP. It would seem that in many ways the left was "slowly digested by the very system it had sworn to contest."[10]

There were certainly limitations to the political left's ability to create the transformative change it sought in Winnipeg. Despite the city's narrow political structures, the timidity of elected representatives, and bitter infighting between the ILP and CPC, all was not lost in the seventeen years of political activity between 1919 and 1936. In a city still dominated by a business elite, ILP and CPC politicians could be mouthpieces for a different voice within the city. Through their positions on city council, the ILP and CPC continued to articulate a vision similar to that of the striking workers of 1919. The city should serve all, they insisted, not just a few; the wealth of the city should be more evenly distributed; there was no need for dire poverty in the midst of such wealth. Whether the issue was streetcar fares or the right to vote, social housing or business taxation, aldermen from these parties consistently articulated counter-hegemonic visions that spoke to the needs of the city's large working class.

There were also very practical benefits to participating in municipal politics. Elections were an opportunity to rally supporters and publicize the vision of the ILP or CPC. They provided these parties with an opportunity to remind their supporters and others about the dangers of the Citizens (or, as was often the case, their opponent on the left), reminding voters of the polarized nature of their city's politics.[11] Both the ILP and CPC talked about how municipal elections provided them with an opportunity to reach out to new potential supporters with the public paying increased attention to politics during the month of the election. This was particularly true of the CPC, which had little access to mainstream media coverage of its activities outside the context of the annual municipal election. Therefore, activities in municipal politics seemed to contribute to rather than distract from action outside the council chamber.

Indeed, it was activities in the council chamber that would contribute to the respective strengths of the ILP and CPC. Before folding into the CCF, the ILP was one of the strongest local parties on the left in the country. Many of its leaders served municipally, it was an urban-oriented party, and the actions it took in city council contributed to a strong base of support throughout the city. Municipal politics, therefore, were a key part of forming the identity of the ILP.

Municipal politics were essential in shaping the CPC's political activities in Winnipeg. While the CPC would eventually elect an MLA in Manitoba, they had a much longer and more consistent presence on Winnipeg City Council. The activities of aldermen such as William Kolisnyk, Jacob Penner, or Martin Forkin made communism real for Winnipeg's North End. People appreciated their hard work, which in turn drew voters and potentially members, to the communist cause. While the demands made by these aldermen were undoubtedly off-putting to some, they likely attracted others who appreciated their unswerving determination.

And finally, the political left was able to achieve some of its legislative agenda—such as raising property taxes for large businesses and providing increased support for the unemployed—when they held a majority of the seats on council. Even without control of council, S.J. Farmer played a key role in defeating W.B. Parker's attempt to obtain a private franchise for central heating. At other times, when they did not hold a majority or the mayoralty, ILP and CPC aldermen were a strong presence on city council, pushing Citizen aldermen to take action on issues for Winnipeg's working class, such as ending the practice of deporting people on relief. While these campaigns were not always successful, they were occasionally able to win victories that were important for the well-being of Winnipeg's working class.

When John Queen entered Stony Mountain Penitentiary to serve his prison sentence for sedition in 1920, very few Winnipeggers would have expected that within fifteen years he would win over 60 percent of the vote in a mayoral election. While much had changed in the intervening years, including Queen's transformation from jailed radical to semi-respectable chief magistrate, the reality of life for Winnipeg's working class had not. Disparities continued to sharply divide the city, with poor living conditions common for the city's working class. The politics of this disparity, the divide between the Citizens and the political left, also had not changed. The struggle against this disparity, against poverty in the midst of plenty, was ongoing. It had been manifested in the General Strikes of 1918 and 1919, in S.J. Farmer's run for the mayoralty in 1919 and ultimate victory a few years later, in the rise of the CPC in Winnipeg's North End, in the debates between the left and the bombastic Ralph Webb, and in Queen's eventual victory along with aldermen from the ILP and CPC.

There is much to learn from the activity of the political left in Winnipeg's municipal politics after the General Strike. There were moments of obstinacy, stubbornness, failure, and divisiveness. There were opportunities missed, times when the left was politically outmanoeuvred. Yet there is also much to celebrate: the pragmatic politics of Queen and the ILP that sought to make life better for Winnipeggers; the unwavering dedication of Penner and Forkin to stand alongside marginalized people such as the unemployed and recent immigrants; and the courage, dedication, and passion of many aldermen, candidates, and behind-the-scenes party workers and members. It was their vision, a vision articulated in 1919 and again throughout the 1920s and 1930s, that sought to re-imagine the city and transform Winnipeg through municipal politics and the council chamber.

ACKNOWLEDGEMENTS

This is a project of many years of interest, archival visits, and countless hours in front of microfilm machines. My interest in the history of Winnipeg originated in a course taught by David Burley at the University of Winnipeg, where I first learned the excitement of digging through archives. It would be continued under the supervision of Ian McKay at Queen's University, whose guidance and teaching greatly expanded my knowledge and understanding of the political left in Canada, and who encouraged my research into the Communist Party of Canada in Winnipeg.

Any researcher is indebted to the many archival and library staff who have provided assistance—in this case at the Archives of Manitoba, City of Winnipeg Archives, Library and Archives Canada, Queen's University, the City of Winnipeg's Millennium Library, the Association of United Ukrainian Canadians Archives, and the Legislative Library of Manitoba. As the manuscript became a book, I also appreciated the support and feedback of the staff at University of Manitoba Press and the anonymous readers whose suggestions and probing questions helped strengthen the book.

Finally, I would like to thank my family. First, my parents, Roger Epp and Rhonda Harder Epp, who instilled in me an interest in history, a recognition of the importance of place, and gave me the confidence and encouragement to turn this work into a book. And finally, to my wife Laurel, for helping me make sense of half-thought-out ideas, joining me on expeditions to find local historical landmarks, and encouraging me through the ups and downs of the writing process. Without your support, this book would not have been possible.

NOTES

INTRODUCTION

1. Strikwerda, *The Wages of Relief*, 3.
2. Frank, "Company Town/Labour Town," 196.
3. McKay and Morton, "The Maritimes: Expanding the Circle of Resistance," 54–5; Frank, *Provincial Solidarities*, 30–1; Naylor, "Southern Ontario," 156; Mitchell and Naylor, "The Prairies," 215.
4. Barrett, "The History of American Communism and Our Understanding of Stalinism," 178.
5. Brennan, "'The Common People Have Spoken With a Mighty Voice,'" 49–86; Black, "Labour in Brandon Civic Politics: A Long View"; Black and Mitchell, *A Square Deal for All and No Railroading,* 27–84; Finkel, "The Rise and Fall of the Labour Party in Alberta, 1917–1942," 61–96; Bright, *The Limits of Labour*.
6. McKay, *Reasoning Otherwise*, 505.
7. Quoted in Mitchell and Naylor, "The Prairies," 216.
8. Reilly, "Introduction to Papers from the Winnipeg General Strike Symposium, March 1983," 7.
9. McNaught and Bercuson, *The Winnipeg General Strike: 1919*, 99.
10. Penner, *Winnipeg 1919: The Strikers' Own History of the Winnipeg General Strike*, xv.
11. Bercuson, *Confrontation at Winnipeg*, 179.
12. J.E. Rea also points to the divergence in unionism between eastern and western Canada (Rea, *The Winnipeg General Strike*, 4. See also, Penner, *Winnipeg 1919*, xiv).
13. Kealey, "1919: The Canadian Labour Revolt," 15; Heron, ed., *The Workers' Revolt in Canada, 1917–1925*, 4; Korneski, "Prairie Fire: The Winnipeg General Strike," 259–66.
14. Heron, ed., *The Workers' Revolt in Canada*, 307.
15. McKay, *Reasoning Otherwise,* 469.
16. Ibid., 493.
17. D.C. Masters, *The Winnipeg General Strike,* 146.
18. Rea, *The Winnipeg General Strike,* 14.
19. Dupuis, *Winnipeg's General Strike*, 130. Norman Penner also has argued that the Strike gave impetus for further political action (Penner, *Winnipeg 1919*, xxi).
20. Bercuson, *Confrontation at Winnipeg,* 198. This perspective is also shared by Errol Black. See also Black, "Labour in Brandon Civic Politics."
21. Bercuson, *Confrontation at Winnipeg*, 205.
22. Artibise, *Winnipeg: An Illustrated History*, 114.
23. Smith, *Let Us Rise!*, 44.
24. See, for example, McCormack, "Arthur Puttee and the Liberal Party, 1899–1904," 141–63.
25. See, for example, Paul Rutherford, "Tomorrow's Metropolis: The Urban Reform Movement in Canada, 1880–1920," in Stelter and Artibise, eds., *The Canadian City*, 435–455.

26. See Korneski, "Liberalism in Winnipeg," 303.
27. Mitchell and Naylor, "The Prairies," 216.
28. Korneski, "Liberalism in Winnipeg, 1890s–1920s," 293.
29. Hiebert, "Class, Ethnicity and Residential Structure," 68.
30. Tulchinsky, *Taking Root*, 63. Winnipeg's Jewish population was the largest per capita of any city in Canada by 1921. Ukrainians lived in four enclaves in the city: the North End, Point Douglas, near the Fort Rouge railyards, and Brooklands (Martynowych, *Ukrainians in Canada*, 138).
31. Jones, *Influenza 1918*, 26–8.
32. Hiebert, "Class, Ethnicity and Residential Structure," 69; Martynowych, *Ukrainians in Canada*, 133; Tulchinsky, *Taking Root*, 166.
33. See, for example, Korneski, "Liberalism in Winnipeg, 1890s–1920s," 230.
34. Hiebert, "Class, Ethnicity and Residential Structure," 80.
35. Martynowych, *Ukrainians in Canada*, 141.
36. City of Winnipeg Health Department, *Report on Housing Survey of Certain Selected Areas: Made March and April 1921*.
37. Tulchinsky, *Taking Root*, 164; Hiebert, "Class, Ethnicity and Residential Structure," 76.
38. Martynowych, *Ukrainians in Canada*, 138.
39. Artibise, *Winnipeg: An Illustrated History*, 130.
40. Ibid., 116; Bellan, *Winnipeg, First Century*, 154–5.
41. Bellan, *Winnipeg's, First Century*, 172.
42. Kendle, *John Bracken: A Political Biography*, 153.
43. Artibise, *Winnipeg: An Illustrated History*, 122.
44. *Municipal Manual 1939*, 200.
45. Bellan, *Winnipeg's, First Century*, 202.
46. *Municipal Manual 1939*, 78.
47. Mitchell and Naylor, "The Prairies," 215.

CHAPTER 1: THE SECOND ROUND

1. Lightbody, "Electoral Reform in Local Government," 310.
2. McCormack, "Radical Politics in Winnipeg: 1899–1915."
3. Ibid. The Labour Representation Committee's platform included calls for practical reforms while stating its ultimate aim was the collective ownership.
4. McKillop, "Citizen as Socialist," 60.
5. *Western Labour News*, 10 July 1919.
6. *Manitoba Free Press*, 8 November 1919.
7. *Winnipeg Tribune*, 6 November 1919.
8. *Manitoba Free Press*, 24 November 1919.
9. *Winnipeg Tribune*, 10 October 1919.

10 *Manitoba Free Press*, 24 November 1919.
11 Anderson, "The Municipal Government Reform Movement," 102.
12 *Manitoba Free Press*, 25 November 1919; 22 November 1919.
13 *Manitoba Free Press*, 24 November 1919.
14 *Manitoba Free Press*, 27 November 1919. Earlier that year, J.W. Dafoe, the editor of the *Free Press,* had been strongly pro-Citizen, providing significant free coverage to the Citizens throughout the Strike. See: Korneski, "Liberalism in Winnipeg, 1890s–1920s," 182–3; Cook, *The Politics of John W. Dafoe and the* Free Press, 98–102.
15 *Manitoba Free Press*, 6 November 1919.
16 *Manitoba Free Press*, 24 November 1919.
17 *Manitoba Free Press*, 27 November 1919.
18 *Manitoba Free Press*, 20 November 1919.
19 Rea, *Parties and Power*, 1; McKillop, "The Socialist as Citizen," 6.
20 *Winnipeg Free Press*, 10 November 1933.
21 Interestingly Alan Artibise has suggested that Winnipeg had better municipal administration than many other Canadian cities because of the sharp divide between the Citizens and the political left. The polarized environment meant that all actions were under intense scrutiny, which resulted, Artibise said, in more transparent and better government (Artibise, *Winnipeg: An Illustrated History*, 146).
22 Artibise, *Winnipeg: An Illustrated History*, 207; Lightbody, "Electoral Reform in Local Government," 314.
23 Indeed, while the Citizens acted essentially like a political party, one of its major complaints against the ILP was the presence of party politics in municipal government. Stanley Knowles, interview with Brian McKillop, 14 June 1969, University of Manitoba Archives (UMA) Ed Rea Collection, MSS 73, Box 1 File 1; "Report Re Manitoba Provincial Elections—1927; Communist Activities," 18 June 1927, Jacob Penner RCMP File 117-89-57 Supp. H, 192; *Winnipeg Tribune,* 19 November 1935.
24 Stinson, *Political Warriors*, 300.
25 Rea, "Political Parties and Civic Power: Winnipeg, 1919-1975," in Artibisead Stelter, *The Usable Urban Past*, 158.
26 *Manitoba Free Press,* 21 November 1919.
27 Wichern, "Historical Influences on Contemporary Local Politics," 41.
28 Smith, "The CCF, NPA and Civic Change," 58–60.
29 Morton, *Manitoba: A History*, 414.
30 *Winnipeg Free Press,* 15 November 1924.
31 Quoted in McKillop, "The Socialist as Citizen: John Queen and the Mayoralty of Winnipeg, 1935," 81.
32 Artibise, *Winnipeg: An Illustrated History*, 144.
33 Quoted in Irvine, "Reform, War, and Industrial Crisis in Manitoba," 241.
34 Mills, *Fool for Christ*, 130–1; Mills, "Single Tax, Socialism, and the Independent Labour Party of Manitoba," 48; Irvine, "Reform, War, and Industrial Crisis in Manitoba," 240–5.
35 Mills, "Single Tax, Socialism and the Independent Labour Party of Manitoba," 56.
36 See Irvine, "Reform, War, and Industrial Crisis in Manitoba," 2–28.

37   McKillop, "Citizen as Socialist," 110; Gutkin and Gutkin, *Profiles in Dissent*, 345. Both McKillop and the Gutkins suggest that the ILP advanced a socialism influenced more by J.S. Mill than Karl Marx. McKillop suggests that many of John Queen's public statements can be found almost verbatim in Mill.

38   Interestingly, though, many Citizen leaders were of British descent but Canadian born. Conversely, most ILP leaders were born in the United Kingdom.

39   Rea, *Parties and Power*, 2–3.

40   Naylor, "Canadian Labour Politics and the British Model, 1920–1950," 289.

41   Rea, "Political Parties and Civic Power: Winnipeg, 1919–1975," 158.

42   Naylor, "Canadian Labour Politics and the British Model, 1920–1950," 294.

43   Wiseman, *Social Democracy in Manitoba*, 11.

44   McNaught, *A Prophet in Politics*, 206.

45   *Manitoba Commonwealth and Weekly News*, 9 November 1934.

46   *Winnipeg Free Press*, 11 August 1934. A few months later, John Queen made very similar remarks in a speech to the Paole Zion Group, saying that there is "one alternative to the distress and misery of the capitalist system and that was socialism" (*Manitoba Commonwealth and Weekly News*, 28 December 1934).

47   "Independent Labour Party of Manitoba Provincial Elections, 1932," LAC, A.A. Heaps Fonds, MG27 III C22, Reel H2271.

48   *Weekly News*, 26 November 1926.

49   *Winnipeg Free Press*, 15 November 1932.

50   *Weekly News*, 8 July 1926.

51   *Weekly News*, 2 May 1930.

52   Naylor, "Canadian Labour Politics and the British Model, 1920–1950," 292.

53   Mills, *Fool for Christ*, 50.

54   *Weekly News*, 8 November 1929; *Weekly News*, 26 October 1928; *Winnipeg Tribune*, 24 November 1934; *Winnipeg Tribune*, 21 November 1934.

55   *Weekly News*, 2 December 1927.

56   "Who are the Citizens?" *Workers Election Bulletin*, 22 November 1932, located in the Communist Party of Canada—Manitoba Archives, Election Bulletins Scrapbook, 1930–1935, no accession number.

57   *Weekly News*, 24 November 1927.

58   McKillop, "The Socialist as Citizen," 109.

59   McKay, *Reasoning Otherwise*, 180; Black and Mitchell, *A Square Deal for All and No Railroading*, 68–9; McCormack, "Radical Politics in Winnipeg: 1899–1915."

60   Bercuson, *Confrontation at Winnipeg*, 59.

61   McCormack, *Reformers, Rebels and Revolutionaries*, 133.

62   Winnipeg General Strike Defence Committee, *Saving the World From Democracy*, 17.

63   McKillop, "The Socialist as Citizen: John Queen and the Mayoralty of Winnipeg, 1935."

64   Jules Preud'homme, "Winnipeg as Seen By a Solicitor," 178, located in Archives of Manitoba (AM), Jules Preud'homme Fonds, MG14 C72 Part 2.

65   Fred Tipping oral history interview with Lionel Orlikow, AM, C831.

66 *Winnipeg Free Press*, 23 November 1934.
67 Bumsted, ed., *Dictionary of Manitoba Biography*, 205.
68 Irvine, "Reform, War, and Industrial Crisis in Manitoba," 21–2.
69 Mills, *Fool for Christ*, 45, 51.
70 Korneski, "Liberalism in Winnipeg," 191.
71 Anderson, "The Municipal Government Reform Movement," 95.
72 *Western Labour News*, 12 November 1920.
73 Mills, "Single Tax, Socialism, and the Independent Labour Party of Manitoba," 37.
74 Ibid., 36.
75 Wiseman, *Social Democracy in Manitoba*, 11.
76 Ross, "Personal Perspective on Bill Ross," 210.
77 *Winnipeg Tribune*, 15 November 1930; *Winnipeg Free Press*, 17 November 1933; *Winnipeg Free Press*, 14 November 1935; Henry Trachtenberg, "Jews and Left-Wing Politics in Winnipeg's North End, 1919–1940," in Stone, ed., *Jewish Radicalism in Winnipeg, 1905–1960*, 135.
78 Co-operative Commonwealth Federation, *The First Ten Years, 1932–1942*, 9.
79 Wiseman, *Social Democracy in Manitoba*, 13.
80 McNaught, *A Prophet in Politics*, 287.
81 Heaps, *The Rebel in the House*, 138.
82 "Resolution on the Situation and Tasks of the P. in District No. 7, 1933," LAC CI Fonds, Reel K286, File 152, 3; "Letter from Charlie to Sam," 22 October 1931, LAC CI Fonds, Reel K281, File 121; "District 7 Report," 18 February 1933, LAC CI Fonds, Reel K286, File 152, 1.
83 "Membership Analysis, Winnipeg," 22 April 1934, LAC CI Fonds, Reel K284, File 140. While these statistics are from a few years after Kolisnyk's career on council ended, they appear to be a fair representation of the Winnipeg communist community during the late 1920s and early 1930s. Interestingly, in the party's document outlining its membership, the English, Canadian, French, and Irish ethnicities were underlined. The CPC routinely attempted to attract more Anglo-Saxon members, with seemingly mixed success. While the CPC in Winnipeg was predominantly Ukrainian, Ukrainians composed only 8.4 percent of the city's total population. See: Artibise, "Patterns of Population Growth and Ethnic Relationships in Winnipeg, 1874–1974," 305. Other ethnic groups with numerous Party members included: thirty Poles, twenty-eight Russians, eighteen Scandinavians, eighteen Jews, and seventeen Germans. There were also a handful of Hungarians, Lithuanians, Scots, Yugoslavians, Icelanders, Finns, Austrians, and Italians.
84 "Membership Analysis, Winnipeg," 22 April 1934, LAC CI Fonds, Reel K284, File 140. Of the 415 members, 226 were unemployed and only 52 were women.
85 "District No. 7 Report, 1935" LAC CI Fonds, Reel K290, File 180; Interview with Andrew Bilecki by Doug Smith, Archives of Manitoba, Doug Smith Collection, C407.
86 This was not an atypical party composition among North American communists. For example, in her study on the CPUSA in Chicago, Randi Storch found that local communist membership in Chicago was "overwhelmingly male, unemployed, proletarian, and ethnic." Similarly to Winnipeg, Storch found that ethnic groups such as Russians, South Slavs, Lithuanians, and Finns were overrepresented, while American-born party members were underrepresented. See Storch, *Red Chicago*, 39–40 and 63.

87 "Resolution on the Situation and Tasks of the P. in District No. 7," LAC CI Fonds, Reel K286, File 152, 3.
88 Roland Penner, interview with author.
89 Quoted in McKillop, "Citizen as Socialist: The Ethos of Political Winnipeg, 1919–1935," 97. McKillop presents biographical information on Penner throughout his thesis, particularly pages 82–5 and 105–11.
90 *The Workers Vanguard*, 17 November 1931.
91 Smith, *Joe Zuken*, 39.
92 Avakumovic, *The Communist Party in Canada*, 77. In comparison, 5,000 marchers attended rallies in both Montreal and Vancouver.
93 The ILP was not impressed by these marches, complaining that "unfortunately, the celebration of (May Day) too frequently is monopolized, or nearly so, by assertive propagandists of policies which do not represent the thought of the vast majority" (*Weekly News*, 1 May 1925).
94 Artibise, *Winnipeg: An Illustrated History*, 133. These boundaries would remain in place until Unicity, the merger of Winnipeg with surrounding municipalities, was founded in 1972.
95 *Winnipeg Tribune*, 16 March 1920.
96 Lightbody, "Electoral Reform in Local Government," 318. While the ward system in Winnipeg helped entrench divides within the city, Lightbody points to the example of Vancouver where an at-large election system introduced in 1936 somewhat depoliticized elections and reduced some of the tensions between left and right.
97 "Two Separate Worlds Within This City of Winnipeg," *The Workers Vanguard*, 17 November 1931.
98 *Weekly News*, 4 December 1925.

CHAPTER 2: THE REIGN OF THE FURIES

1 The issue of holding multiple elected positions was a significant one for the ILP. Alderman Thomas Flye would eventually leave the party due to his opposition to dual position holding. However, several ILP leaders, including S.J. Farmer and John Queen, would serve in both municipal and provincial positions at the same time. They were not the only ones to do this. Ralph Webb would also serve municipally and provincially simultaneously. Opponents of dual position holding argued that an elected official could not adequately serve their constituents if they were working in two legislative bodies at one time.
2 *Manitoba Free Press*, 9 November 1922.
3 *Manitoba Free Press*, 1 November 1922; 2 November 1922; 7 November 1922.
4 Kramer and Mitchell, *When the State Trembled*, 63, 111, and 271.
5 *Manitoba Free Press*, 4 November 1922.
6 Ibid.
7 *Manitoba Free Press*, 18 November 1922.
8 *Manitoba Free Press*, 14 November 1922.
9 *Manitoba Free Press*, 17 November 1922.

10   *The North Ender*, 30 November 1922.
11   *Manitoba Free Press*, 4 November 1922.
12   *Manitoba Free Press*, 14 November 1922.
13   *The North Ender*, 14 November 1922.
14   *Manitoba Free Press*, 23 November 1922.
15   *Western Labour News*, 1 December 1922. In the fall 1922 elections, the ILP member John Kelly became reeve of St. Vital, at the time its own Rural Municipality. Kelly would serve as mayor for two years (1923 to 1924).
16   *The North Ender*, 5 July 1923. Returning to this theme a year later, when S.J. Farmer was running for re-election against Ralph Webb, a *North Ender* editorial commented that "while Col. Webb's message to Winnipeg is 'Forward,' Mayor Farmer is fonder of shouting 'Fore' to his fellow golfers" (*The North Ender*, 27 November 1924).
17   *Manitoba Free Press*, 7 February 1923.
18   Artibise, *Winnipeg: A Social History of Modern Growth, 1874–1914*, 101.
19   Armstrong and Nelles, *Monopoly's Moment*, 94–5 and 156.
20   Ibid., 262 and 301; Nelles, "Public Ownership of Electrical Utilities in Manitoba and Ontario, 1906–1930," 464–83. Interestingly, while public ownership was a key component of political activity for labour politicians in Winnipeg, this was not shared across the country. For example, Nova Scotia mining towns with strong labour representation on council did not seek municipally owned utilities. Instead, these councils in small, single-industry communities pushed for mining companies to provide key services such as electrical and water services. (See: Frank, "Company Town/Labour Town: Local Government in the Cape Breton Coal Towns, 1917–1926," 189.)
21   Armstrong and Nelles, *Monopoly's Moment*, 256 and 134.
22   Doucet, "Politics, Space and Trolleys," 369–77.
23   Weaver, *Shaping the Canadian City*, 38–9.
24   "A Central Steam Heating System for Winnipeg," City of Winnipeg Archives (COWA), PU346 (2), 5.
25   COWA, PU346.
26   *Winnipeg Tribune*, 31 July 1923.
27   *Manitoba Free Press*, 31 July 1923.
28   *Manitoba Free Press*, 8 August 1923.
29   *Manitoba Free Press*, 14 August 1923.
30   Glassco to the Public Utilities Committee, 31 July 1923, COWA, PU 346.
31   John Glassco to Alderman Herbert Gray, 15 August 1923, COWA, PU 346.
32   W.B. Parker to Herbert Gray, 28 August 1923, COWA, PU 346.
33   *The North Ender*, 8 November 1923.
34   *Manitoba Free Press*, 31 October 1023.
35   *Manitoba Free Press*, 15 November 1923
36   *The North Ender*, 22 November 1923.

37 *Manitoba Free Press*, 20 November 1923; *Manitoba Free Press*, 10 November 1923.
38 Smith, *Let Us Rise*, 46.
39 *Winnipeg Tribune*, 17 November 1923.
40 *The North Ender,* 9 September 1923.
41 *Manitoba Free Press*, 10 November 1923.
42 Ibid.
43 *Manitoba Free Press*, 14 November 1923.
44 *Manitoba Free Press,* 19 November 1923.
45 Ibid.
46 *Manitoba Free Press*, 21 November 1923.
47 *Winnipeg Tribune*, 17 November 1923.
48 *Manitoba Free Press*, 24 November 1923.
49 Letter from International Brotherhood of Electrical Workers to Board of Conciliation and Investigation, COWA, L+R 49, 2 June 1924.
50 Letter from James Murdock to S.J. Farmer, COWA Letter 13483, 10 September 1924; Letter from James Murdock to S.J. Farmer, COWA, L+R 49, 8 July 1924.
51 Jones, *Influenza 1918*, 107.
52 *Manitoba Free Press*, 18 December 1923.
53 *Manitoba Free Press*, 29 January 1924.
54 *Manitoba Free Press*, 6 October 1924.
55 *Manitoba Free Press*, 18 November 1924.
56 Jules Preud'homme, "Winnipeg as Seen by the City Solicitor," AM Jules Preud'homme Fonds, MG14 C72, Part 2.
57 *Manitoba Free Press*, 25 November 1924.
58 *Manitoba Free Press*, 22 November 1924.
59 *The North Ender*, 27 November 1924.
60 *Manitoba Free Press*, 31 January 1923.
61 *Manitoba Free Press*, 26 November 1924.
62 *Manitoba Free Press*, 26–27 November 1924.
63 *Manitoba Free Press*, 28 November 1924.
64 *Weekly News*, 2 October 1925.
65 *City Council Minute*s, 1924, Motion 1222.
66 *Manitoba Free Press*, 29 November 1924.
67 *Manitoba Free Press*, 1 December 1924.
68 *Weekly News*, 8 January 1926.
69 *Weekly News*, 8 May 1925.

CHAPTER 3: THE REVOLUTIONARY PARTY ON THE PARLIAMENTARY MAP

1. *The Worker*, 7 May 1932; *The Worker*, 11 May 1929; interview with Roland Penner by the author, 13 December 2007; "Slogans for May Day," Communist Party of Canada—Winnipeg RCMP File 117-91-67, 960.

2. *OBU Bulletin*, 9 December 1926. The newspaper cited was *Freiheit*. The claim was repeated at the time and later. See: Morris, *Look on Canada Now*, 7; "Bill Kolisnyk Honored: A Staunch Fighter," *Pacific Tribune*, found in William Kolisnyk RCMP File 117-89-39, 236. See also: Avakumovic, 136.

3. *Manitoba Free Press*, 1 December 1926.

4. *The Worker*, 21 April 1934; Stewart Smith, "Report to the meeting of the Anglo-American Section, Communist International, 17 July 1935," LAC, CI Fonds, Reel K288 File 169.

5. *The Worker*, 27 January 1934; *The Worker*, 7 March 1935; "Resolution on the Situation and Tasks of District 7, 4 May 1934," LAC, CI Fonds, Reel K287 File 163; Kyle Franz, "Painting the Town Red: The 'Communist' Administration at Blairmore, Alberta, 1933-1936," M.A. thesis, University of Lethbridge, 2007.

6. Endicott, *Raising the Workers' Flag*, 123.

7. "Appendix No. II: Reports by Provinces, December 1934," in Gregory S. Kealey and Reg Whitaker, eds., *RCMP Security Bulletins, The Depression Years, Part I, 1933–1934* (St. John's: Canadian Committee on Labour History, 1993), 433; David Bright, "The State, the Unemployed and the Communist Party in Canada, 1930–1935," *Canadian Historical Review* 78, (December 1997): 560; *The Worker*, 28 November 1935.

8. *The Worker*, 23 December 1933; *The Worker*, 9 December 1933.

9. "Canadian Lander Group—Brigade on Economic Struggles," LAC, CI Fonds, Reel K284, File 139.

10. "The XIII Plenum of the Communist International and the Tasks of the Communist Party of Canada," LAC CI fonds, Reel K286, File 157, 50.

11. "Program of the Communist Party for the Municipal Elections of 1931," LAC, CI Fonds, Reel K282, File 125, 5. With the collapse of the Soviet Union, some historians have argued that documents made available by Russian archives, including the source used here from Library and Archives Canada, demonstrate Soviet influence on communist parties (see John Earl Haynes and Harvey Klehr, "The Historiography of American Communism: An Unsettled Field," *Labour History Review* 68 (April 2003): 65. These sources, however, also demonstrate some of the peculiarities of the local context. Historians such as Randi Storch suggest that rather than proving a top-down theory, these new records allow scholars to see for the first time how the party functioned locally, including meeting minutes, election platforms, and educational materials. See Storch, "Moscow's Archives and the New History of the Communist Party of the United States," *Perspectives* (2000), http://www.historians.org.proxy.queensu.ca/perspectives/issues/2000/0010/0010arc1.cfm.

12. McDermott and Agnew, *The Comintern*, 69; "Bucharin's Report," *The Worker*. 18 August 1928; "Sixth Congress of Communist International," *The Worker*, 18 August 1928; "Report of the Sixth National Convention of the Communist Party of Canada," LAC, Communist Party of Canada Fonds, 31 May 1929–7 June 1929, Reel M7380, 22; Penner, *Canadian Communism*, 98 and 102.

13 *The Worker*, 12 October 1929. For an account of the Sixth Convention of the CPC, during which the Third Period was adopted by Canadian communists, see Smith, *Comrades and Komsomolkas*, 120.

14 Executive Committee of the Communist International, *Capitalist Stabilization Has Ended*, 14; "Sixth Comintern Congress," 110. The term social fascism came from an article written by Joseph Stalin, who described social democracy as the "moderate wing of fascism." (See Angus, *Canadian Bolsheviks*, 242).

15 McDermott and Agnew, *The Comintern*, 98. As early as 1924, Stalin remarked, "fascism is the fighting organization of the bourgeoisie, leaning on the active support of social democracy. Social democracy is objectively the moderate wing of fascism." Quoted in van Ree, *The Political Thought of Joseph Stalin*, 216–7.

16 *Capitalist Stabilization Has Ended*, 11–2.

17 *The Worker*, 1 June 1929.

18 *The Worker*, 5 January 1929.

19 Angus, *Canadian Bolsheviks*, 264.

20 Ibid., 241.

21 Palmer, *Working-Class Experience*, 206.

22 Manley, "Canadian Communists, Revolutionary Unionism, and the 'Third Period,'" 189.

23 Ibid., 175.

24 Palmer, *James P. Cannon*, 10.

25 The traditionalist school is exemplified by such works as: Draper, *American Communism and Soviet Russia, The Formative Years*; Rodney, *Soldiers of the International: A History of the Communist Party of Canada, 1919-1929*; McIlRoy and Campbell, "'Nina Ponomareva's Hats': The New Revisionism, the Communist International, and the Communist Party of Great Britain, 1920-1930," 147–87.

26 "Revisionist" historiography includes works such as: Lyons, *Philadelphia Communists, 1936-1956*; Naison, *Communists in Harlem During the Depression*; and Storch, *Red Chicago: American Communism at its Grassroots*.

27 Haynes and Klehr, "The Historiography of American Communism," 65.

28 Barrett, *William Z. Foster and the Tragedy of American Radicalism*, 275; Thorpe, "Comintern 'Control' of the Communist Party of Great Britain, 1920–1943," 638.

29 Solomon, *The Cry Was Unity*, xxiii.

30 McIlroy and Campbell, "'Nina Ponomareva's Hats,'" 159.

31 Butler, "Mother Russia and the Socialist Fatherland," 2.

32 "Bill Kolisnyk Honored: A Staunch Fighter," *Pacific Tribune* found in William Kolisnyk RCMP File 117-89-39, 236.

33 Krawchuk, *Interned Without Cause*, http://www.socialisthistory.ca/Docs/CPC/WW2/IWC00.htm.

34 Martynowych, *Ukrainians in Canada*, 428.

35 Ibid., 436.

36 "Brief for the Advisory Committee," 9 September 1941, William Kolisnyk RCMP File 117-89-39, 126.

37 "William N. Kolisnyk," William Kolisnyk RCMP File, 117-89-39, 13.
38 "Report Re 'Ukrainian Labour News'—Winnipeg," 4 March 1927, William Kolisnyk RCMP File 117-89-39, 50.
39 Mochoruk, *The People's Co-op*, 16.
40 "Brief for the Advisory Committee," 9 September 1941, William Kolisnyk RCMP File 117-89-39, 126.
41 "Report Re Communist Party of Canada—Winnipeg," 6 December 1926, William Kolisnyk RCMP File 117-89-39, 45.
42 Mochoruk, *The People's Co-op*, 9.
43 Kolisnyk, "In Canada Since the Spring of 1898," 38 and 40.
44 Mochoruk, *The People's Co-op*, 16.
45 Ibid. 26.
46 Betcherman, *The Little Band*, 99.
47 *The Worker*, 11 December 1926.
48 *The Worker*, 13 November 1926.
49 *OBU Bulletin*, 1 December 1927.
50 *The Worker*, 13 November 1926; *The Worker*, 11 December 1926; *The Worker*, 27 November 1926.
51 "Report Re: Communist Party of Canada—Polish Group—Winnipeg," 22 November 1926, in Communist Party of Canada—Winnipeg, RCMP File 117-91-94, 12. An interesting example of the ways that the CPC appealed to ethnic groups as part of their municipal election campaign is illustrated in an article written in the Communists' election press, *The Workers' Vanguard*. In a paper dedicated to the municipal election effort, an article on the Middle East was included that affirmed the Communists' support for self-determination for both the Jewish and Palestinian people. While seemingly out of place in a municipal election campaign, it does indicate the importance the Party placed on appealing to ethnic groups. See "To The Jewish Workers of Winnipeg," *The Workers' Vanguard* November 1929 located in LAC, A.A. Heaps Fonds, MG27 III C7, Reel H2271.
52 *Communist Party of Canada Election Bulletin No. 2* (1927), LAC, A.A. Heaps Fonds, Reel H2271.
53 Ibid.
54 *Weekly News*, 2 December 1927. When communist candidate Leslie Morris was dropped from the ballot, 67 percent of votes were non-transferrable (no second candidate was indicated), 19 percent were given to J.F. Palmer (the Citizen candidate) and only 13 percent went to J.A. Cherniak of the ILP. Although Palmer had been leading Cherniak prior to the redistribution of Morris' votes, his lead had been only 121 votes, so even a small increase in support from communist voters could have won the election for the ILP.
55 *OBU Bulletin*, 1 December 1927.
56 *OBU Bulletin*, 17 November 1927.
57 *OBU Bulletin*, 1 December 1927.
58 *Weekly News*, 10 December 1926.
59 Ibid.

60 "Report Re: Communist Party of Canada—Polish Group—Winnipeg," 22 November 1926, Communist Party of Canada—Winnipeg RCMP File 117-91-94, 12.

61 *The Worker*, 10 December 1927.

62 *The Worker*, 11 December 1926.

63 *Communist Party of Canada Election Bulletin No. 2* (1927), LAC, A.A. Heaps Fonds, Reel H2271. Four years later, the local election paper of the CPC made a similar comment, remarking that "whatever your racial origin may be, the fact that you are a member of the working class is the decisive factor. No one gets higher wages or better unemployment relief because of his nationality. Workers of all nationalities—stick together." See *The Workers Vanguard,* 17 November 1931.

64 Work done by Nelson Wiseman and K.W. Taylor analyzes the relationship between ethnic and class factors in Winnipeg voting records. Their work, which studies elections beginning only in 1945, suggests that ethnic factors were subservient to class factors. See: Wiseman and Taylor, "Ethnic vs Class Voting," 314–28.

65 *The Workers' Vanguard,* November 1929.

66 Tulchinsky, *Taking Root*, 165.

67 "Report Re Civic Elections—Winnipeg, Manitoba, 1924, Communist Party of Canada Activities," 29 November 1924, Matthew Popovich RCMP File 117-91-98, 103.

68 "Minutes of the Political Committee," 15 October 1928, LAC CPC Files, Reel M7380; "Report Re Communist Party of Canada—Winnipeg, Man., W. N. Kolisnyk—Candidate for Alderman—Winnipeg Civic Election—1926," William Kolisnyk RCMP File 117-89-39, 43.

69 Tension between Jewish and non-Jewish communists would continue for many years in Winnipeg. In 1930, Jacob Penner and Leslie Morris expelled four Jewish party members for "a long series of Right-wing anti-Party acts that have marked the work of the Jewish mass organization for some time." See: Angus, *Canadian Bolsheviks: The Early Years of the Communist Party of Canada*.

70 Mochoruk, "'Pop & Co' versus Buck and the 'Lenin School Boys,'" 349.

71 "Minutes of the Political Committee," 15 October 1928, LAC CPC Fonds, MG28-IV4, Reel M7380.

72 Letter from Dan Holmes to Tim Buck, 21 August 1929, LAC, CPC Fonds, MG28-IV4, Reel M7376.

73 Letter from Dan Holmes to Tim Buck, 21 August 1929, LAC, CPC Fonds, Reel M7376.

74 Mochoruk, "'Pop & Co' versus Buck and the 'Lenin School Boys,'" 357.

75 "Report Re 'Ukrainian Labour News'—Winnipeg," 4 March 1927, William Kolisnyk RCMP File 117-89-39, 50.

76 "Minutes of the Political Committee," 15 October 1928, LAC, CPC Fonds, MG28-IV4, Reel M7380.

77 See Endicott, *Raising the Workers' Flag,* 28. Also see a discussion of Finnish communists and their tenuous relationship with the CPC structure in Beaulieu, "A Proletarian Prometheus: Socialism, Ethnicity, and Revolution at the Lakehead, 1930-1935."

78 Betcherman, *The Little Band*, 99.

79 Communist Party of Canada—Winnipeg RCMP File 117-91-67, 984. The ULFTA was formed in 1918 and, while it had branches throughout the country, had its most significant presence in Winnipeg due to the large number of Ukrainians in the city. The relationship

between the ULFTA and the CPC was close, and numerous leaders of the ULFTA (such as Matthew Popovich and John Navis) became leaders in the CPC as well. Nevertheless, there remained tensions between the ULFTA and the CPC over the relationship of ethnicity to the class struggle. See Sangster, "*Robitnytsia*, Ukrainian Communists, and the 'Porcupinism' Debate," 56.

80 Martynowych, "Sympathy for the Devil," 191.
81 Ibid., 508.
82 Fine, "Anti-semitism in Manitoba in the 1930s and 1940s," http://www.mhs.mb.ca/docs/mb_history/32/manitobaantisemitism.shtml; Martynowych, "Sympathy for the Devil," 173–220.
83 *Manitoba Free Press,* 16 November 1929.
84 "Bulletin and Directives on Building Plan for District Seven," LAC, CI Fonds, Reel K284, File 140, 3.
85 "Program of the Communist Party for the Municipal Elections of 1931," LAC, CI Fonds, Reel K282, File 125, 4.
86 *The Worker,* 11 December 1926.
87 Ibid.
88 Quoted in *OBU Bulletin,* 9 December 1926.
89 Letter from Leslie Morris to J.W. Esselwein, 2 December 1926, located in William Kolisnyk RCMP File 117-89-39, 46.
90 "Brief for the Advisory Committee," 9 September 1941, William Kolisnyk RCMP File 117-89-39, 125.
91 Hewitt, "Royal Canadian Mounted Spy," 144–68.
92 *Communist Party of Canada Election Bulletin No. 2* (1927), located in LAC, A.A. Heaps Fonds, MG27 III C22, Reel H2271. Kolisnyk's loyalty to his party was not that different from that expected from ILP members, at least from some portions of the ILP. In 1923, a note in ILP meeting minutes recommends "that our Representatives be requested to subscribe to a plan whereby they must submit to the General Executive any measures they propose to advance." It is not clear what the impetus for this was (had an elected representative done something to displease ILP members?) or to what extent this was ever carried out. See: MG14 D4, ILP Fonds, AM.
93 *Workers Election Bulletin,* 22 November 1932, located in CPC-MA, Election Bulletins Scrapbook, 1930–1935.
94 "W.N. Kolisnyk—Winnipeg," William Kolisnyk RCMP file 117-89-39, 9; "Brief for the Advisory Committee," 9 September 1941, William Kolisnyk RCMP File 117-89-39, 125.
95 "Minute Book of the Centre Branch, Winnipeg," 15 September 1921 and 13 October 1921, Independent Labour Party Fonds, AM, MG14-D4.
96 *Weekly News,* 29 July 1927.
97 In 1927 and 1928 Kolisnyk raised the fate of agricultural labourers, and suggested that the federal government should assist British workers (who had been imported to work on the harvest) return to Britain. Additionally, he argued that no more labourers should be imported because unemployment in Canada was already high. See: Motion 865, 8 July 1927, *City Council Minutes (CCM),* 712. The motion was put forward by Kolisnyk and seconded by John Blumberg and was sent to committee for further study. All city council minutes are

available at the City of Winnipeg Archives; Motion 1134, 4 September 1928, *CCM*, 882; Motion 996, 7 August 1928, *CCM*, 777; See: Motion 208, 20 February 1928, *CCM*, 161; Motion 1041, 19 August 1929, *CCM*, 945. Slave Falls was a hydroelectric project of the City of Winnipeg and, as such, the workers should have been protected by the city's fair wage legislation. This, however, was not the case much of the time, hence the Communist agitation on the issue. The motion on mining and bush camps was ruled out of order.

98 *The Worker*, 12 March 1927.
99 Kolisnyk, "In Canada Since the Spring of 1898," 39.
100 *The Worker*, 13 September 1930.
101 Motion 1135, 4 September 1928, *CCM*, 882. The motion was defeated by ten votes to five.
102 Motion 1067, 20 August 1928, *CCM*, 839. The motion was ruled out of order.
103 Motion 1068, 20 August 1928, *CCM*, 839; Motion 366, 1 April 1929, *CCM*, 330.
104 *Weekly News*, 13 January 1928.
105 *The Worker*, 3 May 1928.
106 *The Worker*, 19 May 1928.
107 *The Worker*, 7 June 1930.
108 *The Worker*, 4 October 1930.
109 *Manitoba Free Press*, 29 April 1930; See also: *Weekly News*, 2 May 1930. The *Weekly News* had a different interpretation of events, suggesting that Kolisnyk said, "Alderman Simpkin favours wood-sawing...and I protested in committee."
110 *Weekly News*, 2 May 1930.
111 *Manitoba Free Press*, 29 April 1930.
112 *Weekly News*, 2 May 1930.
113 Ibid.
114 *Manitoba Free Press*, 29 April 1930.
115 Motion 497, 28 April 1930, *CCM*, 437.
116 *The Worker*, 24 May 1930.
117 *Manitoba Free Press*, 14 May 1930.
118 The number, of course, may be highly exaggerated although this is not necessarily important. Rather, what is interesting in this situation is the link between Kolisnyk's role on council and the broader mass organizations linked to the CPC. See *The Worker*, 3 May 1930.
119 "Report Re: May Day Celebration—Winnipeg—May 1, 1930," Communist Party of Canada—Winnipeg RCMP File 117-91-67, 1997; *The Worker*, 3 May 1930. The *Weekly News* suggested that Kolisnyk "played the role of the martyr excellently." See *Weekly News*, 14 November 1930.
120 *The Worker*, 24 May 1930. An interesting anecdote emerged out of a council meeting in November 1930. Kolisnyk had complained about a plan to dig a ditch using manual labour (as a means to provide more employment) because he said it was a "work test." Immediately Alderman Durward of the ILP rose and read directly from a pamphlet published in the Soviet Union. The pamphlet discussed how the Soviets were employing manual labour to dig ditches as a means of creating employment—the exact proposal that Kolisnyk had just opposed. See *Weekly News*, 28 November 1930.

121 *The Worker*, 26 November 1927.
122 "Report Re: Communist Party of Canada—General—Winnipeg—International Unemployment Protest Demonstration," Communist Party of Canada—Winnipeg RCMP File 117-91-67, 2013.
123 *Manitoba Free Press*, 22 November 1929.
124 *The Worker*, 8 December 1930; *The Weekly News* 2 August 1929.
125 *Weekly News*, 5 December 1930. Simkin won 20.3 percent of the vote in the Ward Two school board race in 1930. A year later, CPC candidate George Ashbrook received only 4.9 percent of the vote in the Ward Two School board race. For the following two elections, the communist vote remained steady at around 5 percent.
126 *Weekly News*, 5 December 1930.
127 "Communism and Its Lessons," *Weekly News*, 2 May 1930.
128 *Winnipeg Tribune*, 19 November 1930.
129 It should also be noted that Kolisnyk missed several council sessions in 1929 due to a severe bout of encephalitis. In his study of communism in Port Arthur and Fort William, Ontario (now known as Thunder Bay), Michel Beaulieu noted that the ILP members of city council blocked attempts for communists to bring their issues forward to council. However, in those communities, communists did not have any elected representatives, pointing to the potential value of Kolisnyk (and other elected communists) as a mouthpiece for the CPC. See: Beaulieu, "A Proletarian Prometheus," 363.
130 *Weekly News*, 5 December 1930.
131 *The Worker*, 15 November 1930.
132 *Weekly News*, 5 December 1930.
133 Ibid.
134 *Manitoba Free Press*, 6 November 1930. Free speech was a key component of communist campaigns in response to Section 98. See Chapter 4.
135 "Personal History File, Page 2," William Kolisnyk RCMP File 117-89-39, 15; "Summary of File for the information of the Advisory Committee on Orders of Restriction and Detention Re: William Kolisnyk," William Kolisnyk RCMP File 117-89-39, 99.
136 Betcherman, *The Little Band*, 99.
137 Letter to the Winnipeg City Central Committee, 31 October 1931, Communist Party of Canada—Winnipeg RCMP File 117-91-67, 1558.
138 "Communist Party of Canada United Front Winnipeg Civic Election Campaign," 22 October 1934, William Kolisnyk RCMP File 117-89-39, 81.
139 Mochoruk, "'Pop & Co' versus Buck and the 'Lenin School Boys,'" 49–50.
140 "Report Re: ULFTA—(Workers and Farmers Cooperative Creamery—Winnipeg)," William Kolisnyk RCMP File 117-89-39, 83; "Brief For the Advisory Committee," William Kolisnyk RCMP File 117-89-39, 123.
141 Quoted in "Brief for the Advisory Committee," 9 September 1941, William Kolisnyk RCMP file 117-89-39, 124; "W. N. Kolisnyk—Winnipeg," William Kolisnyk RCMP File 117-89-39, 13.
142 Kolisnyk, "In Canada Since the Spring of 1898," 40.
143 Mochoruk, *The People's Co-op*, 9.

CHAPTER 4: A VICTORY FOR THOSE ENGAGED IN THE STRUGGLE FOR BETTER CONDITIONS

1. Manley, "Canadian Communists, Revolutionary Unionism, and the 'Third Period,'" 189.
2. Ibid., 167. Manley argues that the local WUL organizers were "good trade unionists" rather than "good Bolsheviks."
3. Quoted in Smith, *Joe Zuken*, 27.
4. Gloria Queen-Hughes interviewed by Paul Barber, January 1970, UMA Ed Rea Collection, MSS 73 Box 1, File 6.
5. *Winnipeg Free Press*, 19 November 1932.
6. "Special Report Re Communistic Activities," 10 November 1931, AM, Communist Activity, 1931-1936, Attorney General Miscellaneous Files, G1542A, File 43.
7. Communist Party of Canada Central Agitprop Department, "Letter to All District and Local Party Organizations," 1931, LAC CI Fonds, Reel K282, File 125.
8. *The Worker*, 26 November 1932.
9. "Letter from Charlie to Sam," 22 October 1931, LAC CI Fonds, Reel K281 File 121.
10. "Directives for the Municipal Election Campaign, 1931," LAC CI Fonds, Reel K282, File 125.
11. *The Worker*, 29 October 1932.
12. "Resolution on Winnipeg Municipal Elections, November 1933," LAC CI Fonds, Reel K286, File 152.
13. "Directives for the Municipal Election Campaign, 1931," LAC CI Fonds, Reel K282, File 125.
14. "Letter from Charlie to Sam," 22 October 1931, LAC CI Fonds, Reel K281, File 121.
15. *North Winnipeg Elector*, 12 October 1935, located in Communist Party of Canada—Manitoba Archvies, Election Bulletins Scrapbook, 1930-1935, no accession number.
16. *Winnipeg Free Press*, 21 November 1933.
17. "Directives For the Municipal Election Campaign," LAC CI Fonds, Reel K282, File 125, 1.
18. *The Worker*, 10 November 1934.
19. "Resolution on the Winnipeg Municipal Elections, November 1933" LAC CI Fonds, Reel K286, File 152, 2.
20. "Program of the Communist Party For the Municipal Elections of 1931," LAC CI Fonds, Reel K282, File 125.
21. *The Worker*, 10 November 1934.
22. "The Mayor-Elect," *Winnipeg Tribune*, 24 November 1934.
23. Pierce [Stewart Smith], *Socialism and the CCF*, 207.
24. "Program of the Communist Party for the Municipal Elections of 1931," LAC CI Fonds, Reel K282 File 125, 4.
25. *Manitoba Free Press*, 16 November 1929; *Winnipeg Free Press*, 23 November 1933.
26. *Winnipeg Free Press*, 21 November 1933.
27. "Bulletin and Directives on Building Plan for District Seven," LAC CI Fonds, Reel K284, File 140, 3.

28 *The Worker*, 7 November 1934; *The Worker*, 21 April 1934.

29 *Voice of Labour*, 29 November 1934.

30 "Resolution on Winnipeg Municipal Elections, November 1933," LAC CI Fonds, Reel K286, File 152, 2.

31 *Winnipeg Free Press*, 30 January 1934.

32 Jacob Penner was by no means the only radical politician to defy decorum. Years earlier, the socialist MLA Charles O'Brien in Alberta, for example, moved an amendment to a resolution in sympathy for Edward VII's widow to include the widows of miners in a recent mining disaster. See: McCormack, *Reformers, Rebels and Revolutionaries*, 64.

33 Penner and Penner, "Recollections of the Early Socialist Movement in Winnipeg," 366–78.

34 Ibid.

35 Penner, "Personal Reflection on Rose Penner," 124.

36 "Report Re Communist Party of Canada—Winnipeg, Man. Penner—Organizer for District," 22 July 1922, Jacob Penner RCMP File 117-89-57, Supp. H, 152.

37 *Weekly News*, 5 January 1934.

38 "Report Re J. Penner," 19 July 1919, Jacob Penner RCMP File 117-89-57 Supp. H, 36.

39 Roland Penner, interview with the author.

40 "Crime Report Re Bolshevism in Winnipeg District," 11 June 1919, Jacob Penner RCMP File 117-89-57 Supp. H, 21.

41 "Cross Reference Sheet, Jacob Penner," 15 August 1929, Jacob Penner RCMP File 117-89-57 Supp. H., 194.

42 Charles Simonite interviewed by Paul Barber, January 1970, UMA Ed Rea collection, MSS 73, Box 1, File 2.

43 "District Circular Memorandum To All Detachments," Martin Forkin RCMP File 119-91-22, 20.

44 Black, "Brandon's 'Revolutionary Forkins,'" 115–8; Black, "The Forkin Letters," 52.

45 Endicott, *Bienfait*, 47. The RCMP intercepted a telegram sent by Forkin urging someone (the name has been redacted) to "rush five hundred unemployed union men to Bienfait carefully routed. Miners fighting for their lives and families." See Martin Forkin RCMP File 119-91-22, 22.

46 Endicott, *Bienfait*, 46; *The Worker*, 2 March 1935; *The Workers' Vanguard*, July 1930; *Winnipeg Free Press*, 12 June 1934; "Re: M.J. Forkin—Communist Party," Martin Forkin RCMP File, 119-91-22, 3; "Report on Conclusion of Case," Martin Forkin RCMP File 119-91-22, 3.

47 "Report on Conclusion of Case," Martin Forkin RCMP File, 119-91-22, 116.

48 Quoted in Petryshyn, "Class Conflict and Civil Liberties," 48–9.

49 "Directives for the Municipal Election Campaign, 1931," LAC, CI Fonds, Reel K282, File 125.

50 "Unite At the Polls On Your Own Behalf," *Workers Election Bulletin*, 11 November 1933, located in CPC-MA, Election Bulletins Scrapbook, 1930–1935.

51 Motion 605, 6 June 1934, *CCM*, 360; *Winnipeg Free Press*, 6 June 1934; *Winnipeg Free Press*, 9 May 1934.

52 Quoted in Butler, "Mother Russia and the Socialist Fatherland," 224.

53 The RCMP estimated that approximately 500 Nationalist Party members lived in Winnipeg. It should be noted that, despite Winnipeg's reputation as a "left-wing city," the Nationalist Party had more members than the Communist Party in the city if these figures are accurate. Kealey and Whitaker, eds., 27; McKillop, "A Communist in City Hall," 46.
54 *Winnipeg Free Press*, 27 February 1934.
55 *Winnipeg Free Press*, 6 June 1934.
56 Ibid.
57 *Weekly News*, 8 June 1934.
58 McEwen, *The Forge Glows Red*, 129.
59 *Winnipeg Free Press*, 21 July 1931.
60 Motion 227, 25 February 1935, *CCM*, 109.
61 *Winnipeg Tribune*, 9 April 1935.
62 Roberts, "Shovelling Out the Unemployed," 12.
63 Roberts, *Whence They Came*, 172.
64 *Winnipeg Free Press*, 9 December 1933.
65 *Manitoba Free Press*, 11 May 1932. Roberts also wrote that some Winnipeg Poles were deported for reputedly being "members of organizations connected with the Communist movement." See Roberts, "Shovelling out the 'Mutinous,'" 98.
66 *The Worker*, 14 May 1932; *The Workers' Vanguard*, July 1930, located in J.S. Woodsworth Fonds, LAC, MG27 III C7, Volume 7, File 13; *The Workers' Vanguard* 17 November 1931.
67 Roberts, "Shovelling Out the Unemployed."
68 Ibid.
69 *Winnipeg Free Press*, 23 April 1935.
70 27 May 1935, Martin Forkin RCMP File 117-91-22, 129.
71 "The Means Can Be Found to Maintain the Unemployed," *Workers Election Bulletin* 22 November 1932, located in CPC–MA, Election Bulletins Scrapbook, 1930–1935.
72 *Workers' Unity*, April 1933.
73 *Report of the Royal Commission on the Municipal Finances and Administration of the City of Winnipeg, 1937*, 6; Goeres, "Disorder, Dependency, and Fiscal Responsibility," 284–5.
74 Goeres, "Disorder, Dependency, and Fiscal Responsibility," 272.
75 *Weekly News*, 5 December 1930.
76 *Workers Election Bulletin*, 22 November 1932 located in CPC–MA, Election Bulletins Scrapbook, 1930–1935.
77 *Winnipeg Tribune*, 17 November 1934.
78 Motion 76, 14 January 1935, *CCM*, 27; *Winnipeg Free Press*, 29 January 1935. The non-contributory unemployment insurance plan received support from the ILP.
79 *Winnipeg Tribune*, 23 November 1933.
80 Jacob Penner, "Communist Councillors Show Good Record for Work in City Council," *The Civic Elector*, 18 November 1935, located in CPC–MA, Election Bulletins Scrapbook, 1930–1935.

81 Penner, "Communist Councillors Show Good Record for Work in City Council," 38–9.
82 *The Worker*, 7 November 1934.
83 Roland Penner, interview with the author.
84 Michael Harris interview with Brian McKillop 24 June 1969, UMA Ed Rea Collection, MSS 73, Box 1, File 3.
85 *Winnipeg Free Press*, 16 November 1933; *Winnipeg Free Press* 15 November 1933.
86 *The Civic Elector*, 18 November 1935.
87 Motion 348, 26 March 1934, *CCM*, 186. The motion was amended to state that an investigation would be made into working conditions.
88 *Winnipeg Typo News*, 31 July 1935; Motion 758, 29 July 1935, *CCM*.
89 *The Civic Elector*, 18 November 1935.
90 Michael Harris interviewed by Brian McKillop 24 June 1969, UMA Ed Rea Collection, MSS 73, Box 1, File 3.
91 *Voice of Labour*, 29 November 1934, 4.
92 "Directives for the Municipal Election Campaign, 1931," LAC, CI Fonds, Reel K282, File 125.
93 Smith, *Socialism and the CCF*, 157.
94 "Resolution on the Situation and Tasks of the P. In District No. 7," LAC CI Fonds, Reel K286, File 152, 4.
95 "Expound Communist Aims in Civic Fight," *Manitoba Free Press*, 15 November 1930.
96 "Letter from Charlie to Sam," 22 October 1931, LAC CI Fonds, Reel K281, File 121, 2.
97 *Winnipeg Free Press*, 21 November 1933.
98 "Resolution on Winnipeg Municipal Elections, November 1933," LAC CI Fonds, Reel K286 File 152, 2.
99 *Weekly News*, 18 May 1934.
100 Penner, *The Canadian Left*, 156.
101 *Weekly News*, 1 December 1933.
102 *Winnipeg Free Press*, 3 January 1934.
103 After returning home from the World Congress in 1935, Stewart Smith rejected the sectarianism he had advocated in 1934, fully adopting Popular Frontism. Two years later he would be elected to Toronto City Council.
104 The Bradshaw Report was completed at the behest of city council by Thomas Bradshaw in 1934. Bradshaw recommended that Winnipeg should decrease business taxes and offset this with a sales tax, a rent tax, and an increase in the price of water and electricity. Since the working class was the most affected by an increase in rent, water, and hydro rates the plan was strongly opposed by both the CPC and the ILP. See City of Winnipeg, *Report of Commission on Assessment, Taxation*, 14–16.
105 *The Worker*, 21 November 1934; "Information on the Election Campaigns and the United Front Tactic," 22 November 1934, LAC CI Fonds, Reel K287, File 161.
106 *The Worker*, 21 November 1934; "Report Re Communist Party of Canada—Winnipeg Civic Election Campaign," 19 November 1934, Communist Party of Canada—Winnipeg RCMP

File 117-91-67, 989. There was a long tradition of one faction of left running candidates against others in Winnipeg to split the vote. In 1910, the Socialist Party of Canada ran a candidate against F.W. Dixon of the Social Democratic Party, stealing enough votes to deny Dixon the victory. See: McKay, *Reasoning Otherwise*, 464.

107 Gutkin and Gutkin, *Profiles in Dissent*, 360.
108 "Communists Propose Another United Front," *Labour Leader*, 3 May 1935.
109 *The Worker*, 21 November 1934.
110 "Report Re: Communist Party of Canada—Winnipeg Civic Election Activities," 8 November 1934, Communist Party of Canada—Winnipeg RCMP File, 117-91-67,988 and 994; *Winnipeg Free Press* 19 November 1934.
111 *Winnipeg Free Press*, 19 October 1935.
112 Joseph Zuken would win Jacob Penner's seat upon his retirement and sat on council from 1961 to 1983.
113 *Canadian Press NewsWire*, 8 May 2000.

CHAPTER 5: FOR FREEDOM'S CAUSE, YOUR BAYONET'S BRIGHT

1 "Synopsis of Reports on Communistic Activities Commencing 5 May 1931", AM, Attorney General Miscellaneous Files, G1542A File 43.
2 Quoted in Penner, *Canadian Communism*, 114.
3 Quoted in Palmer, *Working-Class Experience*, 205.
4 *The Worker*, 5 November 1929.
5 *Winnipeg Free Press*, 15 November 1932.
6 Quoted in McKillop, "Citizen as Socialist: The Ethos of Political Winnipeg, 1919–1935," 97.
7 Letter from Jacob Penner to Norman Penner, December 1956, AM, P599-4.
8 *Manitoba Free Press*, 20 November 1929.
9 Interview with Roland Penner by author.
10 Penner, *A Glowing Dream*, 39.
11 Andrew Bilecki interviewed by Doug Smith. AM, Doug Smith Collection, C409.
12 Stokes, "Fact or Fiction?" http://www.historycooperative.org/journals/llt/57/stokes.html.
13 "Report Re: Uncertain Conditions in Winnipeg," Communist Party of Canada—Winnipeg RCMP Files, 117-91-67, 1408.
14 "Synopsis of Reports on Communistic Activities Commencing 5 May 1931," AM, G1542A, File 43.
15 "Investigation into Communist Movements in Winnipeg and District," Communist Activity, 1931–1936, AM, Attorney General Miscellaneous Files, G1542A, File 43. Future alderman Martin Forkin rejected violence against police. Forkin, who had briefly been a policeman himself, saw the police as a potential source of recruits, not the enemy, saying "we have to appeal to the police as workers with sympathies for fellow workers" (quoted in Endicott, *Raising the Workers' Flag*, 93).
16 Communist Party of Canada—Winnipeg, RCMP File 117-91-67.

17 Vigilant Committee of Winnipeg letter to John Bracken (n.d.), LAC, RG13 Volume 738, 513057.
18 "Synopsis of Reports on Communistic Activities Commencing 5 May 1931," Communist Activity, 1931–1936, AM, Attorney General Miscellaneous Files, G1542A, File 43.
19 "Report Re Communist Party of Canada—General, Alleged Possession of Machine Guns," Communist Party of Canada—Winnipeg RCMP Files, 117-91-67, 1790.
20 Letter from H.J. Martin to Hon. W.J. Major, 6 October 1931; Statement of Emile Luchuk, AM, Attorney General Miscellaneous Files, G1542A, File 43.
21 "Letter re: Communist Activities," Premier's Office Correspondence, 1935, Bracken Papers, AM MG 131 Box 85, File 892.
22 Quoted in Rea, *The Winnipeg General Strike*, 109.
23 Rea, *The Winnipeg General Strike*, 89.
24 Kramer and Mitchell, *When the State Trembled*, 204.
25 LAC CI Fonds, Reel K284, File 140. Since these are figures from the Communist Party they should be treated with some caution, although they do not seem like unreasonable figures. A year earlier, in 1931, the Communist Party recorded 720 arrests (see Endicott, *Raising the Workers' Flag*, 97).
26 *The Workers Vanguard*, 25 November 1931.
27 Penner, *Canadian Communism*, 100.
28 *Winnipeg Free Press*, 7 March 1930; Betcherman, *The Little Band*, 100.
29 *Winnipeg Free Press*, 8 March 1930.
30 Betcherman, *The Little Band*, 100.
31 *Winnipeg Free Press*, 10 March 1930.
32 *Manitoba Free Press*, 29 April 1930.
33 *Winnipeg Tribune*, 17 November 1933.
34 "The Independent Labour Party—Party of Capitalism," *The Workers' Vanguard*, November 1929.
35 "Canadian Labour Defence League Demands Immediate Amnesty For All Worker-Prisoners," *Workers Election Bulletin*, 22 November 1932, located in CPC-MA, Election Bulletins Scrapbook, 1930–1935.
36 "Toronto Is First—But Winnipeg's Turn is Coming," *The Workers' Vanguard*, November 1929, located in LAC, A.A. Heaps Fonds, Reel H2271.
37 *The Worker*, 20 June 1931; John H. Thompson, "The Political Career of Ralph H. Webb," *Red River Valley Historical Society* (Summer 1976): 1–7; Betcherman, *The Little Band*, 146. Toronto was known for its crackdown on communism and leftist groups under Police Chief Dennis Draper.
38 *Manitoba Free Press*, 6 November 1930.
39 Ralph Webb to R.B. Bennett, 25 February 1931, LAC R.B. Bennett Papers, MG16 K Series F, No. 141. Webb sent a similar telegram to Bennett in 1931, stating: "LET US DEPORT ALL COMMUNISTIC AGITATORS STOP IF WE HAVE NOT THE LAWS NOW CANNOT WE OBTAIN THEM THIS SESSION." Quoted in McKillop, "A Communist in City Hall," 43.

40 Quoted in Betcherman, *The Little Band*, 170.

41 Norman Penner, interview with Brian McKillop, 6 June 1969, UMA, Ed Rea Collection, MSS73, Box 1, File 9.

42 "Re Communist Party of Canada—Winnipeg," Communist Party of Canada—Winnipeg RCMP File 117-91-67, 1930; *The Worker*, 29 November 1930; "Statement of the District Board on the Maissonneuve Elections," LAC Comintern Fonds, Reel K284, File 141, 3.

43 "Concentrated Police Forces Raid Workers' Halls and Homes at Behest of Leader of the ILP," *Workers Election Bulletin*, 25 November 1931, located in CPC-MA, Election Bulletins Scrapbook, 1930–1935. The *Workers Election Bulletin* would go on to suggest that while its headquarters were being raided and its literature seized by police, the ILP was enjoying positive coverage from the capitalist press. This served as further evidence, in the minds of Winnipeg communists, that their ILP opponents were part of a capitalist party.

44 *Manitoba Free Press*, 21 November 1931.

45 "Re Communist Party of Canada—Winnipeg," Communist Party of Canada—Winnipeg RCMP File 117-91-67, 1930; "Winnipeg Communist Party Headquarters Were Raided," *The Worker*, 29 November 1930; "Statement of the District Board on the Maissonneuve Elections," LAC Comintern Fonds, Reel K284, File 141, 3.

46 Penner and Penner, "Recollections of the Early Socialist Movement in Winnipeg," 369.

CHAPTER 6: A BOMBSHELL TO MANY CITIZENS

1 *Winnipeg Free Press*, 24 November 1934.

2 By the 1930s, Vancouver had surpassed Winnipeg as the third largest city in Canada and the largest city in western Canada.

3 *Manitoba Commonwealth and Weekly News*, 4 January 1935.

4 In Manitoba's second largest city, the ILP experienced much less success. After peaking in 1928 with four of ten aldermen, the ILP was essentially a "spent force" by the early 1930s. See: Black, "Labour in Brandon Civic Politics: A Long View."

5 *Manitoba Commonwealth and Weekly News*, 4 January 1935.

6 *Winnipeg Tribune*, 10 November 1934.

7 *Winnipeg Free Press*, 17 November 1934.

8 *Winnipeg Tribune*, 15 November 1934.

9 McKillop, "The Socialist as Citizen: John Queen and the Mayoralty of Winnipeg, 1935."

10 Ibid.

11 City of Winnipeg, *Report of Commission on Assessment, Taxation, Etc.*, 16.

12 Ibid., 14.

13 *Winnipeg Tribune*, 10 November 1934.

14 Ibid.

15 *Winnipeg Free Press*, 20 November 1934.

16 McKillop, "The Socialist as Citizen: John Queen and the Mayoralty of Winnipeg, 1935."

17 *City of Winnipeg Municipal Manual, 1935*, 137.

18   *Manitoba Commonwealth and Weekly News*, 30 November 1934.

19   In a post-election article on Mayor-Elect John Queen, the *Winnipeg Tribune* speculated what a labour mayoralty would be like. Of key interest was what Queen would do with the mayoral limousine. Their rather humorous conclusion was that "he'll most likely ride in front with the chauffeur and stop to give friends a lift." See: *Winnipeg Tribune*, 24 November 1934.

20   Kendle, *John Bracken: A Political Biography*, 153.

21   *Annual Report of the Commissioner of Finance*, Winnipeg City Council, 30 and 32.

22   Winnipeg Real Estate Board, *The Tax Burden on Owners of Real Property; Submission to the Royal Commission on Dominion-Provincial Relations by the Winnipeg Real Estate Board* (1937), 10.

23   Brownstone and Plunkett, *Metropolitan Winnipeg*, 11.

24   *Annual Report of the Commissioner of Finance*, 9.

25   *Winnipeg Free Press*, 18 November 1936.

26   McKillop, "The Socialist as Citizen: John Queen and the Mayoralty of Winnipeg, 1935."

27   *Annual Report of the Commissioner of Finance*, 31. Despite increasing operating expenses from $3,653,213 to $4,067,168, the city was able to continue running balanced budgets, largely due to increased business taxes.

28   *Winnipeg Tribune*, 17 November 1934.

29   *Winnipeg Free Press*, 20 November 1936.

30   McKillop, "Citizen as Socialist: The Ethos of Political Winnipeg, 1919–1935," 220.

31   *Winnipeg Free Press*, 21 November 1935.

32   McKillop, "Citizen as Socialist: The Ethos of Political Winnipeg, 1919–1935," 222.

33   Committee on Legislation and Reception Files, City Archives of Winnipeg, CL+R 152 (12).

34   *Winnipeg Free Press*, 21 March 1935. Pitblado also was part of the Citizens' Committee of One Thousand during the 1919 General Strike and co-prosecutor of those arrested for their role in the Strike.

35   *Winnipeg Free Press*, 22 March 1935.

36   Quote from C.C. Ferguson of Great West Life in *Winnipeg Tribune*, 20 March 1935.

37   *Winnipeg Tribune*, 27 March 1935.

38   *Winnipeg Free Press*, 23 March 1935.

39   *Winnipeg Free Press*, 26 March 1935.

40   *Journals of the Legislative Assembly of Manitoba, 1935* (Winnipeg: King's Printer, 1935), 140.

41   *Winnipeg Free Press*, 15 April 1935.

42   Jules Preud'homme, "Re: Business Tax Rates," to G.F. Bentley, 7 March 1936, CL+R 152 (13), COWA.

43   *Annual Report of the Commissioner of Finance*, Winnipeg City Council, 32.

44   *Winnipeg Free Press*, 19 March 1935.

45   *Winnipeg Free Press*, 27 March 1935; *Journals of the Legislative Assembly of Manitoba, 1935*, 140.

46 Strikwerda, *The Wages of Relief*, 44.
47 Ibid., 42–3.
48 Goeres, "Disorder, Dependency, and Fiscal Responsibility," 284.
49 *Winnipeg Free Press*, 26 November 1934.
50 *Winnipeg Tribune*, 17 November 1934.
51 Winnipeg Board of Trade, "Policies and Projects For Putting Men to Work," 26 October 1936. G628 File 1056, AM.
52 *City Council Minutes, 1935*, Winnipeg City Council, 14 January 1935, motion 76, 27. The motion was carried without a roll call of votes.
53 Kendle, *John Bracken: A Political Biography*, 132.
54 *Winnipeg Free Press*, 20 November 1936.
55 Special Committee on Unemployment Relief, *City Council Minutes, 1935*, Winnipeg City Council, 22 April 1935, motion 415, 231.
56 Special Committee on Unemployment Relief, *City Council Minutes, 1935*, Winnipeg City Council, 23 September 1935, motion 966, 524.
57 Special Committee on Unemployment Relief, "Re Eye Glasses for Relief Recipients," *City Council Minutes*, 1936, COWA.
58 *City Council Minutes*, motion 341, 1935, COWA.
59 *City Council Minutes, 1935*, Winnipeg City Council, 4 June 1935, motion 553, 299. Yeas: Lowe, Flye, Anderson, Stobart, Simpkin, and Gray (all ILP) and Forkin and Penner (Communist). Nays: Honeyman, Rice-Jones, Gunn, Andrews, McWilliams, Bardal, Davidson, and Barry (all CEC).
60 "Winnipeg Chamber of Commerce Minutes: Council, Executive, General 1931–1935," MG10 A2 Box 13, Archives of Manitoba.
61 *Winnipeg Free Press*, 16 November 1934.
62 *City Council Minutes,* 1935, Winnipeg City Council, 14 January 1935, motion 82, 29.
63 Unemployed Railwaymen's Association, Letter to Winnipeg City Council, *City Council Minutes,* 1935, motion 1253, 691, COWA.
64 "Suggested List of Works Which Could be Undertaken as Unemployment Relief Projects," Unemployment Relief Works Files, A-14 (24), COWA.
65 *Winnipeg Free Press*, 28 August 1935; *Winnipeg Free Press* 24 June 1935.
66 *Winnipeg Tribune*, 1 November 1935.
67 Strikwerda, *The Wages of Relief*, 40.
68 Ibid., 175.
69 Hewitt, "'We Are Sitting At the Edge of a Volcano,'" 53.
70 *Winnipeg Free Press*, 27 June 1935.
71 *Winnipeg Tribune*, 15 November 1935.
72 *Manitoba Commonwealth*, 19 July 1935.
73 Quoted in Hewitt, "'We Are Sitting At the Edge of a Volcano,'" 60.
74 *Winnipeg Free Press*, 25 June 1935.

75 *City Council Minutes*, no. 87, 1935, COWA.

76 *City Council Minutes*, no. 640, 1935, COWA.

77 *City Council Minutes*, no. 758, 1935, COWA. This vote passed eight to seven. In favour were Aldermen Flye, Lowe, Anderson, Stobart, Forkin, Gray, Blumberg, and Penner. Opposed were Aldermen Rice-Jones, Andrews, Bardal, Honeyman, Davidson, Barry, and Simonite.

78 *Winnipeg Tribune*, 9 November 1936; A.B. Stuart, "letter to Committee on Legislation and Reception," 24 August 1936, CL+R 152 (13), COWA.

79 *City Council Minutes*, 19 October 1936, motion 1092, 700.

80 *City Council Minutes*, 10 August 1936, motion 842, 561.

81 *City Council Minutes*, 8 September 1936, motion 943, 618; *Winnipeg Free Press* 9 September 1936.

82 A.B. Stuart, "Letter to Winnipeg City Council," 24 August 1936, CL+R 152 (13), COWA.

83 *Winnipeg Free Press*, 9 November 1936.

84 *Labor Leader*, 25 April 1935.

85 *Winnipeg Free Press*, 3 January 1935.

86 *Winnipeg Free Press*, 22 May 1935; *Winnipeg Free Press*, 5 April 1935.

87 *City Council Minutes*, no. 789, 1935, COWA; *Winnipeg Free Press*, 3 August 1935.

88 Federation of Civic Employees, "Letter to City Council," 8 April, 1935, Letter 16169, Council Communications, COWA.

89 *Report of Professor M. A. Mackenzie on Actuarial Valuation of Civic Pension Fund As At December 31, 1933*, Winnipeg, 1934. Located in G623 Box 93 File 985, AM.

90 Jules Preud'homme, "Letter to MLAs." G623 Box 93 File 985, AM.

91 "Bylaw 14813," *Bylaws of the City of Winnipeg, 1936*, Winnipeg: Reynolds Printing Press, 1937.

92 *Winnipeg Free Press*, 19 March 1936.

93 Hugh Phillipps, "Letter to Law Amendments Committee," 4 April 1936. G623 Box 93 File 985, AM. Winnipeg firemen, who also belonged to the pension fund, urged the province to accept the bylaw. A letter to the Law Amendments Committee written on behalf of the 307 firemen said that the firemen "earnestly ask your Committee to adopt the suggestion of City Council." See: James Coupar, "Letter to Hon. W. J. Major, Chairman of the Law Amendments Committee," 4 April 1936. G623 Box 93 File 985, AM.

94 *Winnipeg Free Press*, 4 April 1936.

95 Phillipps, "Letter to John Bracken Re: Civic Pensions Bylaw 14813," 25 March 1936, G623 Box 93 File 985, AM.

96 Preud'homme, "Letter to MLAs." G623 Box 93 File 985, Archives of Manitoba. This number was reached because the City had made an initial contribution of $476,300 and, if an employee left municipal employment, they could withdraw their contributions but the contributions that the City for that worker remained in the fund. Preud'homme's calculations concluded that the value of City contributions in the fund was $3,200,420.82 compared with $1,464,673.17 contributed by employees.

97 *Winnipeg Free Press*, 31 March 1936.

98 *Winnipeg Free Press*, 17 March 1936. The Home and Property Owners' Association applauded the threat to fire civic employees if "employees will not listen to reason." *Winnipeg Free Press* 18 March 1936.

99 *Winnipeg Free Press*, 21 November 1936.

100 *Winnipeg Tribune*, 13 November 1936.

101 *Winnipeg Tribune*, 20 November 1936.

102 *Winnipeg Free Press*, 16 November 1936.

103 *Manitoba Commonwealth*, 20 November 1936.

104 John Blumberg quoted in *Winnipeg Tribune*, 3 November 1936.

105 *Manitoba Commonwealth*, 20 November 1936.

106 Artibise, *Winnipeg: A Social History of Modern Growth, 1874–1914*, 40. Artibise suggests that as a result of these rules, the commercial elite were essentially able to ignore the political opinions of much of Winnipeg's population who either could not vote or who only had a single vote. He compares this with provincial politics, where politicians had to work to get the vote of non-Anglo-Saxon voters, as everyone had one vote.

107 *Weekly News*, 6 March 1925.

108 Dagenais, "The Municipal Territory," 208.

109 *Winnipeg Free Press*, 30 March 1936; "Winnipeg Chamber of Commerce Minutes: Council, Executive, General 1936-1940," MG10 A2 Box 14, AM.

110 "Committee Gives Approval to Adult Suffrage in City," *Winnipeg Free Press*, 23 February 1935; *City Council Minutes*, no. 86, 1935, COWA; *City Council Minutes*, no. 142, 1936, COWA; Committee on Legislation and Reception Files, CL+R 152 (12), COWA. Voting rolls would have increased from 99,595 voters to approximately 132,400. It is interesting to think how the addition of over 30,000 voters, all of whom were non-property owners, to the municipal voting rolls could have radically altered the traditional Citizen-dominated political spectrum in the city.

111 *City Council Minutes*, no. 174, 1936, COWA. All CPC and ILP aldermen voted for the motion but Thomas Flye, an independent alderman with connections to labour, did not.

112 *Winnipeg Free Press*, 1 April 1935.

113 "Winnipeg Chamber of Commerce Minutes: Council, Executive, General 1936-1940," MG10 A2 Box 14, AM.

114 *Winnipeg Free Press*, 8 April 1936.

115 Kaplan, *Reform, Planning and City Politics*, 485.

116 *Winnipeg Free Press*, 5 December 1933.

117 Alexander Officer, "Report of the Fifteenth Annual Survey of Vacant Houses and Vacant Suites in the City Also Total Housing Accommodation and Remarks on Housing in General," January 1933, COWA, Public Health and Welfare File 1330.

118 Harris, "Working-Class Home Ownership and Housing Affordability Across Canada in 1931," 128. Winnipeggers paid an average of 26 percent of household income on rent, tied with Montreal for the highest in the country among major urban centres.

119 "Proposed Low-Cost Housing Development For the City of Winnipeg," *Journal of the Royal Architectural Institute of Canada (JRAIC)*, 109–12. It is interesting to note that out of the 16¾-acre site, seven and a half acres were to be dedicated to open parks.

120 "Proposed Low-Cost Housing Development For the City of Winnipeg," 109. Although all buildings were to be accessible by services lanes, there was to be no through traffic through the site.

121 Letter from the North Winnipeg Taxpayers Association to City Council, 15 May 1934, Council Communications File 15909, COWA.

122 The city managed to run "balanced budgets" throughout the 1930s with the exception of money borrowed to pay for unemployment relief. This annual loan amounted to over 10 percent of the city's income. See: *Annual Report of the Commissioner of Finance,* Winnipeg City Council, COWA, 9.

123 *Winnipeg Free Press,* 27 June 1934; Bacher, *Keeping to the Marketplace,* 73.

124 Bacher, *Keeping to the Marketplace,* 76.

125 *Winnipeg Free Press,* 22 June 1934.

126 *Winnipeg Free Press,* 27 December 1934.

127 *Winnipeg Free Press,* 21 February 1935; *Winnipeg Free Press,* 7 March 1935; *Winnipeg Tribune,* 21 February 1935. ILP Aldermen Morris Gray and James Simpkin were joined by the CPC Jacob Penner in support of the proposal. Cecil Gunn, a 'Citizen' alderman, was opposed. Margaret McWilliams, who was not officially a 'Citizen' alderman but often voted with them, abstained.

128 *Winnipeg Free Press,* 19 March 1935.

129 *Winnipeg Tribune,* 7 March 1935.

130 *Winnipeg Tribune,* 12 March 1935.

131 Friesen, *The Canadian Prairies,* 403.

132 R.A. Sara, "Address Before the Technical Bureau, Winnipeg Board of Trade," 8 April 1937, COWA, Housing Folder 10.

133 Kinnear, *Margaret McWilliams,* 117 and 127–8.

134 Area One ran from the Assiniboine River to Notre Dame Avenue and from the Red River to Sherbrook Street. Area Two included from Notre Dame Avenue to the CPR tracks and Burrows Avenue and from the Red River to Sherbrook Street and Main Street.

135 Valverde, *The Age of Light, Soap, and Water,* 132.

136 Ibid., 47.

137 *Winnipeg Free Press,* 19 January 1938.

138 *Report of the Lieutenant-Governor's Committee On Housing Conditions in Toronto,* Urban Policy Archive, Centre for Urban and Community Studies, University of Toronto, http://www.urbancentre.utoronto.ca/pdfs/policyarchives/1934HerbertBruce.pdf.

139 Alexander Officer, House of Commons Special Committee on Housing, Minutes and Proceedings of Evidence, No. 6, 21 March 1935.

140 *City Council Minutes,* 21 October 1935, COWA.

141 *Winnipeg Tribune,* 14 November 1935.

142 *Winnipeg Tribune,* 15 November 1935.

143 *Winnipeg Tribune,* 14 November 1935.

144 *Winnipeg Tribune,* 21 November 1935.

145 *Winnipeg Tribune*, 15 November 1935.

146 *Winnipeg Tribune*, 21 November 1935.

147 "Winnipeg Chamber of Commerce Minutes: Council, Executive, General, 1931-1935," MG 10 A2 Box 13, AM.

148 *Winnipeg Tribune*, 20 November 1935.

149 Beck, "Some Election Practices Worse Than Impersonation," *Winnipeg Tribune*, 16 November 1935.

150 "The Housing Scheme," *The Home Owner*, 15 December 1935, 1, located in Communist Party of Canada—Manitoba Archives, Election Bulletins 1930–1935.

151 "The Housing Scheme," *The Home Owner*, 15 December 1935, located in Communist Party of Canada—Manitoba Archives, Election Bulletins 1930–1935.

152 For example, long-time city Alderman Charles Simonite had previously served on the HPOA executive. With such connections in city hall it is not surprising that the organization wielded significant influence.

153 Jill Wade's study of housing debates in Vancouver illustrates a similar trend in that city, where left-wing politicians, middle-class social reformers, church groups and women's organizations argued for municipal housing schemes and were opposed by the business elite and property owners groups. See: Wade, *Houses for All: The Struggle for Social Housing in Vancouver, 1919–1950*. Other studies which have seriously engaged the history of Canadian housing policy prior to the Second World War include: David Hulchanski, "The 1935 Dominion Housing Act: Setting the Stage for a Permanent Federal Presence in Canada's Housing Sector," *Urban History Review* 15 (1986): 19–39; Richard Harris, "Working-class Home Ownership and Housing Affordability Across Canada in 1931," *Histoire sociale—Social History* 19 (1986): 121–38; Harris, *Creeping Conformity: How Canada Became Suburban, 1900–1960*; John Belec, "The Dominion Housing Act: A Study of the Origins of Canadian Housing Policy,"; Kamal S. Sayegh, *Housing: A Canadian Perspective*.

154 Bylaw 14777," *Bylaws of the City of Winnipeg, 1935*, 127; *Winnipeg Free Press*, 3 October 1935.

155 *Manitoba Commonwealth*, 29 November 1935.

156 "Report of Special Committee on Housing Conditions," COWA, Housing Folder 7. Jill Wade has demonstrated how the frustration with federal housing legislation led community groups to launch campaigns for social housing in Vancouver. See Wade, 74. This appears to be similar to the conditions described here in Winnipeg.

157 *City Council Minutes*, no. 224, 1936, COWA.

158 *Winnipeg Free Press*, 3 March 1936.

159 Winnipeg City Council, "The Need for Housing," in the *City Council Minutes*, 16 May 1938, 387.

160 See: Epp, "Class, Capitalism and Construction," 393–428.

161 *Winnipeg Free Press*, 8 November 1934.

162 *City Council Minutes*, 24 February 1936, COWA.

163 *Winnipeg Free Press*, 2 February 1936; *Winnipeg Free Press*, 3 March 1936.

164 *Winnipeg Free Press*, 15 November 1935.

165 *Winnipeg Free Press*, 5 March 1936.

166 *Manitoba Commonwealth*, 29 November 1935

167 See: Brennan, "'The common people have spoken with a mighty voice,'" 49–86; Warren and Carlisle, *On the Side of the People*, 124; Pitsula, "The Mixed Social Economy of Unemployment Relief in Regina During the 1930s," 120–1.

168 Warren and Carlisle, *On the Side of the People*, 124.

169 Bright, *The Limits of Labour*, 172–7.

170 Finkel, "The Rise and Fall of the Labor Party in Alberta, 1917–1942," 86–7; Masson and Lesage, Jr., *Alberta's Local Governments*, 282.

171 Finkel and Strikwerda, "War, Repression and Depression, 1914–1939," 98.

172 Finkel, "The Rise and Fall of the Labor Party in Alberta, 1917–1942," 87.

173 *Winnipeg Free Press*, 21 November 1935.

174 *Winnipeg Tribune*, 8 November 1935.

175 *Winnipeg Free Press*, 23 November 1935.

176 *Winnipeg Free Press*, 26 September 1936.

177 *Winnipeg Tribune*, 25 November 1936.

178 *Winnipeg Tribune*, 23 November, 1936.

179 *Winnipeg Tribune*, 14 November, 1936.

180 *Manitoba Commonwealth*, 23 October 1936.

181 *Manitoba Commonwealth*, 29 November 1935.

182 The electoral system used by Winnipeg in the 1930s for both aldermanic and mayoralty elections was a transferrable ballot system. Voters would mark their voting preferences and after each ballot the candidate with the fewest votes was dropped from the list and the next preference of each of their supporters was added to the total of the remaining candidates. This process was repeated until a candidate received a majority of the votes.

183 *City of Winnipeg Municipal Manual, 1937*, 138.

184 *Winnipeg Mid-West Clarion*, 30 September 1939. Although this article was written in 1939, it suitably describes the political realities of 1935 and 1936.

185 Quoted in Gutkin and Gutkin, *Profiles in Dissent*, 378.

186 Ibid., 380.

187 *Winnipeg Free Press*, 15 November 1934.

188 *Winnipeg Free Press*, 2 October 1936.

189 McKillop, "Citizen as Socialist: The Ethos of Political Winnipeg, 1919–1935," 241.

190 *Winnipeg Tribune*, 17 November 1936.

CONCLUSION

1 Lloyd Stinson quoted in Lightbody, "Electoral Reform in Local Government," 315.

2 Queen-Hughes would win only 10 percent of the vote in a head-to-head race with popular incumbent and long-time Winnipeg mayor Steve Juba. This remained the highest percentage

of the vote a woman had won in a Winnipeg mayoral race until Susan Thompson was elected in 1992.

3   Bercuson, *Confrontation at Winnipeg*, 176.
4   McKay, *Reasoning Otherwise*, 493.
5   Mitchell and Naylor, "The Prairies," 216.
6   Ibid., 215.
7   McKay, *Reasoning Otherwise*, 493.
8   Quoted in Korneski, "Liberalism in Winnipeg," 192.
9   McCormack, *Reformers, Rebels and Revolutionaries*, 170.
10 McKay, *Reasoning Otherwise*, 457.
11 An example of the different level of polarization between Winnipeg and other Canadian cities is that in Edmonton, one-time labour mayor Dan Knott would run for city council on a pro-business ticket later in the 1930s. It is difficult to imagine a labour leader in Winnipeg running as a Citizen.

BIBLIOGRAPHY

PRIMARY SOURCES

Articles and Books

Bruce, Herbert. *Report of the Lieutenant-Governor's Committee on Housing Conditions in Toronto.* Urban Policy Archive, Centre for Urban Community Studies, University of Toronto. http://www.urbancentre.utoronto.ca/pdfs/policyarchives/1934HerbertBruce.pdf.

Bylaws of the City of Winnipeg, 1935. Winnipeg: De Montfort Press, 1936.

Bylaws of the City of Winnipeg, 1936. Winnipeg: Reynolds Printing Press, 1937.

City of Winnipeg. *Annual Report of the Commissioner of Finance.* Winnipeg, 1936.

City of Winnipeg. *Report of Commission on Assessment, Taxation, etc.* Winnipeg, 1934.

City of Winnipeg Health Department. *Report on Housing Survey of Certain Selected Areas: Made March and April 1921.*

Co-operative Commonwealth Federation, *The First Ten Years, 1932–1942: Commemorating the Tenth Anniversary of the Co-operative Commonwealth Federation at the Seventh National Convention.* Ottawa: CCF National Office, 1942.

Executive Committee of the Communist International. *Capitalist Stabilization Has Ended: Theses and Resolutions of the Twelfth Plenum of the Executive Committee of the Communist International.* New York: Workers Library Publishers, 1932.

Fried, Albert, ed. *Communism in America: A History in Documents.* New York: Columbia University Press, 1997.

Journals of the Legislative Assembly of Manitoba, 1935. Winnipeg: King's Printer, 1935.

Kealey, Gregory S. and Reg Whitaker, eds. *RCMP Security Bulletins, The Depression Years, Part I, 1933–1934.* St John's: Canadian Committee on Labour History, 1993.

Kolisnyk, William. "In Canada Since the Spring of 1898." *Marxist Review* 18 (January-February 1961): 37–40.

Krawchuk, Peter. *Interned Without Cause.* http://www.socialisthistory.ca/Docs/CPC/WW2/IWC00.htm.

McEwen, Tom. *The Forge Glows Red.* Toronto: Progress Books, 1974.

Morris, Leslie. *Look on Canada Now: Selected Writings of Leslie Morris, 1923–1964.* Toronto: Progress Books, 1970.

Penner, Jacob, and Norman Penner. "Recollections of the Early Socialist Movement in Winnipeg." *Histoire Sociale—Social History* 14 (November 1974): 366–78.

"Proposed Low-Cost Housing Development for the City of Winnipeg." *Journal of the Royal Architectural Institute of Canada* (July-August 1934): 109–12.

Report of the Royal Commission on the Municipal Finances and Administration of the City of Winnipeg, 1937. H.C. Goldenberg, Chair. Winnipeg: King's Printer, 1939.

Smith, Stewart. *Comrades and Komsomolkas.* Toronto: Lugus Publications, 1993.

———. *Socialism and the CCF.* Montreal: Contemporary Publishing Association, 1934.

Winnipeg General Strike Defence Committee. *Saving the World From Democracy*. 1920.
Winnipeg Real Estate Board. *The Tax Burden on Owners of Real Property*. 1937.

City of Winnipeg Archives (COWA)
City Council Minutes, 1924–1936.
City of Winnipeg Municipal Manual, 1919–1939.
Housing Folders, 1, 7, 10, 18.
Legislation and Reception Committee Files.
Public Utilities Committee Files, PU 346.
Unemployment Relief Works Files.

Communist Party of Canada—Manitoba Archives (CPC-MA)
Election Bulletins Scrapbook, 1930–1935.

Interview by the Author
Roland Penner. Interviewed 13 December 2007.

Library and Archives Canada (LAC)
A.A. Heaps Fonds.
Communist International Fonds. Microfilm Reels K274-K290.
Communist Party of Canada Fonds. Microfilm Reels M7376-M7413.
Housing Folder 2.
"Letter from 'Vigilante Committee of Winnipeg.'" 18 March 1935. RG13 vol. 738 513057.
Mackenzie King Papers, Reel 3734.
RB Bennett Collection. Microfilm Reel M–1433.

Archives of Manitoba (AM)
Attorney General Miscellaneous Files, Communist Activity, 1931–1936.
Doug Smith Collection. C407—C409.
    Independent Labour Party Fonds, MG14-D4.
    Interview with Fred Tipping, C831.
Jules Preud'homme Fonds. MG14 C72.
Letter from Jacob Penner to Norman Penner. P599–4.
Margaret McWilliams, "An Investigation into Certain Social Housing Conditions in Winnipeg," File 1056 G628.
Premier's Office Files [John Bracken].
Winnipeg Chamber of Commerce Fonds.

RCMP Archival Files
Communist Party of Canada—Winnipeg, File 117–91–67.

Communist Party of Canada—Winnipeg, File 117-91-94.
Jacob Penner, File 117-89-57.
Martin Forkin, File 119-91-22.
Matthew Popovich, File 117-89-39.
William Kolisnyk, File 117-89-39.

University of Manitoba Archives (UMA)
Ed Rea Collection. MSS 73 Box 1, Files 1-9.

NEWSPAPERS

Canadian Press Newswire
Labour Leader
Manitoba Commonwealth
Manitoba Commonwealth and Weekly News
Manitoba Free Press/Winnipeg Free Press
The North Ender
North Winnipeg Elector
OBU Bulletin
The Civic Elector
The Worker
The Workers Vanguard
Voice of Labour
Weekly News
Western Labour News
Winnipeg Mid-West Clarion
Winnipeg Tribune
Winnipeg Typo News
Workers' Unity

SECONDARY LITERATURE

Angus, Ian. *Canadian Bolsheviks: The Early Years of the Communist Party of Canada*. Victoria: Trafford Publishing, 2004.

Armstrong, Christopher and H.V. Nelles. *Monopoly's Moment: The Organization and Regulation of Canadian Utilities, 1830-1930*. Philadelphia: Temple University Press, 1986.

Artibise, Alan. *Winnipeg: A Social History of Modern Growth, 1874-1914*. Kingston: McGill-Queen's University Press, 1975.

———. "Patterns of Population Growth and Ethnic Relationships in Winnipeg, 1874–1974." *Histoire-Sociale—Social History* 9 (November 1976): 297–335.

———. *Winnipeg: An Illustrated History*. Toronto: James Lorimer and Co, 1977.

Artibise, Alan, and Gilbert Stelter, eds. *The Usable Urban Past: Planning and Politics in the Modern Canadian City*. Toronto: Macmillan Company of Canada, 1979.

Avakumovic, Ivan. *The Communist Party in Canada: A History*. Toronto: McClelland and Stewart, 1975.

Bacher, John C. *Keeping to the Marketplace: The Evolution of Canadian Housing Policy*. Montreal and Kingston: McGill-Queen's University Press, 1993.

Barrett, James R. "The History of American Communism and Our Understanding of Stalinism." *American Communist History* 2 (December 2003): 175–82.

———. *William Z. Foster and the Tragedy of American Radicalism*. Chicago: University of Illinois Press, 2002.

Beaulieu, Michel C. "A Proletarian Prometheus: Socialism, Ethnicity, and Revolution at the Lakehead, 1930–1935." PhD thesis. Queen's University Press, 2007.

Belec, John Patrick. "The Dominion Housing Act: A Study of the Origins of Canadian Housing Policy." PhD Thesis, Queen's University, 1988.

Bellan, Ruben. *Winnipeg, First Century: An Economic History*. Winnipeg: Queenston House Publishing Company, 1978.

Bercuson, David J. *Confrontation at Winnipeg: Labour, Industrial Relations, and the General Strike*, 2nd edition. Kingston: McGill-Queen's University Press, 1990.

Betcherman, Lita-Rose. *The Little Band*. Ottawa: Deneau, 1982.

Black, Errol. "Brandon's 'Revolutionary Forkins,'" *Prairie Forum* 20 (2, 1995): 255–79.

———. "Labour in Brandon Civic Politics: A Long View," *Manitoba History* 23 (Spring 1992).

———. "The Forkin Letters." *Manitoba History* 56 (October 2007). http://www.mhs.mb.ca/docs/mb_history/56/forkinletters.shtml.

Black, Errol, and Tom Mitchell. *A Square Deal for All and No Railroading: Historical Essays on Labour in Brandon*. Edmonton: Athabasca University Press, 2000.

Brennan, J. William. "'The Common People Have Spoken With a Mighty Voice': Regina's Labour City Councils, 1936–1939." *Labour/Le Travail* 71 (Spring 2013): 49–86.

Bright, David. *The Limits of Labour: Class Formation and the Labour Movement in Calgary, 1883–1929*. Vancouver: UBC Press, 1998.

———. "The State, the Unemployed, and the Communist Party in Calgary, 1930–1935." *The Canadian Historical Review* 78 (December 1997): 537–65.

Brownstone, Meyer, and T.J. Plunkett. *Metropolitan Winnipeg: Politics and Reform of Local Government*. Berkeley: University of California Press, 1983.

Buckner, Phillip, and R. Douglas Francis, eds. *Canada and the British World: Culture, Migration and Identity*. Vancouver: UBC Press, 2006.

Bumsted, J.M., ed. *Dictionary of Manitoba Biography*. Winnipeg: University of Manitoba Press, 1999.

Butler, Nancy. "Mother Russia and the Socialist Fatherland: Women and the Communist Party of Canada, 1932–1941, with specific reference to the activism of Dorothy Livesay and Jim Watts." PhD thesis. Queen's University, 2010.

Constant, Jean Francois, and Michel Ducharme, eds. *Liberalism and Hegemony: Debating the Canadian Liberal Revolution*. Toronto: University of Toronto Press, 2009.

Cook, Ramsay. *The Politics of John W. Dafoe and the* Free Press. Toronto: University of Toronto Press, 1963.

Draper, Theodore. *American Communism and Soviet Russia, The Formative Years*. New York: Viking Press, 1960.

Dupuis, Michael. *Winnipeg's General Strike: Report from the Front Lines*. London: The History Press, 2014.

Endicott, Stephen. *Bienfait: The Saskatchewan Miners' Struggle of '31*. Toronto: University of Toronto Press, 2002.

———. *Raising the Workers' Flag: The Workers' Unity League of Canada, 1930–1936*. Toronto: University of Toronto Press, 2012.

Epp, Stefan. "A Communist in the Council Chambers: Communist Municipal Politics, Ethnicity, and the Career of William Kolisnyk." *Labour/Le Travail* 63 (Spring 2009): 79–104.

———. "Class, Capitalism and Construction: Winnipeg's Housing Crisis and the Debate Over Public Housing, 1934–1939." *Histoire Sociale—Social History* 86 (November 2010): 393–428.

———. "'Fighting for the Everyday Interests of Winnipeg Workers': Jacob Penner, Martin Forkin and the Communist Party in Winnipeg Politics, 1930–1935." *Manitoba History* 63 (Spring 2010): 14–26.

Fine, Jonathan. "Anti-Semitism in Manitoba in the 1930s and 1940s." *Manitoba History* 32 (Autumn 1996). http://www.mhs.mb.ca/docs/mb_history/32/manitobaantisemitism.shtml.

Finkel, Alvin. "The Rise and Fall of the Labour Party in Alberta, 1917–1942. *Labour/Le Travail* 16 (Fall 1985): 61–96.

———. *Working People in Alberta*. Edmonton: Athabasca University Press, 2012.

Frank, David. "Company Town/Labour Town: Local Government in the Cape Breton Coal Towns, 1917–1926." *Histoire Sociale—Social History* 27 (May 1981): 177–196.

———. *Provincial Solidarities: A History of the New Brunswick Federation of Labour*. Edmonton: Athabasca University Press, 2013.

Franz, Kyle. "Painting the Town Red: The 'Communist' Administration at Blairmore, Alberta, 1933–1936." M.A. thesis, University of Lethbridge, 2007.

Friesen, Gerald. *The Canadian Prairies: A History*. Toronto: University of Toronto Press, 1984.

Goeres, Michael R. "Disorder, Dependency, and Fiscal Responsibility: Unemployment Relief in Winnipeg, 1907–1942." M.A. thesis, University of Manitoba, 1981.

Gutkin, Harry, and Mildred Gutkin. *Profiles in Dissent: The Shaping of Radical Thought in the Canadian West*. Edmonton: NeWest Press, 1997.

Harris, Richard. *Creeping Conformity: How Canada Became Suburban, 1900–1960*. Toronto: University of Toronto Press, 2004.

———. "Working-Class Home Ownership and Housing Affordability Across Canada in 1931." *Histoire Sociale-Social History* 19 (May 1986): 121–38.

Haynes, John Earl, and Harvey Klehr. "The Historiography of American Communism: An Unsettled Field." *Labour History Review* 68 (April 2003): 61–78.

Heaps, Leo. *The Rebel in the House: The Life and Times of A.A. Heaps*. London: Niccolo Publishing Company, 1970.

Heron, Craig, ed. *The Workers' Revolt in Canada, 1917–1925*. Toronto: University of Toronto Press, 1998.

Hewitt, Steve. "Royal Canadian Mounted Spy: The Secret Life of John Leopold/Jack Esselwein." *Intelligence and National Security* 15 (Spring 2000): 144–68.

———. "'We Are Sitting At The Edge of a Volcano': Winnipeg During the On-to-Ottawa Trek." *Prairie Forum* 19 (1994): 51–64.

Hiebert, Daniel. "Class, ethnicity, and residential structure: the social geography of Winnipeg, 1901–1921." *Journal of Historical Geography* 17 (1991): 56–86.

Hinther, Rhonda L., and Jim Mochoruk, eds. *Re-Imagining Ukrainian Canadians: History, Politics and Identity*. Toronto: University of Toronto Press, 2011.

Hulchanski, David. "The 1935 Dominion Housing Act: Setting the Stage for a Permanent Federal Presence in Canada's Housing Sector." *Urban History Review* 15 (June 1986): 19–39.

Irvine, Duncan. "Reform, war, and industrial crisis in Manitoba: FJ Dixon and the framework of consensus, 1903–1920." M.A. thesis, University of Manitoba, 1981.

Jones, Esyllt. *Influenza 1918: Disease, Death and Struggle in Winnipeg*. Toronto: University of Toronto Press, 2008.

Kaplan, Harold. *Reform, Planning and City Politics*. Toronto: University of Toronto Press, 1982.

Kealey, Gregory. "1919: The Canadian Labour Revolt." *Labour/Le Travail* 13 (Spring 1984): 11–44.

Kendle, John. *John Bracken: A Political Biography*. Toronto: University of Toronto Press, 1979.

Kinnear, Mary. *Margaret McWilliams: An Interwar Feminist*. Montreal and Kingston: McGill-Queen's University Press, 1991.

Korneski, Kurt. "Liberalism in Winnipeg, 1890s–1920s: Charles W. Gordon, John W. Dafoe, Minnie J.B. Campbell, and Francis M. Beynon." PhD thesis. Memorial University of Newfoundland, 2004.

———. "Prairie Fire: The Winnipeg General Strike." *Labour/Le Travail* 45 (Spring 2000): 259–66.

Kramer, Reinhold, and Tom Mitchell. *When the State Trembled: How A.J. Andrews and the Citizens' Committee Broke the Winnipeg General Strike*. Toronto: University of Toronto Press, 2010.

Lightbody, James. "Electoral Reform in Local Government: The Case of Winnipeg." *Canadian Journal of Political Studies* 11 (June 1978): 307–332.

Lyons, Paul. *Philadelphia Communists, 1936–1956*. Philadelphia: Temple University Press, 1982.

Manley, John. "Canadian Communists, Revolutionary Unionism, and the 'Third Period': The Workers' Unity League, 1929–1935." *Journal of the Canadian Historical Association* 16 (1994): 167–91.

Martynowych, Orest. *Ukrainians in Canada: The Formative Years, 1891–1921*. Edmonton: Canadian Institute of Ukrainian Studies Press, 1991.

Masson, Jack, and Edward C. Lesage, Jr. *Alberta's Local Governments: Politics and Democracy*. Edmonton: University of Alberta Press, 1994.

Masters, D.C. *The Winnipeg General Strike*. Toronto: University of Toronto Press, 1950.

McCormack, A. Ross. "Arthur Puttee and the Liberal Party, 1899–1904." *Canadian Historical Review* 51 (June 1970): 141–63.

———. "Radical Politics in Winnipeg: 1899–1915." *MHS Transactions* 3 (1972–1973). http://www.mhs.mb.ca/docs/transactions/3/radicalpolitics.shtml#70.

——. *Reformers, Rebels, and Revolutionaries: The Western Canadian Radical Movement, 1899–1919*. Toronto: University of Toronto Press, 1977.

McDermott, Kevin, and Jeremy Agnew. *The Comintern: A History of International Communism from Lenin to Stalin*. Basingstoke: Macmillan Press, 1996.

McIlroy, John, and Alan Campbell. "'Nina Ponomareva's Hats': The New Revisionism, the Communist International and the Communist Party of Great Britain, 1920–1930." *Labour/Le Travail* 49 (Spring 2002): 147–87.

McKay, Ian. *Reasoning Otherwise: Leftists and the People's Enlightenment in Canada, 1890–1920*. Toronto: Between The Lines, 2008.

McKillop, A.B. "A Communist in City Hall." *Canadian Dimension* (April 1974): 41–50.

——. "Citizen as Socialist: The Ethos of Political Winnipeg, 1919–1935." M.A. thesis, University of Manitoba, 1970.

——. "The Socialist as Citizen: John Queen and the Mayoralty of Winnipeg, 1935." *MHS Transactions Series* 3 No. 30 (1973–4).

McNaught, Kenneth, *A Prophet in Politics: A Biography of JS Woodsworth*. Toronto: University of Toronto Press, 1959.

McNaught, Kenneth and David J Bercuson. *The Winnipeg General Strike: 1919*. Don Mills: Longman Canada Ltd, 1974.

Mills, Allen. *Fool for Christ: The Political Thought of JS Woodsworth*. Toronto: University of Toronto Press, 1991.

——. "Single Tax, Socialism, and the Independent Labour Party of Manitoba: The Political Ideas of F.J. Dixon and S.J. Farmer." *Labour/Le Travail* 5 (Spring 1980): 33–56

Mochoruk, James. *The People's Co-op: The Life and Times of a North End Institution*. Halifax: Fernwood Publishing, 2006.

Morton, W.L. *Manitoba: A History*. Toronto: University of Toronto Press, 1957.

Naison, Mark. *Communists in Harlem During the Depression*. Chicago: University of Illinois Press, 1983.

Nelles, H.V. "Public Ownership of Electrical Utilities in Manitoba and Ontario, 1906–1930." *Canadian Historical Review* 57 (December 1976): 464–83.

Palmer, Bryan. *James P. Cannon and the Origins of the American Revolutionary Left, 1890–1928*. Chicago: University of Illinois Press, 2007.

——. "Rethinking the Historiography of United States Communism." *American Communist History* 2 (December 2003): 139–73.

——. *Working-Class Experience: The Rise and Reconstitution of Canadian Labour, 1800–1980*. Toronto: Butterworth and Co., 1983.

Penner, Norman. *Canadian Communism: The Stalin Years and Beyond*. Toronto: Methuen, 1988.

——. *The Canadian Left: A Critical Analysis*. Scarborough: Prentice Hall Canada, 1977.

——. *Winnipeg 1919: The Strikers' Own History of the Winnipeg General Strike*, 2nd edition. Toronto: James Lorimer and Company, 1975.

Penner, Roland. *A Glowing Dream: A Memoir*. Winnipeg: J. Gordon Shillingford, 2007.

——. "Personal Perspective on Rose Penner." In *Jewish Radicalism in Winnipeg, 1905–1960*, ed. Daniel Stone. Winnipeg: Jewish Heritage Centre of Western Canada, 2002.

Petryshyn, J. "Class Conflict and Civil Liberties: The Origins and Activities of the Canadian Labour Defense League, 1925–1940," *Labour/Le Travail* 10 (Autumn 1982): 39–63.

Pitsula, James M. "The Mixed Social Economy of Unemployment Relief in Regina During the 1930s." *Journal of the Canadian Historical Association* 14 (2004): 97–122.

Rea, J.E. *Parties and Power: An Analysis of Winnipeg City Council, 1919–1975*. Winnipeg: Department of Urban Affairs, Province of Manitoba, 1976.

———. *The Winnipeg General Strike*. Toronto: Holt, Rinehart and Winston of Canada, Ltd, 1973.

Reilly, Nolan. "Introduction to Papers from the Winnipeg General Strike Symposium, March 1983." *Labour/Le Travail* 13 (Spring 1984): 7–10.

Roberts, Barbara. "Shovelling Out the 'Mutinous': Political Deportation from Canada Before 1936." *Labour/Le Travail* 18 (Fall 1986): 77–110.

———. "Shovelling Out the Unemployed." *Manitoba History* 5 (Spring 1983): 12–24.

———. *Whence They Came: Deportation from Canada, 1900–1935*. Ottawa: University of Ottawa Press, 1988.

Rodney, William. *Soldiers of the International: A History of the Communist Party of Canada, 1919–1929*. Toronto: University of Toronto Press, 1968.

Sangster, Joan. "*Robitnytsia*, Ukrainian Communists and the 'Porcupinism' Debate: Reassessing Ethnicity, Gender, and Class in Early Canadian Communism, 1922–1930." *Labour/Le Travail* 56 (Fall 2005): 51–89.

Sayegh, Kamal S. *Housing: A Canadian Perspective*. Ottawa: Academy Books, 1987.

Smith, Andrea B. "The CCF, NPA, and Civic Change: Political Forces Behind Vancouver Politics, 1930–1940." *BC Studies* 53 (Spring 1982): 45–65.

Smith, Doug. *Joe Zuken: Citizen and Socialist*. Toronto: James Lorimer & Company, 1990.

———. *Let Us Rise! An Illustrated History of the Manitoba Labour Movement*. Vancouver: New Star Books, 1985.

Solomon, Mark. *The Cry Was Unity: Communists and African-Americans, 1917–1936*. Jackson: University of Mississippi, 1998.

Stelter, Gilbert A., and Alan Artibise, eds. *Shaping the Urban Landscape: Aspects of Canadian City-Building Process*. Ottawa: Carleton University Press, 1982.

———. *The Canadian City: Essays in Urban and Social History*, 2nd edition. Kingston and Montreal: McGill-Queen's University Press, 1984.

Stinson, Lloyd. *Political Warriors: Recollections of a Social Democrat*. Winnipeg: Queenston House, 1975.

Stokes, Lawrence D. "Fact or Fiction? German Writer A.E. Johann, a Winnipeg Communist, and the Depression in the Canadian West, 1931–1932." *Labour/Le Travail* (Spring 2006): 131–42.

Stone, Daniel, ed. *Jewish Radicalism in Winnipeg, 1905–1960*. Winnipeg: Jewish Heritage Centre of Western Canada, 2002.

Storch, Randi. "Moscow's Archives and the New History of the Communist Party of the United States." *Perspectives* (2000). http://www.historians.org.proxy.queensu.ca/perspectives/issues/2000/0010/0010arc1.cfm.

———. *Red Chicago: American Communism at its Grassroots*. Chicago: University of Illinois Press, 2007.

Strikwerda, Eric. *The Wages of Relief: Cities and the Unemployed in Prairie Canada, 1929–1939*. Edmonton: Athabasca University Press, 2013.

Struthers, James. *No Fault of their Own: Unemployment and the Canadian Welfare State, 1914–1941*. Toronto: University of Toronto Press, 1983.

Thompson, John H. "The Political Career of Ralph H Webb." *Red River Valley Historical Society* (Summer 1976): 1–7.

Thorpe, Andrew. "Comintern 'Control' of the Communist Party of Great Britain, 1920–1943." *The English Historical Review* 113 (June 1998): 637–662.

Tulchinsky, Gerald. *Taking Root: The Origins of the Canadian Jewish Community*. Toronto: Lester Publishing, 1992.

Valverde, Mariana. *The Age of Light, Soap and Water: Moral Reform in English Canada, 1885–1925*. Toronto: McClelland and Stewart, 1991.

Van Ree, Erik. *The Political Thought of Joseph Stalin: A Study in Twentieth-Century Revolutionary Patriotism*. New York: Routledge Curzon, 2002.

Wade, Jill. *Housing for All: The Struggle for Social Housing in Vancouver, 1919–1950*. Vancouver: UBC Press, 1994.

Warren, Jim and Kathleen Carlisle. *On the Side of the People: A History of Labour in Saskatchewan*. Regina: Coteau Books, 2005.

Weaver, John. *Shaping the Canadian City: Essays on Urban Politics and Policy, 1890–1920*. Toronto: Institute of Public Administration of Canada, 1977.

Wichern, P.H. "Historical Influences on Contemporary Local Politics: The Case of Winnipeg," *Urban History Review* 12 (June 1983); 39–43.

Wiseman, Nelson. *Social Democracy in Manitoba: A History of the CCF-NDP*. Winnipeg: University of Manitoba Press, 1986.

Wiseman, Nelson, and K.W. Taylor. "Ethnic vs Class Voting: The Case of Winnipeg, 1945." *Canadian Journal of Political Science* 2 (June 1974): 314–28.

INDEX

A

Anderson, Victor, 120, 122, 126, 141
Ashbrook, George, 167n125

B

Barry, James, 95, 133
Bennett, R.B., 112, 114, 132–33
Bilecki, Andrew, 109
Blumberg, John: dealings with CPC, 77, 79, 98; on free speech issues, 94; as Jewish ILP member, 32; length of civic service, 19, 145; and On-To-Ottawa trekkers, 125; on paying part of salary to ILP, 74; on police repression, 113; seconding motion on agricultural labourers, 165n97
Blumenberg, Sam, 6
Bobiwski, Stanley, 68, 69
Bracken, John, 110, 111, 122, 123, 127, 128
Bradshaw Report, 104, 117–18, 171n104
Buck, Tim, 73, 77, 94

C

Calgary municipal government, 139
Canada, Government of, 123, 132–33, 137
Canadian Nationalist Party, 95, 170n53
Citizen Group: background and mandate of, 22–25; and business taxes, 121–22; and central heating facility, 47–49; changing ward system, 37–39; connection to WEC, 41–42, 46; CPC tactics against, 67, 113; and deportations, 97; and Depression relief, 123, 124; and housing, 131–32, 133, 136–37; and labour issues, 126; on 1922 council, 44; and 1922 election campaign, 40–43; and 1923 election campaign, 49–51, 52; and 1924 election, 56–57; mayoral campaign of 1934, 104–5; political use of fear of revolution, 111–12; during S.J. Farmer's second term, 52, 53–54. *See also* Webb, Ralph
Citizens' Committee of One Thousand, 3, 6, 20–21, 22, 112
Civic Labour League (CLL), 138–39
Comintern, 61–63, 63–64
communism: Citizens' Group view of, 25; and Popular Front, 103; and Third Period, 61–63, 69, 97, 101–2; traditionalists v. revisionists, 63–64
Communist Party of Canada (CPC): attacks on ILP, 77–80, 84, 94, 98, 102–3, 113, 114, 147–48, 174n43; attitude toward royalty, 97–98; background of, 33–35, 91, 157n83; and change of wards, 37–39; election of W. Kolisnyk, 59–60, 68, 71, 72–74, 82–83; and electoral reform, 131; ethnic troubles within, 68–72, 87; fight for free speech, 93–96; Jewish-Ukrainian tensions in, 69–70, 164n69; legacy of council work, 145–46; mayoral campaign of 1934, 118; and municipalization of services, 138; in 1923 election, 50; in 1926 election, 66–67; in 1936 election, 143; offer of support to J. Queen, 104; paranoia about, 106–7, 110–11; police intimidation and oppression of, 86, 107, 109, 110–11, 112–15, 173n25; and public housing, 137; record in municipal politics across Canada, 60–61; revolutionary goals of, 15, 88–89, 107–11; rise of as municipal force, 5, 15, 58; rivalry with ILP, 16, 58, 59, 66–67, 68–69, 73, 86; support for labour, 76, 98–101, 148–50; tactics against Citizen Group, 67, 113; tactics of 1930s, 84–85, 87–88; and Third Period, 62, 77–80, 84, 101–2, 108; use of propaganda, 86–87; view of class, 34–35. *See also* Kolisnyk, William; Penner, Jacob

Co-operative Commonwealth Federation (CCF), 33, 103

Coulter, Garnet, 143

D

Dafoe, J.W., 32, 148, 155n14

Davidson, Frederick, 53, 133

deportations, 96–97, 114, 170n65

Depression. *See* Great Depression

Dixon, F.J., 26, 28, 40

Dixon, F.W., 172n106

Dominion Labour Party (DLP), 25–26

Draper, Dennis, 113, 114

Durward, Robert, 59, 76, 166n120

E

Edmonton municipal government, 139

Eight Men Speak (play), 94–95

electoral reform, 35, 130–31

employment/unemployment: in 1920s, 12–13; during the Depression, 14, 98–100; and Queen government, 136; relief for, 1, 76–77, 98, 99, 123–24, 127

Evans, W. Sanford, 131

Ewen, Thomas, 70, 80

F

fair wages motion, 126

Farmer, S.J.: and A. Puttee, 9; biography, 31–32; and central heating facility, 47–48, 49; as federal candidate, 29; and founding of ILP, 26, 27, 28; impact of his mayoralty, 14–15, 40, 43–44, 148, 150; and 1919 election, 18–19, 21; and 1922 election campaign, 42; and 1923 election campaign, 50–52; and 1924 election campaign, 54, 55–56, 159n16; and Norman Dam, 52; second term as mayor, 52–54; and Slave Pact, 52–53, 148; and Winnipeg Electric Company, 44, 46

fascist politics, 72, 95

Federation of Civic Employees (FCE), 76, 127, 128–29

Flye, Thomas: and deportations, 96; and electoral reform, 131; and free speech issues, 94; harassed by CPC, 69, 77, 86; long-time service of, 19; and R. Webb, 102

Forkin, Martin: biography, 92–93; in election campaigns, 87, 88, 89, 102–3, 104; and FCE dispute, 127; on free speech issues, 96; gets elected, 84; length of civic service, 15, 145; and public housing, 137; on royalty, 97–98; support for labour, 99, 100, 101; view of municipal government, 144; and violence against police, 172n15

G

General Strike. *See* Winnipeg General Strike

Gray, Charles, 1, 20, 21

Gray, Morris, 123, 124, 125

Great Depression, 13–14, 25, 76–77, 98–100, 122–24

Gunn, Cecil, 121, 136, 140

H

Heaps, A.A., 4, 18, 40, 44, 114

Holmes, Dan, 70, 73, 97

Home and Property Owners' Association, 118, 127, 136–37

Honeyman, Egbert, 121

house farming, 135–37

housing, 1, 2, 11, 14, 131–37

Hyman, Marcus, 32–33, 80

I

Independent Labour Party (ILP): attitude toward royalty, 97–98; background and mandate of, 25–33; Britishness of, 26–27; and central heating facility, 47–49; and change of wards, 37–39; and control of council members, 74, 165n92; cooperates with Kolisnyk on council, 75–76, 77; and deportations, 97; and Depression relief, 122–24; election platform of 1930s, 88; as enemy of CPC, 77–80, 84, 94, 98, 102–3, 113, 114, 147–48, 174n43; and free speech issues, 94, 95, 96; Jewish wing of, 32–33; legacy of council work by, 145–46; legacy of Queen mayoralty, 143–44; and 1922 election, 40, 42; and 1924 election, 54, 56–57; and 1934 election, 116, 117–18; and 1936 election, 140–43; and On-To-Ottawa trek, 125–26; revolutionary aims of, 27–28, 111; rivalry with CPC, 16, 58, 59, 66–67, 68–69, 73, 86; support for labour, 98–99, 100, 101, 148–50; view on electoral reform, 35; votes received in mayoral elections, 119; work relief programs, 124–25. *See also* Farmer, S.J.; Queen, John; Queen government

International Brotherhood of Electrical Workers (IBEW), 52–53

Ivens, William, 4, 19, 77, 91

J

Jacob, Robert, 49–51, 72

K

King George V's Jubilee, 97–98

Kolisnyk, William: biography, 64–66; CPC control of on council, 72–74; defeated in 1930 election, 81; elected as alderman, 59–60, 66; interned, 115; legacy of, 82–83; length of civic service, 15; life after council, 81–82; nomination fight in 1928, 70–71; and police intimidation, 112, 113; and post-revisionist communism, 63–64; RCMP reports on, 65, 66, 73, 79, 82; reaction to his victory, 68, 69–70; and Third Period ideology, 77–79, 80–81; work on council, 74–77, 80–81, 165n97, 166n120, 167n129

L

labour movement: and 1919 Winnipeg mayoral election, 18–21; and 1934 Winnipeg mayoral election, 116, 118; in early Winnipeg elections, 18; and General Strike, 8; and Queen government, 126–27; support from Communists for, 76, 98–101, 148–50; Trades and Labour Council, 25–26, 29, 47–48

Lowe, William, 122, 141

M

Manitoba, Government of: and business tax increase, 122; and civic pensions dispute, 128; and Depression relief, 123, 124; and electoral reform, 131; and government buying of services, 138; and public housing, 133, 134

Manitoba Conference of the Unemployed, 124

Manitoba Free Press: and 1919 Winnipeg mayoral election, 20, 21; and 1922 election, 41, 42; and 1923 election, 49; on S.J. Farmer, 43, 56; on W. Kolisnyk, 59. *See also Winnipeg Free Press*

Market Square, 95–96

May Day parades, 36, 58, 79, 158n93

McEwan, Tom, 95–96, 108

McKerchar, John, 42, 47, 56, 104, 105, 117–18, 123, 143

McLean, Dan, 56, 67

McWilliams, Margaret, 133–34

Mill, John Stuart, 26

Montreal municipal government, 45–46

Morris, Leslie, 67, 70, 73, 80

N

National Unemployed Workers' Association (NUWA), 99

Non-Partisan Association (NPA), 23

Norman Dam, 52

The North Ender, 42, 44, 50

O

One Big Union (OBU), 20–21, 25, 76, 77, 128, 129

On-To-Ottawa trek, 125, 138

P

Parker, B.W., 47–49

Penner, Jacob: as anti-fascist, 95; biography, 89–92, 90; CPC leadership view of, 34; dedication of park to, 105; and deportations, 96–97; election of, 84; and FCE dispute, 127; fight for free speech, 94–96; as focus of anti-communist talk, 114; interned, 115; and J. Queen, 29; length of civic service, 15, 145; and public housing, 137; on royalty, 97; style in council meetings, 89; support for labour, 99–100, 101; and Third Period ideology, 97, 103; view of revolution, 108–9, 115

Penner, Roland, 91, 100, 108–9

Pitblado, Isaac, 121, 175n34

Popovic, Matthew, 59, 69, 70

Preud'homme, Jules, 29, 54, 127, 128

Pritchard, William, 4

Prominent Functionaries of the Communist Party (PROFUNC), 115

Puttee, Arthur, 8–9

Q

Queen, John: biography, 29–31, 30; at CCF convention, 33; on change of wards, 37; on disparity of rich and poor, 27–28; first elected, 18; legacy of his mayoralty, 16–17, 143–44; as mayor from 1938 to 1942, 143, 145; and 1919 election, 19; and 1922 election, 40; and 1934 election, 103–5, 117; and 1935 election, 140; and 1936 election, 141–42; and On-To-Ottawa trekkers, 125–26; in prison, 150; on public housing, 133, 135; and unemployment measures, 77, 98, 123, 127; and Winnipeg General Strike, 4, 8, 9, 29. *See also* Queen government

Queen government: and business tax increase, 120–22; and civic pension plan, 127–29; and Depression relief, 122–24; and electoral reform, 130–31; and labour issues, 126–27; municipalization of services, 137–38; and public housing, 133–37; and work relief programs, 124–25. *See also* Queen, John

Queen-Hughes, Gloria, 31, 86, 145

R

RCMP (Royal Canadian Mounted Police): and CPC plots, 110–11; and M. Forkin, 92; and On-to-Ottawa trek, 125; report on 1926 election, 68; reports on J. Penner, 92; reports on W. Kolisnyk, 65, 66, 73, 79, 82; spying on CPC, 86, 107, 109

Regina municipal government, 138–39

Rice-Jones, Cecil, 133

Richardson, James, 13–14

Ross Queen, Katherine, 31

Russell, R.B., 4, 128, 129

Russian Revolution, 29

S

Section 98 of Criminal Code, 93–94

Seven Sisters dam, 45

Shapack, Rose, 91, 100

Simkin, Saul, 80, 113, 167n125

Simonite, Charles, 92

Simpkin, James: and business taxes, 122; and central steam-heating facility, 47; and election campaigns, 80; and Great Depression, 27, 124; and labour issues, 101, 126; and W. Kolisnyk, 77, 79

Simpson, W.B., 26, 27, 48, 96, 102

Slave Pact, 52–53, 75, 148

Smith, Stewart, 60, 102, 103, 108

Social Democratic Party (SDP), 26, 29

Soviet Union, 61, 63

Sparling, J.K., 40–42

Special Committee on Housing Conditions, 137

Special Committee on Unemployment Relief, 123–24

Steek, Garth, 105

Stobart, Matthew, 122, 135

streetcars, 41–42, 44–46

Sullivan, J.G., 23, 48, 53–54

Sydor, Harry, 81–82

T

taxation, 1, 21, 120–22

Tipping, Fred, 31, 39

Toronto municipal government, 46

Towers, Graham, 120

Trades and Labour Council (TLC), 25–26, 29, 47–48

U

Ukrainian Labour Farmer Temple Association (ULFTA), 71, 164n79

Ukrainian nationalists, 71–72, 82

unemployment. *See* employment/unemployment

United Farmers of Manitoba, 27

V

Vancouver municipal government, 45

Vigilante Committee of Winnipeg, 110

W

Wade, Orton, 97, 109

Webb, Ralph: anti-communism of, 113–14; characterized by W. Kolisnyk, 79; as Citizen leader and mayor, 23–25, 24; CPC threats against, 110, 111; and free speech issues, 94, 95, 96; and 1924 election campaign, 54–56; in 1925 election, 38–39; and 1926 election, 58; in 1936 election, 141; and On-To-Ottawa trek, 125; as supposed ally of ILP, 102; on Winnipeg housing, 131

Weekly News: British slant of, 27; on class warfare, 28; on communism, 103; on CPC, 67, 77, 80; denounces J. Penner, 95; election coverage of, 4; on electoral reform, 130; on ILP, 57; and unemployment policy, 98; on W. Kolisnyk victory, 68

Western Labour News, 18, 32, 44

Winnipeg, 9–14, 35–39, 120, 122, 139–40

Winnipeg Building Trades Council (BTC), 135–36

Winnipeg Civics Association, 49

Winnipeg Electric Company (WEC), 41–42, 44–45, 46, 75, 138, 145

Winnipeg Free Press: on Depression relief, 123; on J. Penner, 103; and labour disputes, 126; mayoral campaign of 1934, 117; on need for public housing, 134; and 1935 election, 140; on police intimidation of CPC, 113; on riot at Market Square, 95. *See also Manitoba Free Press*; and typographical union strike, 101

Winnipeg General Strike: and changes to wards, 37; effect on 1919 Winnipeg mayoral election, 18, 20, 21–22; effects of, 1, 6–9, 29; as factor in 1926 election, 68; and leftist party tensions, 25; overtones of in 1922 election, 40–41, 42–43; and question of public ownership of utilities, 45; role in ILP-CPC rivalry, 80; and Section 98 of the Criminal Code, 93; seen as a beginning not end, 146–47; used to scare people off the left, 112, 113

Winnipeg Hydro, 45, 48

Winnipeg Tribune, 101, 126, 136, 141

Woodsworth, J.S., 8, 9, 33

The Worker: election coverage, 86, 89; on ILP, 80, 81, 97; on J. Penner, 100; and Market Square, 79; on municipal politics, 60; and revolutionary zeal, 108; on Slave Pact, 75; and Third Period ideology, 62; and W. Kolisnyk, 66, 68, 73, 74

Workers' and Farmers' Cooperative Association, 65

Workers' and Farmers' Cooperative Creamery, 81, 82

Workers' Unity League (WUL), 84–85

Z

Zuken, Joseph, 86, 145, 172n112